AN AESTHETIC OCCUPATION

The Immediacy of Architecture and the Palestine Conflict

DUKE UNIVERSITY PRESS   Durham and London   2002

AN AESTHETIC OCCUPATION

Daniel Bertrand Monk

© 2002 DUKE UNIVERSITY PRESS

All rights reserved

Printed in the United States of

America on acid-free paper ∞

Designed by Amy Ruth Buchanan

Typeset in Quadraat by G & S

Typesetters, Inc.

Library of Congress Cataloging-in-

Publication Data appear on the last

printed page of this book.

Le Yael. Ki ge'ulati hi.

IMMEDIACY: THE QUALITY

OR CONDITION OF BEING

IMMEDIATE; FREEDOM

FROM INTERMEDIATE OR

INTERVENING AGENCY;

DIRECT RELATION OR

CONNECTION; DIRECTNESS

CONTENTS

AG	Attorney general
AS(pol)	Assistant secretary for political affairs
CID	Criminal Investigations Division
CO	Colonial Office
CZA	Central Zionist Archives
ETR	Ernest Tatham Richmond
FO	Foreign Office
HMG	His Majesty's Government
HWR	Admiral Herbert W. Richmond
ISA	Israel State Archives, Jerusalem, Israel
JMA	City of Jerusalem Municipal Archives, Jerusalem, Israel
MMR	Margaret Mary Richmond [née Muriel Lubbock]
OETA	Occupied Enemy Territory Administration
PEF	Palestine Exploration Fund

PEFQ Palestine Exploration Fund, *Quarterly Statement*
PRO   Public Record Office, Kew, London, England
SMC   Supreme Muslim Shari'a Council
ZO   Zionist Organization

al-Aqsa Arabic, literally "the more remote," but referring to the entire Muslim religious complex encompassing the Dome of the Rock and the Aqsa Mosque in Jerusalem

Ateret Cohanim Hebrew, literally "the Priestly crown," the name of a religious nationalist organization whose purpose is to settle Jews in East Jerusalem and the Muslim quarters of the Old City

bayan Arabic, "proclamations, reports," but also meaning "patency, obviousness"

al-Buraq Arabic, also *al-Buraq al-Sharif*, or "noble Buraq." The name of Muhammad's steed, it is by tradition also the name given by Muslims to the site Jews commonly refer to as the Western, or Wailing Wall in Jerusalem. Muslim tradition holds that it is at this site that Muhammad tethered Buraq on his night journey, known as the 'Isra to the Aqsa.

Hakeren Lemorshet Hakotel Hama'aravi Hebrew, for the Western Wall Heritage Foundation

al-Haram al-Sharif Arabic, literally "the noble enclosure or compound," the term refers to the same compound as the Aqsa, i.e., the Muslim Sanctuary contained of the original Herodian walls once bounding the Hebrew Temple in Jerusalem. In its center stands the Dome of the Rock

Jam'iyyat Hirasat al-Masjid al-Aqsa wa'l-Amakin al-Islamiyya al-Muqaddasa bi'l Quds Arabic, for the Society for the Protection of the Aqsa Mosque and the Islamic Holy Places in Jerusalem

Lajnat al-Difa' 'an al-Buraq al-Sharif Arabic, for Defense Committee for the Buraq al-Sharif, variously translated by the Shaw Commission as the Defense Committee for the Noble Buraq

al-Majlis al-Shar'i al-Islami al-A'la Arabic, for the Supreme Muslim Shar'ia Council, also known as the Supreme Muslim Council and the SMC

Majlissiyyun Arabic, referring to the political faction associated with the Supreme Muslim Council of Palestine, and by default, with the Husayni family

ma'mur awqaf Arabic, referring to the regional official responsible for management of Muslim religious trusts

Mizrah Hebrew, literally an "orient," referring to a plaque placed on a wall in Jewish households for the purpose of orienting prayer toward Jerusalem

Nabi Musa Arabic, for "the Prophet Moses," but also referring to a Muslim shrine located between Jerusalem and Jericho at which an annual festival was held each spring

al-Nakba Arabic, literally "the catastrophe," but referring to the Palestinian national dispossession in 1948

Reshut Hamekomot Hak'doshim Hebrew, for the Holy Places Authority

shari'a Arabic, Muslim canonical law

Shaykh al-Islam Arabic, for the Mufti of Istanbul, who was also the chief of the Ottoman religious establishment. Also referred to as Şeyhülislâm (Turkish).

Simchat Torah Hebrew, for the Jewish holiday celebrating the completion of a full cycle of the Pentateuch's reading, and the inauguration of a new one

Sukkot Hebrew, for the Jewish Feast of the Tabernacles, celebrating the exodus from Egypt

Va'ad Hale'umi Hebrew, Jewish National Council during the Mandate era

waqf Arabic, Muslim religious trust. Plural: *awqaf*. According to Ottoman land laws, one of six categories of land ownership in Palestine. In Mandatory Palestine, waqf properties were administered by the Supreme Muslim Shari'a Council, or SMC.

When T. E. Lawrence published *The Seven Pillars of Wisdom*, he addressed the thorny problem of transliteration with characteristic flippancy. Asked by his editor if "Nuri, Emir of the Ruwalla" bore any relation to the "chief family of the Rualla," or to the "Rueli" referred to elsewhere in the text, Lawrence replied: "Should have also used Ruwala and Ruala." Similarly, when asked if other inconsistencies in transliteration were intentional, the author responded: "Rather!" Anyone who has had to transpose the words of one language into the letters of another can immediately appreciate the temptation to which Lawrence succumbed. (After all, his sarcasm attests to a fundamental incongruity between tongues that no system can completely overcome.) But they will also recognize in Lawrence's inconsistent transliteration a coherent orthography of disrespect, by which I mean a perfectly consistent system of naming, premised on the notion that the titles of others exist only for him.

The arguments I advance in this book have something to do with the paradox exhumed by Lawrence. But I chose not to perpetuate that contradiction deliberately in the transliteration of the Arabic and Hebrew names, terms, and phrases that dot its pages. Instead, when I have included Arabic sources I have tried to follow the conventions of the *International Journal of Middle East Studies* as closely as possible. Hebrew posed a different problem. Since there is no generally accepted convention for the transliteration of modern Hebrew that would make sense to anyone but linguists, I've presented Hebrew words consistently, following what I think to be common sense: the letter *Chet* = Ch, *Khaf* = Kh, and *Kuf* = K. The *Sh'va Nach* appears as an apostrophe and the *Sh'va Na* is an E. I absorb the *Hei Hayedi'a* into the following word, just as I've done in this sentence. (This is a simple system, and I'm sure it can't be any worse than the orthographically correct but incomprehensible signs to "Petah Tiqwa" one sees on the highway as one exits Ben-Gurion airport, which is itself presented on the same road signs as "Natba'g".) More generally, I've avoided the use of diacritical marks (other than the Arabic hamza ʾ and the ʿ ayn) except when absolutely necessary. And I've abandoned proper transliteration altogether when a term is better known under a commonly accepted spelling in English. (For example, I spell the Hebrew pseudonym for the author Asher Ginsberg as it appears in most bibliographies: Ahad Ha'am.) In some instances, I have opted to live with the translations established by others in order to avoid confusion. (Thus, the organization known as "Lajnat al-Difaʿ ʿan al-Buraq al-Sharif" appears as the "Defense Committee for the Noble Buraq," following the name given it by a parliamentary commission in 1930). Last, I've left the transliterations of others intact when I cite them, but I've added my own in brackets in those instances when the discrepancy might be confusing to the reader.

An *Aesthetic Occupation* was written during the interval spanning two notorious political incidents in Jerusalem: the so-called archaeological tunnel episode of September 1996 and the crisis that followed upon Israeli Likud party leader Ariel Sharon's self-declared "visit of peace" to the Haram al-Sharif/Temple Mount exactly four years later. Nevertheless, this is not a timely work in the conventional sense of the term. To the contrary, the very idea of "timeliness"—the notion that during such moments of crisis, the truth of a political situation presents itself directly and without mediation—is one that I call into question in the pages that follow. More to the point, this is a political biography of that same idea, a history of its participation in the same violent struggle it would explain.

There is a significant conceptual difference between writing a history that assumes we understand, prima facie, the workings of monuments and holy sites in the perpetuation of a conflict, and one that examines how the conflict *itself* has fashioned and refashioned its own explanation of the monument's political role, in the process disclosing its own understanding of history. In my case, the difference between these two projects can be measured in years. In order to write a version of *An Aesthetic Occupation* consistent with the second project, I necessarily abandoned a series of previous drafts that conformed to the first project and the accusatory historiographic norm I now see it sustains. The book that follows this preface, then, is a repudiation of my own earlier understanding of this conflict, as well as the dissertation in which I first began to elaborate it. I can think of no higher praise for my teachers, Claudia Brodsky and Anthony Vidler, than that their teaching and example enabled this to happen. In fact, I'm certain they were wondering why it took me so long.

Any excuses I may have mustered in my own head for leaving the project as it then stood—that is, for failing to address questions of architecture in the history of the conflict's self representation—were politely done away with by the opportunity offered me for study and reflection by the Committee for International Peace and Security of the Social Science Research Council, which awarded me a MacArthur Foundation fellowship in international peace and security in 1975. The ensuing two fellowship years were spent, first, at the Institute of War and Peace Studies, Columbia University, and next at the Center for Critical Theory and the Art Department at Duke University, with very long research intervals spent in London and Jerusalem to boot. I am grateful to Jack Snyder at Columbia, and to Fredric Jameson, Richard Powell, and Annabel Wharton at Duke, for their assistance and encouragement at their respective institutions. I also want to express my heartfelt thanks to the MacArthur Foundation and the members of the SSRC's Committee on International Peace and Security, particularly Peter Katzenstein, R. B. J. Walker, and Steve Smith. I don't think they could possibly suspect how important it was for me to listen to them account for the way the world of security studies itself accounts for the kind of crisis of which I wanted to write a critical history.

During this same period of research and study, I had a series of conversations with Ilan Pappe of Haifa University, Yaron Ezrahi of the Israel Democracy Institute, and Elias Sanbar of the Sorbonne and the *Revue d'études palestiniennes* that were crucial to the development of this project. Though none of these remarkable scholars knew it at the time, these discussions caused me to shuttle between London and Jerusalem to pursue new directions in research. Inspired by them to jump back into the archives, I repeatedly imposed on the hospitality of family and friends wherever I landed. In London, my doppelganger, Daniel Monk of Keele University, provided a much-appreciated haven, as did "our American cousin," Mark Nagel. In Jerusalem, Shimon Piltzer did the same. No less significantly, during his bachelor days Shimon made the piles of newspapers that accumulated in his loft my own personal archive.

This book relied upon a large number of archival and primary sources to make its case; behind each citation there was a guardian angel. In Israel the assistance offered by the respective staffs of the Israel State Archives, the Central Zionist Archives, the Archives of the Jerusalem Municipality, the Jewish National Library, and the Central Archives for the History of the Jewish People proved invaluable. In the United Kingdom, my work was greatly facilitated by the goodwill of the staffs of the Public Record Office, the British Library, the Middle East Centre at St. Antony's College, Oxford, and the Pembroke and Kings College Libraries at Cambridge. I am also indebted to Andras Riedlmayr of the Aga Khan Program of the Architecture and Fine Arts Library at Harvard University for sharing with me his copy of Mimar Kemalettin's memorandum on the reconstruction of the Aqsa, and to Asli Niyazioglu for helping me read it.

This book also relies upon primary sources that presently have no archival home, though they deserve one. Chief among these are the Ernest Tatham Richmond papers, which were made available to me through the kindness of his grandchildren: Sally Morphet, Emma Shackle, Sophie Richmond, and Sam Richmond. They have shown me every conceivable courtesy, and, chiefly, the courtesy of allowing this to be the first published study to rely extensively on the E.T. Richmond papers. I will remain forever grateful to them for the trust they have placed in me.

During the last four years, many people responded helpfully to public presentations of the research that would become this book; their remarks proved to be vivid reminders of the fact that people continue to live and suffer the history I treat here. I particularly want to thank the Architectural Association in London and its director, Mohsen Mostafavi, as well as the Politics and Social Theory Group at Warwick University and MIT's History, Theory, and Criticism Program for their engaged and sometimes spirited commentary on this project. I am equally grateful to Kenneth Frampton for all our spirited debates. All of these encounters triggered significant modifications in the text, and the revisions were in turn read by colleagues who have taught me by the example of their sharing how perverse the words "intellectual property" really are. None of what I finally committed to print would have ever left my desk were it not for the careful scrutiny given to my arguments, in one form or another, by K. Michael Hays, Sidra deKoven Ezrahi, Herman Lebovics, Mike Davis, W. J. T. Mitchell, Eric Zakim, Mary Rawlinson, and Alona Nitzan-Shiftan. (Mike Davis and Alessandra Moctezuma also provided the "essential aloha"—whatever that means—and Gene Lebovics the indispensable comfort food. David Szulanski, a brilliant poet, contributed the necessary *ṭarab* via email). Most importantly, Sara Lipton began every day of the last three years by telling me to "knock 'em dead," and ended by reviewing my pathetic efforts to do away with historical characters all too skilled in rising from the grave. She, more than anyone else, is responsible for anything good the reader may find in this book. An early draft of chapter 1 appeared in AA Files. I'm extremely grateful to its editor, Mary Wall, for her generous assistance in its preparation for publication, as well as for the criticism she offered.

Each of my two academic home bases, the State University of New York at Stony Brook and Harvard University's Graduate School of Design, helped expedite this project's publication. Through the generous support and encouragement of Jorge Silvetti, chair of the Architecture Department of the Graduate School of Design at Harvard, and of the school's dean, Peter Rowe, I benefited from the research assistance of Geoffrey Taylor. At Stony Brook, Dean Paul Armstrong and the chair of the Art Department, James Rubin, made it possible for me to benefit from the help of Hedi Ben-Aicha, Karen Levitov, and Katherine Carl. I want them each to know—mentors and students alike—that I realized I was being coaxed along at every step by gifted intellects. Yet I alone am responsible for any errors in the text, and particularly for any errors in translation or transliteration.

In the end, this book demanded of me that I learn how to practice a kind of emotional reserve that is utterly unnatural to me—a refusal to adopt an immediately discernible location toward the very claims whose history I wished to trace. I have come to realize, however, that this apparent standpoint of reserve was in reality the standpoint of heartbreak: to refuse to make oneself completely at home in this conflict, is necessarily to make oneself at home in the *telling* of this conflict, and particularly, in the literary salon, where (to paraphrase a unique intellect) this struggle squeezes sense out of its victims' fortunes by repeatedly calling for new ones. To those who have shared their lives and their love with me, the price of this self-imposed dislocation has been all too apparent. But I want them to know that it is they who have always shown me the way forward; my parents most of all. Having suffered real dislocations (and not just intellectual ones), Abraham and Raquel Monk have taught me that "the only life that can be lived responsibly in the face of such despair" is one that is all the more strongly oriented toward redemption. In their case, this meant a secure future for their children. Following their loving example, I dedicate this book to my own daughter, Julia. I know that both my own mother, and Julia's mom, will not fail to understand that in throwing this message in a bottle into the sea on her behalf, I'm also dedicating this work to them.

INTRODUCTION:

THE FOUNDATION

STONE OF

OUR EXISTENCE,

WITHOUT

EXAGGERATION.

The claim to immediate political impact will not just turn out to be a bluff: it will also be exposed as the attempt to liquidate an almost hopeless situation by a series of completely hopeless maneuvers. In short, it resembles nothing so much as Baron Münchhausen's claim that he pulled himself out of a swamp by his own hair.

—Walter Benjamin, "Critique of the New Objectivity"

JERUSALEM, 16 SEPTEMBER 1996. In a gesture he would later claim was "demanded by sovereignty," Israeli Prime Minister Benjamin (Bibi) Netanyahu orders the opening of a new gate to an archaic tunnel, an ancient conduit passing from the precincts of the Western Wall, or Buraq, northward to the Muslim quarter of the city. Within hours, violence ensues, leaving at least seventy people dead. The occupied territories are then sequestered, and for the first time since the establishment of the Palestinian Authority, Israeli troops trade fire with Palestinian security forces. Among the many casualties of this "archaeological tunnel" crisis, observers argue, are the Oslo peace accords themselves.[1]

Soon after these events take place, a critical reckoning begins. Commentators on the conflict begin to rewrite the unresolved recriminations hurled by participants at the time, as if from a critical perspective born of long experience with such accusations, a worldview that situates the tunnel affray within larger taxonomies of the conflict. For example, shortly after the week of violence passes, Dr. Abdul Qader Tash, editor-in-chief of the *Arab News* and columnist for the Jeddah daily *al-Madinah*, concludes: "Israel is trying hard to convince the world that the explosion of Arab anger following the opening of the now infamous tunnel under the al-Aqsa Mosque was totally unjustified."[2] Tash presents with palpable skepticism the argument of the Israeli government "that the Palestinians exploited the incident to rouse the Muslim world against Israel"; in his own understanding of the origin of the violence, Tash echoes the position of then Crown Prince Hassan of Jordan, who on the first day of the tunnel crisis argued that Israel had provoked the violence by its insensitivity to Muslim and Arab sensitivities.[3] In contrast with this view, in the pages of *Time* magazine another analyst, Pulitzer prize–winning columnist Charles Krauthammer, argues that even though the opening of the tunnel "was denounced from Turtle Bay to Timbuktu as a desecration of Islamic holy sites in Jerusalem," the reality is that the "Western media were simply taken in by a lie . . . put out by the PLO and the Arab League": "At Arafat's urging, the League issued within 48 hours of the tunnel's opening a declaration calling the tunnel 'part of an Israeli Zionist plot to destroy the Aqsa mosque [and] set up the Temple of Solomon.'"[4]

In the face of such acrimony, it is all too easy to overlook how much already has to be agreed upon in order for this crisis to assume familiar contours at the hands of its interpreters. For violence to pass into self-evidence, several axioms have to be shared by friends and enemies alike. First, everyone has to participate in the intuition of something "immediate": namely, the presumption that in architecture a political reality presents itself to view directly and without mediation.[5] Convinced of this immediacy, no one, here, disputes the fact that the same construction "demanded by sovereignty"— the tunnel—also occasions the "explosion of Arab anger." They only disagree on the trigger, in the process disclosing the second point of tacit agreement between them: for the tunnel to be subsumed within a familiar history of such crises, the interpreters of the conflict have to concur that this is an immediacy confirmed by use, or in other words, that the monument is a fuse with which one can ignite a human bomb. Tash argues that the Israeli decision to open the tunnel is self-evidently an act of instigation that backfired, subsequently forcing its leaders to "placate and deceive the world and to contain the fury their arrogance [had] aroused."[6] Conversely, reaching much the same conclusion expressed by Ehud Olmert (the city of Jerusalem's mayor) when he accused President Arafat of engaging in "insane incitement" [in Hebrew, "hasata meturefet"], Charles Krauthammer accuses the Palestinian Authority of perpetrating an "incendiary libel, calling on Palestinians 'to express their anger' over this 'aggression on al-Aqsa Mosque' and 'desecration of Holy Places.'"[7] In these exchanges no one challenges the idea that the tunnel can be deployed—this time like artillery—against the peace process. The commentators only disagree about which culprit sets off the weapon, thereby introducing the last, paradoxical area of tacit consensus between them: for the tunnel to become only one crisis in a series of others—in a "state of emergency" that "is not the exception but the rule" for this conflict—those authorized to speak for politics have to concur that the transparency of their political circumstances is confirmed/ratified reflexively, in the self-evidence of an "incendiary" politics of blame.[8] In contesting one another's claims for the tunnel's uses, opponents turn to those claims *themselves* and suggest that the immediacy of their political situation is confirmed in architecture's *representation*. For example, Krauthammer argues that the media unselfconsciously ratified a piece of "modern propaganda with medieval resonance"—in his words, a "blood libel," which, in converting an archaeological find into a religious-nationalist fetish, obscured the nature of the mass violence that actually took place; Tash in turn directly accuses Krauthammer of perpetrating a metalepsis—a substitution of cause for effect—which not only turns "facts upside down," but in doing so repeats the founding "lie" of Israel's very existence. Finally revealing that what is at stake in accusations about architecture is the proper representation of history itself, Tash argues: "Of course, it is not strange for Israel or its apologists to play such games with truth. Its claim to be rightfully in Palestine, the very basis of its existence is built upon a historical distortion. This

3

latest attempt to delink the issue of the tunnel from that of their claim for the mythical Temple is but another trick to deceive those who are unaware of the relevant history."[9]

■

This is a book about the career of architecture in the prehistory of the present conflict between Israelis and Palestinians, a record of all the work that had to be done in order for the so-called archaeological tunnel episode to achieve its unquestioned political "immediacy" in the telling of this struggle. I do not intend to chronicle the constructions and demolitions of the kind that Edward Said has described as the very "atoms" of this conflict's existence—although an accounting of these is also desperately overdue—but to offer instead a history of the assumption that in this conflict architecture constitutes such an "atom" at all.[10] Because I am aware that these claims have a long pedigree in the perpetuation of a conflict, and are even sustained by those who seek only to end it with justice, in *An Aesthetic Occupation* I present a history of the argument for a politics of monuments at its modern point of elaboration, during the period of British suzerainty in Palestine known as the Mandate era.[11] More specifically, this study traces the progressive normalization of that argument, its problematic passage to transparency and ubiquity in the representation of a struggle, a passage so complete that even my own effort to estrange it might now appear strange.

Of necessity, *An Aesthetic Occupation* is at the same time a historiographic exploration of the accumulation of such claims since the time of the Mandate, a record of how they have been maintained by subsequent participants in this conflict, as well as by those authorized to speak for its history. I offer a history of what the conflict *itself* has presented as the career of architecture in this conflict, not in order to ratify or deny those claims, but in order to document the historical development of that style of interpretation, even in what might pass for transcendental perspectives on the quarrel. I am concerned with a history of struggle that has presented itself to itself in a way that has required it to assert and reassert the identity between certain privileged representations of architecture and the actuality they would name. My concern is born of urgency, since (as subsequent crises indicate) this unquestioned practice clearly persists into the present, as a conceptual precondition for any thinking about the dynamic of this conflict, or about its resolution.

Most important, perhaps, in this work I am committed to asking if there is not a certain truth in the enduring untruth of this conflict's normative presentations of architecture's political self-certainty, its meaning-in-itself. My suspicion—one I elaborate during the course of this study—is that in the repeated but normalized failure of this conflict to explain *how* its truth is confirmed as immediate in the architecture it privileges, we see something of the character of history itself—in the irreducible actuality of that failure. Think of it this way: the kinds of political immediacy accorded to architecture in this struggle—the demolitions, new settlements, threatened mosques, and projected temples that are presumed to signal something more than performative brutality—give form to history through the category of the negative, precisely by their very intimate distance from it. As Theodor Adorno has noted, at its [most] "realist" of extremes (and with the perception of architecture as a political "atom" we have reached such limits), "identitarian thought" presents itself as the "covering image of [a] prevailing dichotomy." [12] Inasmuch as it "thwarts the reconcilement for which it mistakes itself," [13] the conflict's repeated calls to immediacy actually ratify the universality of mediation.

Before I go on, let me note—unambiguously—that the aims of this inquiry are not so much philosophical as political. My contribution is unabashedly polemical. In attempting to analyze precisely what has always been second nature to the combatants and interpreters of this history—that is, the very form of the icons and figures that, in the apparent immediacy of their significance, putatively provoke or retroactively explain the mass actions privileged in the telling of this history—I enter into and display a dimension of a conflict that the same combatants think themselves able to control, but which to no small degree *defines* them as custodians of a certain vision of historical causality. [14] In pragmatic terms, this means that where this struggle's participant-observers look to architecture and invoke the transparency of the political, I point (with alarm) to a conflict unable to account for itself to itself.

This is not the first book to attempt an analysis of the place of monuments in the representation of this conflict's history. In fact, there has been virtually *no* accounting of the modern struggle over Palestine and Israel that has not (been forced) to tread over much of the same territory I cover here. However, they do so *in passing*. Not in the sense that they mean to imply the irrelevance of those issues, but on the contrary, in the sense that in many analyses of this conflict, a putative logic of manifestations (the immediacy of architecture) presents itself as something that so clearly accounts for history that it itself seems to require no historical accounting.

In passing: a recent popular religious history of Jerusalem explains present circumstances as if they were a species of "hierophany"—a long-standing mythology of sacred presences, capable of being explained by a higher science of manifestations.[15] For example: if, during the heart of the archaeological tunnel crisis, Benjamin Netanyahu explained his policy imperatives by stating that in the shaft he had touched "the foundation stone of our [national] existence, without exaggeration," then in her *Jerusalem: One City Three Faiths* Karen Armstrong sustains much the same logic of adumbration under the rubric of that logic's explanation.[16] Drawing on the religious history of Mircea Eliade and the Chicago school, Armstrong argues that the persistence of an archaic understanding of images, holy sites and symbols (of a kind, it is implied, no longer experienced in the modern Occident) constitutes an "underlying current" of modern experience in the holy city. This "sacred geography," as she describes it, makes it difficult for members of the "cult" of Jerusalem "to see the city objectively, because it has become bound up with their conception of themselves."[17] As Armstrong concludes that "the question of Jerusalem is explosive because the city has acquired mythical status," she not only links violence to a hierophany of the first order (the hierophany of people who, like Bibi, *say* they believe in manifestations, regardless of whether they mean it or not), but simultaneously introduces a tacit hierophany of a second order, arguing that politics now manifests itself in the mythology of manifestations.[18]

In passing, second, in the sense that historical analyses of this conflict do not generally question the existence of the hierophanies of a second order of the kind presented by Armstrong, only the uses to which that species of immediacy has been put: as with the commentators on the tunnel crisis, who presuppose the political transparency of the monument in their debates over its deployment, the historiography of Palestine and Israel folds a tacit logic of manifestations into controversies over its "application," into debates concerning the monument's career over the long haul of a struggle. And, as in analyses of the tunnel affray, so in many attempts to identify general patterns of history and historical consciousness in this contest, there are redemptive and accusative presentations of the way the immediacy of architecture is certified by its "utility." For example, in *Palestinian Identity*, Rashid Khalidi attempts to plot the historical construction of Palestinian national consciousness (via subtle readings of the Palestinian people's "narratives" and "nominations" of identity), even as he tacitly sustains (and relies upon) a logic of manifestations in the treatment of that effort. Presenting much the same vision of the secular/national uses of sacred geography as that found in the pages of the Israeli tourist brochure for the archaeological tunnel, Khalidi's argument states: "It is easy to see why Jerusalem should have been the touchstone of identity for all the inhabitants of Palestine in the Modern era as in the past."[19] Despite its apparent affiliation with a constructionist politics of identity, in philosophical terms Khalidi reprises a popular version of a phenomenology of Spirit, an idealist vision of history according to which Spirit—in the form of consciousness—actualizes itself and reaches progressively higher stages of self-consciousness in the paradox of its own exteriorization.[20] It is precisely this "redemptive" vision of the uses of Jerusalem—not the fact that it may be used—that is contested by other chroniclers of this conflict, who see claims for the relation of consciousness to matter as a recurring and dangerous fetishism that actually confirms architecture as a symbolic weapon. For instance, in his *City of Stone: The Secret History of Jerusalem*, Meron Benvenisti argues that the putative redemptive "touchstone" of historical consciousness described by Khalidi is in reality nothing more than "a gigantic quarry from which each side [Palestinian and Israeli] has mined stones for the construction of its myths—and for throwing at each other."[21] Repeating much the same type of charge as that issued by the Arab League in 1996, which spoke of the archaeological tunnel as an immediate manifestation of Israeli expansionism, Benvenisti hypostatizes this same immediacy into a principle of history, arguing that in order to truly understand the enigma of the city's relation to the conflict one has to "leave the quarry of history" behind, and face the "earthly Jerusalem."[22] Strangely, neither Khalidi nor Benvenisti sees the more pressing demand to write the history of the "touchstone" and the "quarry"—the historiography of the irreducibly reciprocal claims for the lieux de mémoire and the "invented traditions" they themselves reprise.[23] Instead, as each affirms the absolute correspondence between consciousness and things by pointing to the practical outcomes of that correspondence, together they reaffirm a common logic of stones—a principle of manifestations—that is constitutive of the historical condition they themselves analyze.[24]

In passing, last, in the sense that the editor of a remarkable series of theoretically oriented studies of this conflict astutely recognized—I believe for the first time—that it is "fueled by claims that challenge our philosophical thinking," even as his own efforts to introduce a moral philosophy of this struggle confirm a normative, unquestioned, presumption of a causal relation between politics and the representation of "sacred geographies"[25]: In its first sentences, Tomis Kapitan's *Philosophical Perspectives on the Israeli Palestinian Conflict* passes over and thus tacitly preserves the very style of presupposition that I attempt to historicize here. Presenting the same sort of immediacy-in-representation that characterized Tash's and Krauthammer's sense of the archaeological tunnel (that is, assuming that a representation is in itself that which sanctions reflexive philosophical speculation on the conflict), Kapitan writes that a place, transubstantiated into a "terra Sancta," can instigate or account for a violent history because it "evokes powerful passions involving identity, honor, and the propriety of cultural claims."[26]

In this book I never get past what others say "in passing." To examine how the culture of this conflict has accounted for its own perpetuation in terms of a tacit science of appearances—the hierophanies, touchstones, quarries, reflections that establish an identity between history and its representations—is to begin to grasp its historical logic. This is a logic of *adequation*, an idea that actuality fits into the concepts invoked to house it without leaving a remainder, or, conversely, that symbols or objects overtake—are "adequate to"—the reality they name.[27] The crux of the matter, however, is that as history has a problem keeping up appearances in this fashion, "mere immediacy" already "presupposes abstract temporal sequence."[28] With each new summons of the "concrete," this logic of adequation—the assertion of a "prepared and objectified form of the concepts" discernible even in cynical interpretations of others' cynicism—shows itself be as irreducible as it is impossible.[29] Motivated by the abstract nature of the appearances they themselves privilege, the participants and interpreters of this conflict confirm a negative dialectic—the inevitable inadequacy built into any project of adequation—in their repeated, prolonged, and deadly efforts to arrive at the inverse: a reliable politics of inherences.[30]

The result, I argue, is not only a reification of history, but a prolonged history of reifications. In the successive theories of representation of Armstrong, Khalidi, Benvenisti, and Kapitan, what one witnesses "in passing" is not only a normative philosophy of history, but a palimpsest of this conflict's own course. First, to invoke a "magical" or religious vision of adequation— as Armstrong appears to when she speaks of others' continuing faith in manifestations—is to pay tribute to a moment in the prehistory of this conflict when that same demystification of myth became its own myth, and an interpretive science of "sacred geographies" disclosed itself to be indistinguishable from what it sought to extinguish: the belief in an immediately intuited history, confirmed in architecture. Second, to invoke an "operative" vision of adequation—according to which politics is presumed to *make use* of that same science of manifestations as a façade for its own secular imperatives—is, similarly, to pay tribute to the moment in this conflict when history tacitly reasserted the structure of adequation even while presuming to offer a critique of it: specifically, in claims that the truth of a political condition could be immediately discerned in architecture's uses. Seen in this light, the respective "touchstones" and "quarries" of Khalidi and Benvenisti are archaeological artifacts of an instrumental reason that—in a turn actually taken during the conflict—erected itself as a monument to the dissolution of a vulgar "science" of magical adequations, and in so doing, sustained the same "science" as a mimesis of enlightenment. Third, to maintain a "reflexive" theory of adequation—in interpretations of others' representations of the monument's utility—is to repeat the reflexive turn that took place in this history. Kapitan's philosophical endeavor recalls the actual moment in this struggle when inquiries into the politics of figuration themselves became a new figuration of the political. In that turn, when politics explained that architecture's adequacy to history was vested in representations of that adequacy all along, this history normalized (the rule) of its own formalization as a constitutive feature of its violent perpetuation. In this way, history would be advanced by pointing to architecture's representation.

All of this suggests that it is time to think differently about time, because with this final sacralization of the secular, "reflexive" theory of adequation —with its passage to transparency—the same old "sacred geography" discloses itself as the uncanny dead end of a history of successive immediacies, reasserts itself as the homeopathic magic that was always already present even in the most critical, reflexive, representations of this conflict.[31] To "pay tribute to" the crises of adequacy that I have just described, then, is not to say that the past influences the present, or, following Nietzsche, that "recurrence is eternal," but rather that in a real sense we continue to inhabit a paradoxically present prehistory. "Where we perceive a chain of events [the angel of history] . . . sees one single catastrophe which keeps piling wreckage upon wreckage."[32]

There is a critical dimension to this understanding of history, if one is willing to sift through the ruins. Where the problematic relation between history and its aspect is ideologically disavowed (and thus, perpetuated) in a politics of monuments, the shape of history is successfully recalled in the "negative of its trace."[33] Here, the architecture that is perpetually summoned to immediacy actually presents itself as a *cipher* of history, not because it simply marks this conflict's discursive and dramaturgical limits, but because it "potentiates from within the requirement of its objective transformation."[34] Architecture *itself* assembles and reassembles the constellation of possible positions actually assumed by participants in this conflict, who confront the element of the nonidentical within architecture as if that element were the trace of the agency of the Other, that is, as if each threat to an immediately intuited reality confirmed by an object emanated from an opposing presentation of immediacy, rather than from the fact that the object's "identity" only introduces itself "in its otherness to all identification."[35] (This is, quite frankly, the heart of my argument, and it is also what I am thinking of when I refer to a reification of history that is told by a history of reifications: first, a perpetual intrusion of the nonidentical in that which identifies history by way of its manifestation; and second, the "practical" accommodation of that intrusion in an apotropaic fashion, as if it were a menace already constituted from within the ranks of the political.)

Sigmund Freud deduced the political power of an apotropaic or menacing representation from its consequences, arguing that "what arouses horror in oneself will produce the same effect upon the enemy against whom one is seeking to defend oneself."[36] If, for Freud, the apotropaic image is the *cause* of a certain psychopathology (representing the priority of the subconscious in the domain of the political, i.e., of history), the process I have just described implies instead that apotropaism is the name one would have to give to an inverse *effect*.[37] In other words, the apotropaic does not signal the practical career of a dialectically organized unconscious, as Freud once believed. (Dialectical because, as he would discover, the menacing meaning of the apotropaic figure transmogrifies into its contrary, something quite reassuring).[38] Rather, as it is expressed in these normative explanations of the apotropaic, that putatively "intrusive" unconscious—assembling itself according to a logic of simultaneous displacement and condensation, play and cogency, around an image—actually reveals itself to be the subjective mark of an objective, but thoroughly abstract, condition: it is the trace left on people's practices by a figure's refusal to gain identity with what it is supposed to represent. "This paradoxical issue is a harsh fact of life for those who we might think had other business," but the problematic that emerges between history and its dedicated manifestations presented itself concretely —as an ongoing and menacing crisis—to the actors who participated in the same politics recalled, abstractly, and ahistorically, "in passing."[39]

Each one of the forms of adequation I have described comes to the fore in a historical moment, and these moments structure this book. The problem of a "magical" vision of adequation is the very real historical crisis of scriptural geography. During the "long" nineteenth century described by Eric Hobsbawm (which, in the case of Jerusalem we can date from Napoleon's invasion of Egypt in 1798 to England's conquest of the city in December 1917), the scientific study of holy sites was coextensive with a series of geopolitical imperatives, indeed, with the project of imperialism as a whole.[40] This is familiar territory. And yet, in the familiarity of the normative explanations of that coincidence—which see the forms and sites of divinity advanced in evangelical scriptural geography as nothing more than reflections of secular imperatives—what one witnesses is the irreducibility of the same dialectic confronted by the scriptural geographers of an imperial age. In part 1 of this work, which is entitled "Stone," I argue that, here, in the dissolution of a "science" of manifestations under the sign of ideology, history actually bequeathed the logic of manifestations unscathed to a modern conflict: in the myth of architecture's political and secular immediacy.

The dilemma of an "operative" adequation is the historical crisis of architecture—or more properly, of those involved in a politics of monuments that I analyze in part 2, entitled "Tile." According to normative periodizations of this conflict, during the first stage of British hegemony in Palestine, the enveloping political conflict between Arabs and Jews involved a series of demonstrations, riots, and maneuvers over holy sites, culminating in the Buraq, or Wailing Wall riots of August 1929. This is also familiar territory.[41] However, when we explain this history by saying that monuments were used by one or both sides as the "touchstones" of political identity, or "quarries" of incitement, we exhume the insuperable poetics of *agency* that confronted the combatants themselves. (What motivates the architecture that motivates violence?) Here, I argue, in the erosion of architecture's instrumentality under the sign of its motivation, the politics of monuments bequeathed the play of hierophanies to politics "proper," in a "reflexive" theory of adequation. None of the contradictions that were raised by an operative understanding of architecture's adequacy to history was resolved or sublated (in the sense of a Hegelian *Aufhebung*); they were only normalized in the argument that it was possible to see and account for history directly, not in the *uses* of monuments, but in the *claims* for those uses.

Finally, the crisis of a "reflexive" theory of adequation is the constitutive and concrete paradox of politics, as it is usually conceived. Following the tragic violence of 1929, political opponents in Palestine found themselves called upon to press home their respective national imperatives via interpretations of the causes of the conflict itself, in arguments before commissions of inquiry on the origins of violence and in pamphlets propagandizing those same assertions. (This is a pattern that would be repeated several times, most notably in 1930, and again during the partition commissions of 1937 and 1938 that came on the heels of the *thawra*, or Palestinian national revolt

11

that began in 1936.) Then it became a normative practice to argue that the other side's strategic "designs" (this is the word actually used) could be read directly, in their representations of monuments—in actual pictures of architecture that were seen as instantiations of the politics they named. Clearly, this is also familiar ground to present interpreters of the conflict, for whom this reflexive vision of adequation seems to boil down to a question of the contested "propriety of cultural claims."[42] However, in reifying the representation of the political into a self-proximate politics of representation (which fails to question its own premises), the present rehearses the conflicted aesthetics of a tortured past. In part 3 of this study—called "Paper"— I suggest that with the gazetteers and their pictures, the irreducible dialectics of the image—its refusal to present itself solely as a social fact or as an autonomous form—resolved itself into a myth of the immediacy of history's mediation: a paradoxical figure of realpolitik that recalls architecture to objectivity over and over again.[43]

This, then, is the history I propose to tell, though indirectly, and some would say backward: a history of figures/monuments, which in their inadequacy to the norm of adequacy they are asked to sustain, immanently reconvene the abstract actuality of a conflict, courtesy of the recriminations of their political interpreters—a history of apotropaic response upon apotropaic response to a dialectical image, in a perverse politics that, finally, becomes indistinct from art criticism. This is a history, finally, of one of the most prolonged and favored excuses for suffering, because it has so often been hiding in plain sight—and has so long figured materially—as the explanation of suffering.

But to what end? What could be the purpose of such a history, if not to take away the excuses for an anguish that is now routine? In proposing an immanent critique of the architecture of this conflict, and in that way highlighting the constitutive (though normalized) incapacity of this struggle to account for itself, I concede that I offer few prospects for my own intervention in it. Eschewing any hope for a policy-relevant study, the reality is that I am trying, instead, to call things by their proper name.[44] To assume anything else, it seems to me, would be to break faith with the victims of this conflict's favored excuses for its own inevitability, and to acquiesce to a normative "actionism" that pays tribute to the same history of alibis by advancing a vulgar myth of its interruption.[45]

In trying to call things by their proper name, then, I am also attempting to question Israel and Palestine's history, precisely where it seems most self-evident, objective, universal, and inexorable. Because there, in the far-from-immediate immediacy of the architecture that feeds the tacit historicism of those who speak for the present state of affairs, I see the inevitable incompleteness of peace, regardless of what present or future accords may achieve at the practical level. I am, finally, contesting the today of this conflict for the sake of its past. Because in the enduring prehistory performed in the "archaeological tunnel"—and specifically, in what would pass for the historiography of the inevitability of the crisis that came with it—what emerges instead is the opposite: the story of an immense effort to conflate the excuse for suffering with the inevitability of suffering, a collusion between form and violence in a series of aesthetic occupations that stretch back to antiquity without any end in sight: "The current amazement that the things we are experiencing are 'still' possible . . . is *not* philosophical. This amazement is not the beginning of knowledge—unless it is the knowledge that the view of history which gives rise to it is untenable." [46]

THE FOUNDATION STONE

I. STONE

When an ordinary preacher of to-day uses the traditional
phrases of religion—when he speaks of hell, of Jerusalem,
of union with the Body of Christ, of the warfare between
flesh and spirit, and the contrast between earth and heaven
—he is at once understood to be dealing merely in metaphors. But to [General Gordon] . . . such phrases as these
have a meaning as literal as they had to Dante. Hell for him
is a veritable abyss of fire; the new Jerusalem is a veritable
city in the heavens; and the Jerusalem of the earth is a spot
so sacred, that the configuration of the ground it stands
upon is a *hieroglyph* designed by God.
—W. H. Mallock, "General Gordon's Message"

The Bleak Confusion of Golgotha . . . is not just a symbol of
the desolation of human existence. In it transitoriness is
not signified or allegorically represented, so much as, in its
own significance displayed as allegory.
—Walter Benjamin, *The Origin of German Tragic Drama*

IN JANUARY 1883 General Charles Gordon (1833–1885) arrived in Ottoman Palestine with the intention of identifying the precise topographic position of Golgotha (derived from the Aramaic *gulgulta*, meaning "the place of skulls"), the place of Christ's passion on the cross and presumed by Victorians to be close to the vicinity of his tomb. One of those select figures whose careers were irreverently chronicled by Lytton Strachey in his *Eminent Victorians*, this same "Chinese Gordon" had helped to quell the Taiping Rebellion in 1864, had reconstructed England's fortifications along the Thames, and, directly prior to his arrival in Palestine (while posted in the Seychelles), had engaged in a series of bizarre researches on the exact position of the Garden of Eden.[1] In the year following his investigations in Palestine, Gordon met his end in the Sudan, where, after seeking to quell the Mahdist revolt of Muhammad Ahmad, he was killed, and then posthumously beheaded during the siege of Khartoum. From that moment onward he was assumed within the pantheon of English imperial martyrs.[2]

This "Warrior of God, man's friend and tyrant's foe," as Tennyson's epitaph dubbed him, was a religious visionary so consumed with spiritual fervor that he was seemingly incapable of committing his thoughts to script without initialing "the apotropaic initials D.V. [*Deo volente*] after every statement in his letters implying futurity."[3] Yet, with both seriousness and deliberation, Gordon transposed the seventeenth-century English cleric Joseph Hall's (1574–1656) devotional articulation of an allegorical union between the body of Christ and the "members" of his religious fellowship into an ecstatic pantheism: a kind of fetishism premised upon a belief in the actual, phenomenal "in-dwelling" or penetration of Christ within the corpus of his followers.[4] A general hermeneutic strategy presented itself to Gordon in consequence of the symmetries established by this concrete union. As the elements of material reality—the landscape, the specific aspect of objects in the natural world, the geographic position of Golgotha itself—necessarily were the coded signs of divinity, then it was also apparent that the divine (or the position of divinity) could quite literally be surveyed. It has been said of Hall's own original hermeneutic that it presumed "a sermon lay behind every stone,"[5] but it would be equally fair to say that the inverse was true of Gordon, who sought to petrify the figures of Scripture into actual marks on the land.[6]

Though generally interpreted as a particularly colorful and quixotic episode within the history of that brand of evangelical imperialism inaugurated by Shaftesbury and ending, perhaps, with Lloyd George, Arthur Balfour, and Wyndham Deedes, General Gordon's private excursus into the scriptural geography of Palestine in 1883 marks instead a significant turn in the history of those conjoined aesthetic, discursive, and epistemological imperatives that Edward Said has aligned with the term "orientalism"—the "Western style for dominating, restructuring, and having authority over the Orient."[7] Marked by a "distribution of geopolitical awareness"[8] into the space of representation, orientalism as a discipline establishes dominance over an imaginary domain and rehearses there, within the space of representation, the West's historical cathexis with the actual Orient of material history.[9] Gordon's eventual "rediscovery" of Golgotha and the manner of his proof for discerning its location signal a critical moment in the restructuring of orientalism's discursive and figural practices. Though still deeply imbricated in what Said has termed the "imaginative geography" of nineteenth-century pilgrimage literature, Gordon's mission stands on the brink of the performative and "instrumental" imperatives that would dominate orientalism in its modern forms. As with the instrumental orientalists whom he anticipates, the aim of Gordon's unusual cartography is to impress the Orient into "urgent actuality."[10] More specifically, immanent within Gordon's science of manifestations—built into the insufficiency of his efforts to resolve the material world into a form of magical inherences—are the workings of a way of talking about history that would dominate modern Palestine during much of the period of British dominion there.

The general's recovery of a topographic feature that could give meaning to the Gospels' designation of Golgotha as the "place of the skull" (actually grounding Golgotha in the landscape as a motivated feature) was formulated in a simple sketch. Gordon prepared an image-in-plan so startling that, once understood, it would not only redeem the scriptural past, but explode into his present, forcing it to "become the now [*Jetzt*] of contemporary actuality."[11] Relying on original topographic surveys of Jerusalem prepared by Charles Warren of the Palestine Exploration Fund (PEF) upon the close of the Crimean War, Gordon traced the peculiar pattern of contour intervals in Warren's plan of the city (as it would appear) without what the general referred to as the cumulative "debris" of oriental history—that is, architecture. Beneath the shroud formed by the contemporary Ottoman city of Jerusalem, Gordon claimed, lay the previously concealed anamorphic figure of Christ on the cross. And at the head of this strange topographic rune, on a hill to the north of the city, lay Golgotha, the actual place of the figure's skull (figures 1 and 2): "I refer to Sir Charles Warren . . . for the explanation of the plan of Jerusalem without debris. . . . His plan shows very clearly the human figure, and only wants the skull hill to be considered with it to

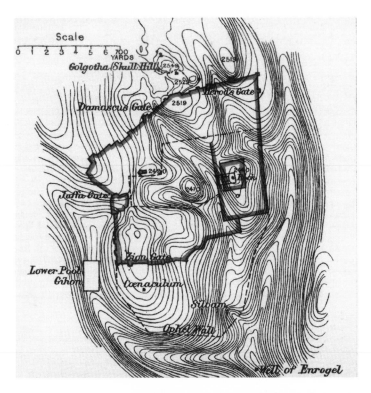

FIG. 1 C. G. Gordon's map of Jerusalem, showing the figure of Christ in the contour intervals of the terrain. Reprinted from C. G. Gordon, *Reflections in Palestine* (London, 1884), pl. 1.

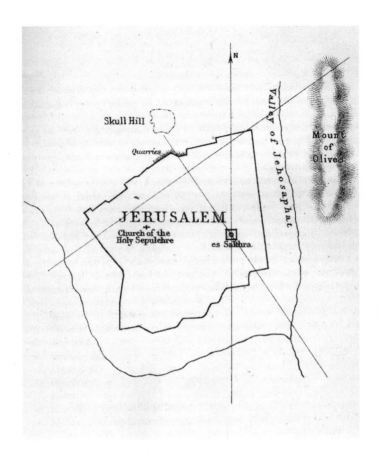

FIG. 2 C. G. Gordon's sketch of the human figure superimposed upon the map of Jerusalem. Reprinted from Charles George Gordon, "Notes on Eden and Golgotha," PEFQ, 1884.

complete it. . . . I think the cross stood on top of the skull hill, in the centre of it." [12]

Several strands of a vast historical project converge upon, merge within, and are in a sense fulfilled with Gordon's "revelation" of the anamorphic figure of Christ on the cross. In the passage of time spanning the publication of Chateaubriand's *Travels* (1812) and Volney's *Ruins of Empire* (1806) at the beginning of the nineteenth century, and the subsequent topographic descriptions of Palestine outlined in Daniel Clarke's *Travels in Various Countries* (1812), James Fergusson's *The Holy Sepulchre and the Temple of Jerusalem* (1865), Claude Reignier Conder's *Tent Work in Palestine* (1878), and culminating with Gordon's own posthumously published *Reflections in Palestine* (1884), Golgotha became the site of a geopolitical contest over its own figuration. In the space of a century, English and American scriptural geographers dislodged Golgotha from its firmly established geographic position—the site of the Church of the Holy Sepulchre, which was and remains a monument firmly in the possession of Eastern and Catholic Churches—and, by questioning the identification of the site with Golgotha on scientific and topographical grounds, successfully sublimated Calvary to the landscape itself. Moreover, this displacement both signaled and was effected through a systematic effort to supplant the privileged tropic function of Golgotha as the archetype of allegory, the very place where, as Benjamin has noted, "transience is rendered allegorical," and to represent the "petrified primordial landscape" of Jerusalem itself in a redemptive fashion, as symbol. [13]

Architecture appears at the nexus of this contest over Golgotha. During the course of the nineteenth century, the Calvary of Chateaubriand and Lamartine passes over from an established emblem of "mournful loss" (that sign of irretrievable history perpetually reconfirmed by the relation of a fixed monument to a petrified oriental landscape surrounding it) into something qualitatively different. If, for Chateaubriand, who, significantly, represented himself as the last of the pilgrims, the features of Jerusalem—the terrain and the architecture of a city marked by "flat terraces or domes . . . [that] resemble sepulchers" [14]—presented themselves only as functional fragments of an allegory intended to forever recapitulate the significance of events on Golgotha through the perceived rigor mortis of contemporary oriental forms, then for Robert Curzon, James Fergusson, Claude Conder, and their English and Protestant compatriots, the same perceived immutability of the Orient potentially reaffirmed Golgotha's symbolic function. It was precisely the "petrified unrest" of the landscape and the architecture of Jerusalem (to paraphrase Benjamin once again) that confirmed, not simply "the desolate confusion of the place of skulls," but also a Golgotha of historical redemption.[15]

I have no wish to fold the Golgotha of Walter Benjamin's theory of allegory onto the Golgotha of Gordon as an end in itself. Instead, I would like to point out the historical relation between them. For Benjamin, the decisive distinction between allegory and symbol, was not, as Goethe had argued, a distinction between particulars and universals, but one of time.[16] Referring to the work of Friedrich Creuzer, whose emphasis on the "momentary quality," of the symbol, approached what he called "the real state of affairs," Benjamin related the symbol and allegory to each other in a dialectic that pointed, by way of its abstraction, to the abstraction of history itself: "Whereas in the symbol destruction is idealized and the transfigured face of nature is fleetingly revealed in the light of redemption, in allegory the observer is confronted with the *facies hippocratica* of history as a petrified primordial landscape. Everything in that history that, from the very beginning, has been ultimately, sorrowful, unsuccessful, is expressed in a face— or rather in a death's head."[17] In working through his own temporal distinctions, however, Creuzer, in his *Symbolik und Mythologie der altern Volker* (1810), had been attempting to arrive at a lexical differentiation between Orient and Occident. The former, for Creuzer, was a "symbolic world," and the latter, its "syllogistic" counter. (Efforts at this type of distinction would continue unabated throughout the nineteenth century, as Edward Said has convincingly shown.) In summary, the spirit of romanticism's assault on allegory and baroque figural convention that Benjamin subjected to a dialectical critique in his *Trauerspiel* study, also extends to the orientalism, or "practical" romanticism, from which it is in many respects indistinct.[18]

The Calvary of scriptural geography participates in a politics of failed inherences that is similarly dialectical to the exclusion of its resolution. With the geographers' and travelers' efforts to dissociate Golgotha-as-allegory from Golgotha-as-symbol, a strange historical condition emerges. The moment of ecstatic recovery that is both desired and in some sense willed into existence by the romantic's invocation of a self-proximate symbol of redemption in a nature beyond history, cannot but be condemned to the status of a "second nature" (a "fallen nature"), in all its brutality, precisely because it enters into a chain of eternal samenesses that works through the very idea of a "natural history."[19] In its own fate, then, the failure of a politics of intrusion against the established figuration of Golgotha becomes an allegory for history. Pointing to the most remarkable secular presentations of Christ's passion within an emblematics of history, Benjamin notes: "Where

man is drawn towards the symbol, allegory emerges from the depths of being to intercept the intention, and to triumph over it."[20] Conversely, the
established emblematics of allegory of Chateaubriand and Lamartine not
only ratify a status quo of territorial possession, but, as the negation of all
that exists (of all that follows Golgotha), also stake a claim for the ownership of the name of redemption as well: "from the perspective of death, the
product of the corpse is life," after all.[21]

In *Orientalism* Edward Said has implicitly confirmed an allegorical politics
of the monument, and more specifically, of Golgotha. For example, he notes
that by the end of Lamartine's voyage to Palestine in 1833, when this human
"bundle of predispositions" has "achieved the purpose of his pilgrimage
to the Holy Sepulchre, that beginning and end point of all time and space, he
has internalized reality enough to want to retreat from it back into pure con-
templation, solitude, philosophy, poetry."[22] This is a significant point, because it was precisely in order to call into question this type of contemplative
investment that, throughout the nineteenth century, the English scriptural
geographer necessarily assumed a role akin to that of the *intriguer* in Benjamin's baroque dramas, willfully undermining the "earthly mournfulness
of allegorical interpretation" through a rhetoric of "devilish jocularity" directed against the established emblematics of the monument.[23] Clearing the
path toward an alternative aesthetics of intervention, modern travelers to
Palestine from Robert Curzon onward railed against what they perceived to
be both the phenomenal and tropic cornerstone of allegory, the martyrium
at the center of the Church of the Holy Sepulchre.[24] Edward Clarke expresses
this antagonism most clearly in his own description of the church:

> Quaresmius, by an engraving for the illustration of the mode of burial
> then practiced, has shewn, according to a model familiar to the learned
> monk, from his residence in the Holy Land where such sepulchres now
> exist, the sort of tomb described by the Evangelists. But there is nothing
> of this kind in the Church of the Holy Sepulchre. . . . In order to do away
> with this glaring inconsistency, it is affirmed that Mount Calvary was
> levelled for the foundations of the church; that the word . . . *mons*, does
> not necessarily signify mountain, but sometimes a small hill; that the
> sepulchre of Christ, alone remained after this levelling had taken place,
> in the centre of the area; and that this was encased in marble![25]

This then was the modern skeptic's strategy: as he revealed that architecture necessarily confirmed that the presumed position of a Golgotha was
artifice, he affirmed that another recoverable, latent, and authentic Calvary

could be redeemed in an ever present topography that only needed to be brought "out of infinite distance into infinite closeness."[26] Stating that, "from [the] elevated summit [of the Mount of Olives] almost all the features of the city may be discerned," the message of Clarke's own disbelief was that "the features of Nature continue the same, though works of art have been done away."[27] And the same theme was elaborated in various and productive forms. Following the toponymic strategy employed by Edward Robinson in his *Biblical Researches in Palestine*, the massive *Survey of Western Palestine* conducted by the PEF not only produced accurate maps of the Holy Land (some of which were subsequently used by the British army in its conquest during the campaign of 1917–1918), but also compiled a series of indices relating contemporary Arabic place names to sites described in the Bible or the Gospels.[28]

Similarly, James Fergusson's researches on the ancient topography of Jerusalem not only raised questions concerning the authenticity of the Church of the Holy Sepulchre but necessarily pointed in the direction where an alternative and authentic Golgotha would have to lie. Fergusson combined topographic speculation with architectural history and concluded that a transference of holy sites had taken place during the Middle Ages, a fraud in which the original martyrium of Christ (in his view, the Dome of the Rock itself), had been taken over by the Muslim conquerors of Jerusalem. In his view, Christian clerics had consequently erected a dummy monument (the present Church of the Holy Sepulchre), whose own proxy status had been obscured by time. For the Anglican visitor, the payoff of Fergusson's theory was that the site of the Hebrew Temple and the site of the passion were now conflated into one. As far as Fergusson was concerned, the morphology of Dome of the Rock confirmed this view. The monument could not have been erected by Muslims, he suggests, because it displays " a beauty of proportion and appropriateness of detail which we do not find in their [Islamic] works."[29] Fergusson's conclusions were in turn popularized by George Grove of the PEF, and by Dr. William Smith in his *Dictionary of the Bible: Comprising Its Antiquities, Biography, Geography, and Natural History* (1858).[30]

So successful were the endeavors of these revisionists that by the latter half of the nineteenth century, no special knowledge of scriptural geography, architecture, or evangelical history were required in order to articulate this new fetishism of landscape. For example, in her *Wanderings over Bible Lands and Seas* (1873), Elizabeth Rundle Charles succinctly reiterated the original "intriguers" formula, stating that the time-worn paths of Palestine were in themselves the most holy of sites, since "the ways traced out almost

25

unconsciously by the feet of men outlive the laborious erections of their hands."[31]

However, at the same time as this enveloping and infinitely productive mystical imperialism assimilated the aspect of geographic research, cartography itself advanced inexorably toward the resurrection. In the very rigor of their methods, the same series of surveys, archaeological researches, and topographic analyses that unseated the Golgotha "encased in marble," all seemed to anticipate Gordon's moment of ecstatic recovery. So, in 1878, following the moment when the PEF's own Claude Reignier Conder concluded that Golgotha (the "place of skulls") had to be a "rounded knoll" actually shaped like a skull (on the toponymic assumption that place-names in Jerusalem were not arbitrary but logically had to correspond in form or use to what they designated), all that was required to complete the motivation of landscape not only into the emblem of divinity but also into divinity's material trace, was the introduction of Gordon's novel hermeneutic strategy: his willful petrification of the figures of biblical prose into material presences.[32]

This is not to suggest that this next step was uncontested. An essay in the *Palestine Exploration Fund Quarterly* (published the year after Conder records the discovery of this "northern" Calvary) advised future researchers against "trying to find a rock shaped like a skull." This article, probably intended as an admonishment of Conder, the field director of the PEF, is remarkable for its conclusion that the toponymic "skull hill" could only be a fiction, a "piece of very beautiful symbolism."[33] However, in the imperative of recovery that overtakes the search for a Golgotha of landscape, the cautions of the essayist appear too late. At the moment when he warns against the possibility of attaining the skull, the retrieval of the entire corpse is imminent. Only five years later, in his posthumously published "Notes on Eden and Golgotha," Gordon completed the logic of manifestations that had been developing in his compatriots' critique of others' vulgar logic of manifestations, noting that "the mention of the Place of the skull in each of the four Gospels is a call to attention. . . . [I]f the skull is mentioned four times, one naturally looks for the body, and if you take Warren's or others' contours with the earth or rubbish removed showing the natural state of the land, you cannot help seeing that there is a body, that Schick's conduit is the oesophagus, that the quarries are the Chest, *and if you are venturesome you will carry out the analogy further.*"[34]

In its implausibility as a religious achievement, Gordon's anamorphic figure implies a historical, secular victory; when viewed in relation to the history of European intentions in the eastern Mediterranean, the historical passage from the Golgotha of the French Catholic Chateaubriand to the Calvary of the British and [eccentrically] Protestant Gordon is not incidental. As I have already intimated, each phase of this passage exists in a complex historical relation with the highly nuanced practices of great power politics in the Ottoman Empire during an era dominated by what was then called the Eastern Question.[35] If, as many scholars have argued, Napoleon's attempt to outflank his European rivals in Egypt may be seen as the inaugural event of this new age of empire, it is because from that time onward the strategic imperatives of the great powers toward one another would henceforth be played out deep within the Ottoman Empire, through the surrogacy of regional leaders, and at times, as an extended dramaturgy or war of gestures. England, France, Russia, and later, the Austro-Hungarian Empire, Bismarck's Germany, and Italy, each sought ways to consolidate their respective positions while attempting to deny the others' advances.[36]

This condition of perpetual and fluid maneuver at the level of international politics coincided with the passage toward the intensified ideology of engagement that Edward Said has described as orientalism's "worldliness": a preconscious political instrumentality of contemporary European researches in the Orient, which, in a fashion similar to the diplomatic contest, also attempted to maintain "a flexible relational superiority" toward its object.[37] Elsewhere Said explains the connection between such practices and imperialism as one akin to the relation between culture and society as a whole, so that the latter might be understood as the condition of possibility for the former.[38] Here, the argument goes, the realm of necessity (society) creates the aspect of a sphere beyond itself (culture), as a precondition for its own perpetuation.[39]

Reading cultural production as the manifest content of latent historical forces, other scholars have, in a similar fashion, looked to the progression of emblematic texts I have already cited—the published researches of Clarke, Fergusson, and Conder on scriptural geography, leading to Gordon's own "recovery" of Golgotha—and treated these as ideologically coextensive with the so-called Eastern Question itself. For example, in *Digging for God and Country: Exploration in the Holy Land, 1799–1917*, Neil Asher Silberman relates Daniel Clarke's researches to contemporary geopolitical circumstances, noting that he arrived on the shores of Palestine in one of Lord Nelson's supply ships.[40] Various scholars have also associated Fergusson's researches on the architecture of the Hebrew Temple and the Dome of the Rock to the Syrian Crises of the 1830s, since it was during the decade of

A HIEROGLYPH DESIGNED BY GOD

Ibrahim Pasha's governorship of Palestine that a surveyor named Frederick Catherwood was permitted to enter the Haram al-Sharif in Jerusalem, the enclosure within which the Dome of the Rock stands and where the Jewish Temple once stood. He subsequently produced plans on the basis of which Fergusson arrived at the remarkable conclusion that this monument had to be the original martyrium of Jesus, rather than the Church of the Holy Sepulchre.[41] Barbara Tuchman, in a well-known history of England's engagement with Palestine, refers to the work of the PEF's engineers, post-Crimea, as a classic instance of Bible and sword "working together unmistakably"; in those labors, she sees the "epitome of British experience in Palestine, always a double thing composed of biblical nostalgia and imperial thrust."[42] Similarly, Naomi Shepard has related Conder's completion of the survey of Palestine to worsening Anglo-Ottoman relations following the Eastern Crises of 1877–1878 and to renewed fears that Russia would attempt to reassert its prerogatives in Palestine.[43]

And yet, the very demand that we acknowledge the seemingly obvious intrusion of politics into this history of figuration is itself far from obvious, because the claim for the political transparency of such presentations of Golgotha (or even the argument for a latent politics behind manifest appearances) is *itself* also part of a continuing history of "symbolic" recuperations of Golgotha. Looking back to the history of Palestine during the nineteenth century, and specifically of the cartographic sciences that lead inexorably toward Gordon's Calvary, one witnesses an overlay of sorts. As the symbolic recuperation of divinity lapsed into an allegory for mundane history of imperial imperatives, that same process tacitly sustained the argument for the symbolic immediacy of architecture—propped up a science of manifestations—in the belief that the monuments of Jerusalem, and even the city itself, were the unmediated reflections of a secular realpolitik. (A realpolitik that endures as the irreducible given of twentieth- and twenty-first-century historiography of those efforts.) Architecture becomes the brute immediacy of the political. Strangely, when seen from this perspective the logic of orientalism can well be seen as one of socially necessary "appearances"—of ideology—but to the degree that it sustains the syntagmatic, architectonic, relation of equivalences between latent histories and manifest appearances, so can its critique; that is, the critique of orientalism becomes a new species of orientalism.[44]

My argument, then, is that immanent within the history of the failure of history to inhere in its repositories is the secret preservation of the belief in such inherences. For Chateaubriand, the same "synchronic essentialism" that maintained the rigor mortis of evangelic history as an active presence, simultaneously presented itself as the mark of oriental despotism.[45] For Clarke, Curzon, and their compatriots, the same "inauthentic" holy sites venerated by the Catholic and Eastern Churches were, nevertheless, the "authentic" manifestations of European and Russian political imperatives, the very mirrors of modern political duplicities. By 1918, upon the conquest of Palestine by the British, C. R. Ashbee, the first civic adviser to the governor of Jerusalem could claim that he was able to read the city's various religious compounds as a reflection of the entire political history of the Eastern Question leading to the fall of the Ottoman Empire during World War I:

> Coming into the City from the old pilgrim route, Mons Gaudii, we notice how the ancient Jerusalem is all but obliterated; we see the once Golden dome no longer, we see a bastard Florence, a bastard Nuremberg, a bastard Moscow, an imitation Louvres, a Bavarian suburb and an imitation Oxford. . . . All modern building seems to have been strangely prophetic of the War. The Austrians and the French have perhaps shown most reserve. The Italians lavish wildly their surplus funds from the Boxer indemnity, the Russians have spread themselves rather naively over vast areas of land, the Germans with a hard pretentiousness have established their worship of Caesar or made in the Weisenhaus a Bavarian enclave; incidentally they have selected the most commanding military points. The English in a sort of cold and aristocratic aloofness have shut themselves up in a college court of their own. All have been alike in their use of mechanism, without any reference to the finer life of the City; all with the possible exception of the Moslem, who has not yet discovered it."[46]

Having arrived at the specter of the anticipatory function assigned to architecture's anterior reflection—in other words, having come to the paradox articulated by Ashbee when he retroactively reads monuments as prefigurations of a global conflict—I do so with a purpose other than finding fault with the ideology of history (an ideology of manifestations) that attends the telling of this history. Once again, my aim is not to police the figures of this historical conflict, but to write a fragmentary history of the same figures. What is most significant in presenting a history of the representation of history as a brandished monument, or as an apotropaic gesture, is the very usefulness of the civic adviser's sublimation of the monument into a "reflection" of concrete political events, as contrasted with Gordon's willful "petrification" of Christ's reflection into matter. If historiography reveals that Gordon's myth of recuperation is in some sense *instrumental*—in other words, that it is a "tool" or "reflection" of political history—then conversely, Gordon's Golgotha brings to crisis this same comfortable epistemology of immediacy—revealing in modern pronouncements about what such mystical petrifications really mean in political terms—the *mythic* character of historiographic scrutiny's own instrumental reason, its own resolution of history into expedient forms of causality.

Consequently, between the petrification of history and its arrested reflection one encounters the originary historical features of the abstraction of which I am attempting to provide an initial glimpse here: a vision of adequation suspended, dialectically, between its magical and operative figuration. During the nineteenth century the same scientific attitude that would nullify the allegory of the monument, and in its logic render landscape symbolic (redeem it as immediately present), effectively brought to light a historical actuality within which the same instrumental reason that cast light on the myth of Golgotha inaugurated its own myth and, as such, lapsed into an allegory of history, a ruin of its own strategic imperatives. At the same time, however, a hope for symbols survived in those ruins. In the very "self-consciousness" of the failure of that project of recovery, a secular myth of the monument's political transparency was also being erected all along, an operative vision that sees each recovery of the sacred as nothing more than the historical triumph of the profane. The secular critique of hierophanies is itself hierophany. In the Golgotha of scriptural geography redemption withers "under an undialectically mythical glance, the glance of Medusa."[47]

II. TILE

These changes give some, though not a complete, idea of
the tendency for the building continually to adapt itself to
new conditions. This tendency still continues, as it has continued for twelve centuries and more. And though, through
this process of change and adaptation much have been lost
that might in other circumstances have been preserved—
and though, to that extent, it is to be regretted—it may yet,
on the other hand, be welcomed by many as an unmistakable sign of a determination to maintain the building, if
not altogether in its original, at least in some form, and as a
proof of continued vitality in the ideas and beliefs that the
building has, except for the short period of the Frank occupation, symbolized without interruption from the seventh
century to the present day. For change has been a condition
of the building's existence and of its continued power to
represent those ideas. Had there been no change the building would have disappeared.

—Ernest Tatham Richmond, *The Dome of the Rock in Jerusalem*

In profane matters the instrument derives its worth from the end, and is valued for the most part only so far as it is a means to that end; and consequently we change the instrument as the end demands, and finally when the end is no longer pursued the instruments automatically fall into disuse. But in sacred matters the end invests the instrument with a sanctity of its own. Consequently there is no changing or varying the instrument; and when the end has ceased to be pursued the instrument does not fall out of use, but is directed towards another end; in the one case we preserve the shell for the sake of the kernel, and discard the shell when we have eaten the kernel; in the other case we raise the shell to the dignity of the kernel and do not rob it of that dignity even if the kernel withers, but make a new kernel for it.

—Ahad Ha'am, "Sacred and Profane"

How could they have an inkling of beauty who saw in everything only matter?

—G. W. F. Hegel, "The Spirit of Christianity and Its Fate"

34   IN SEPTEMBER 1934, fifty years after General Gordon "discovered" the anthropomorphic Calvary to the north of Jerusalem, and seventeen years after Great Britain gained suzerainty over the Holy Land, Ernest Tatham Richmond, the director of Palestine's Department of Antiquities, published a tract on the sites of the crucifixion and the resurrection.[1] "In the course of this book," he would later record, "I destroyed any yet lingering belief in General Gordon's fantastic 'Garden Tomb,' as the true site."[2] Richmond's tract is actually a metahistory of that "lingering belief," following in the tradition of L. H. Vincent's "Garden Tomb: L'Histoire d'un mythe" and C. W. Wilson's *Golgotha and the Holy Sepulchre*—two studies that cast a skeptical eye on the already skeptical eye that Anglo-American geography itself had cast upon the traditional holy sites.[3] But if Vincent, in particular, only contested that venerable tradition of skepticism "in passing," as he challenged the authenticity of the so-called Garden Tomb by reminding the world that the logic evinced by its supporters was not altogether distinct from the "rabbinically tainted" mysticism of Gordon, Richmond differs from Vincent in a crucial sense: his is a retrospective glance upon the entire theory of the monument's adequacy to history of which that tradition of skepticism was a part.[4] To him, what was actually cast into doubt by the "traditional" holy sites is the idea that history presents itself—in all its immediacy—in the secular uses to which those same icons have been put. For him, the truth of the holy sites, properly understood, simply liquidated a modern reduction of architecture to mundane utility of a political sort.

In its specific organization, Richmond's The Sites of the Crucifixion and the Resurrection (1934) is actually a prolonged rejoinder to Wilson, who had attempted to outline the most significant historical and archaeological questions that would force themselves upon any modern attempt to authenticate the original site of the Holy Sepulchre.[5] In its broader intentions, however, Richmond's pamphlet is an assault on the normative historical consciousness that attends modern arguments for or against the traditional sites to begin with, and as such it approaches an Ideologiekritik of Wilson's "questions."[6] Wilson, for example, suggested that the arguments favoring the traditional sites necessarily rested upon an unsubstantiated belief in a "continuous tradition" of knowledge, the supposition of a collective memory that permitted Jerusalem's Christians to identify the exact site of Golgotha for Emperor Constantine three hundred years after the crucifixion. (Following from this, he also suggested that much also depended on the "attitude of the early Christians towards holy places," since modern researchers would have to explain the paradoxical passage from the aniconic worship of the Jewish followers of Jesus to the "cult" of monuments that emerged with the construction of the Church of the Holy Sepulchre in the fourth century C.E.)[7] Richmond acknowledges these points but suggests that implicit in any demand for evidence of a "continuous tradition" is a similarly unexamined presumption of inauthenticity, or (continuation of) a normative tradition of suspicion which held that Constantine fabricated religious monuments and fostered a "fetishistic cult of Holy Places" to serve as instruments of his own, secular ends, and that the Church perpetuated this "reprehensible course" into the present (for example, in the archaeological researches of Vincent and the archaeologists of the École biblique): "Briefly, the suggestions [of the skeptics] amounted to this: that no one really knew or cared where the sites were; that Constantine acted for political ends; and that the Church acted in a manner that was at once fraudulent and materialistic."[8]

For Richmond, the demystification of myth inaugurates its own myth, a myth of utility which, in destroying a certain noble conception of the monument's function, in itself has political uses. In other words, the stink of the political emerges from the modern cult of utility and the instrumental reason that attends it and not from an originary fetishism of monuments in the past. Seen in this light, Richmond's pamphlet assumes the character of an allegory of noxious modernity, or that "great fog," as he describes it. And this allegorical dimension betrays itself in the use of the term "materialistic," which in Richmond's lexicon is regularly a cipher for the contemporary political circumstances in which he was implicated. In the parable of materialism that Richmond constructs, each of the relevant contemporary actors assumes a role directly analogous to the dramatis personae in the tacit conspiracy of monuments Richmond debunks, that is, Constantine, the Catholic Church, and even the "Romanist" archaeologists of the École Biblique, all of whom (according to the normative skepticism of which Richmond is skeptical) contrived to motivate the already motivated relation between people and icons to their own ends.

This requires some elaboration. Before assuming the position of director of the Department of Antiquities in 1927, Richmond had served in the first British civil administration in Palestine, from 1920 and 1924. He is actually best known (some would say "notorious") for his work during that brief period when, as assistant secretary for political affairs (A.S. Pol.) under High Commissioner Herbert Samuel, he functioned as the government's principal liaison with Palestinian political and religious elites.[9] During his tenure in that office, and in a context of some intrigue and political confusion, Richmond worked to elevate Muhammad Hajj Amin al-Husayni to the position of grand mufti of Palestine, and to constitute a Supreme Muslim Council (SMC) (what Richmond called a "Central Moslem Authority") under the presidency of the same Hajj Amin.[10] The new grand mufti and the SMC quickly assumed important roles in the organization of Palestinian political affairs, advancing the independent aspirations of Palestinian Arabs and their opposition to Zionism. Architecture assumed an important position in that enterprise. With Richmond's active assistance, these Majlissiyyun—or members of the faction of the SMC and the Husaynis—undertook international fund-raising efforts for the restoration of the Haram al-Sharif in Jerusalem, a project which, in its appeal as a defense of Jerusalem's Muslim holy sites from Zionism, often relied on claims that Jews were poised to take over the Aqsa for the purpose of rebuilding the Solomonic Temple.[11] The grand mufti, the SMC, and their adjuncts were also important participants in political struggles between Arabs and Jews over the Buraq, or Wailing Wall, a contest that, according to most observers, culminated in the mass violence of August 1929.[12] Richmond resigned the secretarial post in the spring of 1924, having come to the conclusion that in its commitment to the Jewish national home policy, England had become the servant of a materialist Leviathan for which Zionism was the vanguard in the East.[13] Given his perceived partisanship in Palestinian politics, Richmond's reappointment to the post of antiquities director in 1927 was made specifically contingent upon his willingness to promise Lord Plumer, the successor to Herbert Samuel as high commissioner, that he would refrain from any further political involvement in the country's affairs.[14]

The end of the overtly political Richmond, however, roughly coincided with charges of what his detractors called "Richmondism." By the time he penned his treatise on holy sites—two years following the mass violence that shocked the country in 1929—Richmond was only too aware of the fact that just like Constantine and the Catholic Church of the skeptics' imagination, the grand mufti and the SMC were accused of using monuments ("in a manner at once fraudulent and materialistic") for self-interested political purposes, in this case mobilizing the Palestinian masses against Zionism.[15] Moreover, Richmond also knew that like Père Vincent and the archaeologists of the École biblique, he himself was suspect of gerrymandering antiquity to mischievous ends[16] and, far worse, that according to the revisionist Zionist journalist Itamar Ben-Avi he was a "man of mystery" who secretly used the users of monuments to wreak havoc upon the country:

> I do maintain that, as the "Lawrence of Palestine," he is our "Man of Mystery," whose actions are not seen but known, not written but felt, everywhere and in every way. In short, "Richmondism" with all that it thus signifies, now permeates the air of our local Government, and I do not even shrink from throwing upon his shoulders, more than upon those of any others, the responsibility for the "Wailing Wall Atrocities" —dreamed, nay willed by him, though he was physically absent momentarily from the scenes of operations.[17]

Even these accusations that Richmond is the mastermind who "uses" those who use monuments to mobilize others falls prey to his critique of materialism, however. Insofar as such accusations subsume mass behavior within a means-ends rationale, they merely—in Richmond's mind—perpetuate the vulgar logic of modernity itself. For Richmond, the relation between the theory of "uses" advanced by religious skeptics in the case of the Catholic holy sites, and the skepticism advanced by the Zionist "accusers" in the matter of the Wall is not analogical but historical. Their skepticism, as he understands it, is the epistemology appropriate to a creeping materialism in history, a crude though metastasizing worldview that can only present things in its own likeness. As he elaborated his own opposition to this type of thinking, Richmond shows himself to be a Christian idealist who merged three models.[18] Like A. W. N. Pugin, or Thomas Carlyle, Richmond condemned the intrusion of "Mammonism" (as the normative consciousness of a capitalist modernity) into a world previously marked by an *authentic* relation between essences and appearances; a world in which "all visible things," according to Carlyle, are not traces or reflections of material causes, but present themselves instead as "emblems [in which] matter exists only spiritually, and to represent some Idea, and *body* it forth."[19] Following Hilaire Belloc, whose writings he studied closely, Richmond argued that this process began with the Protestant Reformation, and that Mammon's expropriation of the vestments of transcendence (its reduction of essences to appearances) was consequently not the outcome of a structural historical change—the formation of industrial capital—but rather the result of an *agency* aided by the "servile state," an exploitation of the many by the few.[20] Much like G. K. Chesterton and Hilaire Belloc, Richmond located this agency within "a Jewish oligarchy, only partially assimilated into English life."[21] However, in parallel with the thought of a contemporary Catholic cleric named Dennis Fahey, Richmond globalizes this phenomenon.[22] In an idealist recapitulation of the "Conspiracy of the Elders of Zion," Richmond believed the "International Jewish Money Power," the Russian Revolution, and Zionism were part of a unitary plot to reduce Spirit (*Geist*) to a history of its manifestations, in a process that "implied the ultimate destruction both of Christianity and of Islam."[23] As he explained in an anonymously published essay of 1926: "In the new world order thus foreshadowed, the Jewish race, itself the veritable Messiah, modernized in thought and detached from any supernatural belief, will sit, as it were, at the golden tables feeding upon Behemoth and Leviathan, or in other words, upon the fruits of the whole earth and the harvest of its seas gathered by the labour of a Gentile world, which we may imagine to have been reduced to servile conditions by a cultivated materialism."[24]

In its reasoning, then, Richmond's reprehensible anti-Semitism bears a romantic pedigree. A Judaism "modernized in thought and detached from any supernatural belief" is tantamount to an abrogation of Spirit (*Geist*), a fetishism of means.[25] Like the Hebrews in Derrida's brilliant reading of Hegel's *Spirit of Christianity and Its Fate*, Richmond's Jew is consequently "stranger to the symbol" because the "split between the infinite and the finite" performed in a signifying object "blinds him, deprives him of all power to represent to himself the infinite concretely."[26] This blindness, Derrida explains, reconstitutes apotropaism as a historical principle in Hegel's thought: the Jews' lack in turn refigures/reduces all "sensible representation" to "a materialist weapon": "seeing in the sensible representations only wood and stone—matter—he [the Jew] easily rejects them as idols."[27] However, if in Hegel's thought the Jews' negative relation to representation is triumphally eclipsed by the genius of Christianity (precisely because of its capacity to arrive at "the intermediate schema of an incarnation in wanting"), in the modernity that Hegel never lived to see, Richmond in turn sees the potential eclipse of that historical triumph.[28] In the materialism that refused to acknowledge the *devotional* function of an entire culture's monuments "to things unseen," Richmond argued, lay a new civilization's servile iconism to things "seen."[29] The postwar world, then, was suspended in a tenuous balance between an authentic vision of adequation (an understanding of the devotional uses of material symbols that was maintained by the amalgam of Islam and Catholicism that Richmond described as "Mediterranean Culture") and an inauthentic one perpetrated by an "Anglo-Saxon-Judaic World" intent upon reifying its own secular logic of utility as if it were reason per se.[30] Seen in this light, Richmond's critique of materialism is historically significant because it represents the precise moment at which the operative project of adequation renders itself ideologically transparent, but cannot configure its own dissolution as the inauguration of an alternative, reflexive politics of adequation.[31] Richmond never abandons the idea that history is confirmed as immediate in monuments' uses. He only rejects the uses to which that idea has been put.

A complex understanding of architecture emerges in tandem with Richmond's effort to divorce an operative vision of adequation from crude instrumentality. As he assaults a contemporary modernity by arguing for a distinction between the fetishism of matter and a phenomenology of Spirit (i.e., matter as the manifestation of an immanent idea), he subjects architecture to a similar "stereotomy": in an apotropaic fashion, Richmond attempts to present the monument as a "mark" that is as solid as stone, "re-marked in its essential traits as the same," and to deny the element within it that is errant and "freed from all determined bonds of origin."[32] Elaborated in his private, anonymous, pseudonymous, and public writings between 1919 and 1929, the most comprehensive presentations of this conception appeared, first, in his study of the Dome of the Rock (written in 1919 and revised for publication in 1923–1924) but were reworked later, in his pamphlet on the Christian holy sites written in 1931. In these works one immediately perceives that Richmond's idealist vision of history precludes any iconic—or magical—understanding of adequation; that is, precludes any reassertion of a simple identity between the mutable and the immutable in an object (à la Gordon). To the contrary, in Richmond's view the iconic position was actually the one maliciously projected onto Catholicism by "befogged Western heretics" like Wilson, who, in falsely debunking a putative "magical" understanding of adequation—that is, in "demystifying" an idolatry nowhere actually present in traditional Christian devotion to holy sites—tacitly assert an *arbitrary* relation between the symbol and its meanings.[33] Richmond recognizes that to assert such a relation of contingency between history and its clothing is, paradoxically, to reassert a kind of iconism (precisely where one has denied it), since the skeptics' arguments concerning a worldly "cult of holy places" presupposes the equation of architecture with secular politics. Eschewing this regressive understanding of the symbol and its uses, Richmond does not argue for an *identity* between monuments and the historical truth they "body forth" but asserts instead that in holy sites immutable Spirit is immanent within mutable matter, rendering the relation between them as one of *necessity*. For Richmond, the immediacy confirmed by architecture is a *function* of its instrumentality in the perpetual reassertion of an idea:

> None of the efforts made to decry ancient traditions and to deride ancient usages have succeeded, either in shaking the validity of ancient tradition or in uprooting from the minds of men the natural and normal instinct to venerate these venerable sites. . . . Should the present building collapse, or should it, like its predecessors, be destroyed, it cannot be doubted that another would, in due time, rise from the ruins, once more to make manifest the veneration in which men must always hold the sites of the Crucifixion and the Resurrection of Our Lord.[34]

Along with this presentation of architecture's *historical* purpose comes a critique of the arguments of a dominant materialism concerning how people "use" architecture, and/or conversely, concerning how architecture, in its significance, can activate people. These were arguments, as it turns out, that were already implicit in Wilson's original question concerning the "continuous tradition of knowledge" and in his query about the creation of a "cult of holy sites." (Needless to say, Richmond also believed these to extend into contemporaneous political circumstances. For this reason they needed to be debunked.)[35] In the first place, the question of the "continuous tradition" posed by Wilson was, in reality, a question of agency. Understanding the "veneration of venerable" monuments as a form of volition in the "minds of men," Richmond calls into question the implicit mass psychology of the skeptics. In effect, Richmond challenges the presupposition that the mass is always already constituted by a thirst for obedience or a passive horde mentality that permits cynical elites to manipulate the faithful through the use of transitional objects, in this instance, holy sites. Like Freud, whose thinking he would in every other way probably have reviled, Richmond asks instead "what makes the masses into masses" to begin with.[36] The answer, he concludes, lies in the question. At the moment when the skeptics' vision of the masses is disclosed to be at one with a materialist understanding of causality, Richmond suggests, one can no longer see holy sites as the implements for the manipulation of the few by the many, but rather as the points of an organic transitivity used by the few to *become* a coherent many. A very different understanding of architecture's purpose from that of the skeptics is contained here. For Richmond, the immediacy of history, as the very idea of the proximity of the masses' "archaic inheritance," sustains itself self-consciously in a people's active nurturing of the spiritual potential in the sensual; in other words, in the way they uphold the vestiary relation between architecture and what it commemorates as a relation of immanence. Any skepticism concerning the "continuous tradition of knowledge," in Richmond's understanding of events, is nothing less than part of a modern effort to obscure the uninterrupted perpetuation of this type of organic agency in the Christian and Mediterranean worlds:

> They [the early Christians] knew that future generations would desire to visit these places in order to gain the satisfaction and the advantages that fall to normal human beings who, following a natural instinct, use material memorials for the purpose of keeping alive memories that are precious to them. They knew that Jesus Himself had made use of the sensible to convey the spiritual. They were aware, as we are aware, that the spirit is stimulated through the senses. These writers of the Gospels would have regarded it, no less than normal people must still regard it, as folly to suggest that carefully to note the sites, as they noted them, was contrary to the spirit of the Gospels they themselves wrote, and to suggest that, in so doing, they were acting in a manner that was out of harmony with the teaching of Jesus as recorded by one of them (John iv, 21ff). They, like normally intelligent and healthy humanity in subsequent ages, including our own, would not have confounded two distinct orders of ideas, on the one hand the veneration of a site associated with events of transcendent importance, and on the other its superstitious adoration.[37]

In the same instant when Richmond locates architecture's adequacy to history in the monument's activation of the idea it renders manifest, Wilson's (and his successors') question about a "cult of holy sites" suddenly presents itself in a new light, as a query about the *motivation* of symbols. If, from the skeptics' perspective, the paradox of an originally aniconic Jewry erecting iconic memorials to Jesus could only be resolved by casting doubt upon the authenticity of those same memorials, toponymy presented itself to them as a viable method for researching scriptural geography because it presupposed a field beyond human intention, or "superstition" as they most often referred to it. To Richmond, however, this is precisely why toponymy revealed itself as a suspect strategy. In his view, any attempt to authenticate holy sites by asserting a necessary identity between topographic features and the names originally assigned to them—in the way, for example, that Gordon's Golgotha was presumed to be genuine because it was a hill shaped like a skull—was itself to surrender to vulgar iconism.

The path to this iconic belief in the identity between a place-name and its topographic or functional character was paved by the skeptics' distrust of architecture, or, in Richmond's words, by their "fantastic suggestion" that people, through their labor, motivate the significance of monuments rather than discover eternal motivation in them.[38] Against the skeptics' (toponymic) myth of demystification (and in consonance with his idealist/structuralist understanding of *logos*) Richmond argues that the very significance of the sites associated with evangelical history is itself what *guaranteed* their progressive distantiation—by architecture—from the realm of the merely existent. Describing the Church of the Holy Sepulchre in precisely this way, Richmond suggests that the building was nothing less than the ongoing elaboration, over sixteen centuries, of an originary structuring activity, an objectification that began when Constantine's architects "decided to isolate the Sepulchre from the non-essential rock that surrounded it"[39] (figure 3). As a gesture that clearly precluded any confusion of "two distinct orders of ideas"—that is, a phenomenology of Spirit and the fetishism of things themselves—Richmond believed that this isolation of the "essential" from the "nonessential" was precisely how early Christians sought "to give adequate architectural expression to their natural veneration for these sites."[40] Progressive transformations had to be understood in much the same way. For Richmond, the perpetual refiguration of architecture confirmed its status as the mutable mark of the immutable, the very clothing of Geist:

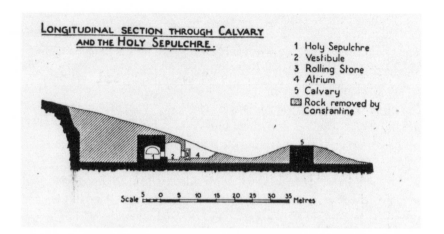

FIG. 3 Cross-section of the Church of the Holy Sepulchre (according to E. T. Richmond), indicating the way that Constantine's architects "decided to isolate the Sepulchre from the non-essential rock that surrounded it." Reprinted from Ernest Tatham Richmond, *The Sites of the Crucifixion and the Resurrection* (London, 1937), 32.

That conviction [of the early Christians that "adequate" architectural expression to their "natural veneration" for holy sites should be permitted to stand in Jerusalem] has remained firmly rooted in the minds of Christians for more than fifty generations; so firmly, that it has always succeeded in *remanifesting* itself, in some sort of architectural form, even after the worst disasters due to natural causes, as well as the most savage demolitions, due to religious animosity and fanaticism. Thus that conviction has always proved *indestructible*; and it has never been possible entirely to thwart the act of giving some sort of architectural expression to the desire that it has always generated.[41]

Arriving in this way at a world of imperishable "convictions," Richmond teases an idealist understanding of the monument's function out of the wreckage of a materialist theory of adequation. He tells the story of a *projection*: arguing that the proponents of a normative, though flawed, theory of architecture's uses are forced by the paradoxes built in to their own representations of the monument's utility to revert to a vulgar idolatry. By its own inadequacy to the measure of adequacy it purports to name, this idolatry in turn ratifies the very "indestructibility" of what the skeptics presumed themselves to have canceled: the commensurability of architecture to reality, in its *historical* function as the vestment of transcendental truths.

43

But the inverse is simultaneously true. Viewed historically, Richmond's presentation of a materialism that privileges what it disavows is actually a projection of *his own* failure to establish a stereotomic distinction between architecture as the legitimate raiment of Spirit and what he elsewhere refers to as "drapery," "camouflage," or "humbug," to denote the intrusion of the arbitrary into a necessary semantic relation between idea and form, kernel and shell.[42] The trail of Richmond's writings and political interventions between 1919 and 1929 constitute the record of an immense effort to assert a proper theory of architecture's uses, that is, to interpret architecture's job as the constructive anticipation of Spirit. Richmond considered this an urgent task. And yet, in each of his attempts to assert this crucial alignment, the emergence of a contingent relation between buildings and their meaning, *where only a motivated one had been presumed to exist*, similarly guaranteed that the question of "uses"—that is, of agency—could only assert itself as a contradiction in Richmond's thought. To this crisis he assigned the name "politics," effectively treating the moment of architecture's errancy—the corruption of semantic motivation—as the mischief of others. The paradox, here, is that in assigning blame in this fashion Richmond gives priority to a form of agency he otherwise denies. Richmond cannot allege the "remanifestation" of Geist in the Mediterranean world without invoking (and indeed, privileging) the actuating "draperies" of a Anglo-Saxon-Judaic political conspiracy; one that maneuvers the significances of monuments, transforming them into the instruments of its own ends.

If Richmond's pamphlet on the sites of the crucifixion is, as I suggest, actually an allegory of contemporary events, this is not simply because the dramatis personae of his own exposition (Constantine, the Church, and Catholic archaeologists) correspond to the various figures who accuse and are accused of "using" architecture to political ends in the Palestine of his own day, himself included. The pamphlet is an allegory, more importantly, because despite their messianic promise of a "fulfilled" time (to paraphrase Benjamin), the successive logical triumphs against skepticism that are achieved there actually pay suit to history as the persistence of the condition in which "no one can really live in fulfilled time."[43]

I was walking on the walls of Jerusalem one day, on my way
to the Haram, when I stumbled on Mercutio and the Zionist. The Temple area lay below us, and the Dome of the Rock
was glittering in the evening sun.

"Will they ever get onto that work?" said Mercutio. "I
mean in earnest. They have played with it for so many years
now. Richmond in his memorable Report, I believe, asked
for £E70,000, and in five years you have how much, £E900?
It's a great pity those funds were ever turned over to the
Wakf."

"Should we administer them any better?" said I.

He shrugged his shoulders. "But why did they ever
do it?"

"It was chivalry on the part of the High Commissioner,"
said the Zionist. "Being a Jew, he did not wish to mix himself up in Moslem affairs."

"That is where he and you make a great mistake," said Mercutio. "He should have been the British High Commissioner first and the Jew afterward. The Moslems were quite ready for guidance; the chance is gone now."

"You might at least give us credit for our good intentions . . . but after all why should we be interested in this building?"

Why indeed? Yet there it stood in its thirteen hundred years of majesty and loveliness.

"Alas," said Mercutio, "even if you have no history have you no eyes? Must God appoint unto them that boast in Zion ashes for beauty?"

"Well," said I, "I wish they'd carry out the Richmond Report and get the great work started."

"Perhaps they might have done," said Jacob Funkelstein acidly, "if they had let Mr. Richmond go on with the job he is fitted for instead of pitchforking him into politics"; for the Zionist does not like Ernest Richmond.

Mercutio was at him with his rapier.

"Ernest Richmond," said he, "is the sheet anchor of Zionism in Palestine." . . . "Can't you see that it is he, and he alone, that gives the Arabs confidence in an administration that for them would otherwise be wholly Zionist. The fact that here is an Englishman . . ."

"Wholly anti-Semite," said the Jew.

"Wholly devoted to Arab interests, an Englishman, too, of fearless and outspoken honesty—the fact that such a man is set in a place of power is for them a standing sign of the impartial justice of the British Raj."

"A preposterous paradox."

"Just as much a paradox as the preposterous Balfour Declaration whose Arabic tail you people perpetually ignore, but the lash of which you will some day feel. If it weren't for Ernest Richmond, you'd be having your throats cut, and don't you make any mistake about it."

"But what has an architect to do with politics, anyway?"

"There again you go so wrong. It is because you Jews have no sense of plastic art, never have had, and never will have, that you are blind to the meaning of the Dome of the Rock."

—C. R. Ashbee, *A Palestine Notebook*

OVER FIFTEEN YEARS before Ernest Tatham Richmond penned his pamphlet on the sites of the crucifixion and the Holy Sepulchre, he had already reached the conclusion that the fate of contemporary civilization lay in the Orient.[1] There, he believed, the reassertion of a moral correlation between appearances and truth—a "remanifestation," in his language—would expose the duplicity of an Occident corrupted by a materialist ethos, and in doing so, rescue the West from ruin.

Richmond first framed this view in 1912, when, after a long stint as a civil servant and architect in Egypt, he wrote "A Dialogue [Imaginary] about Foreign Dominion."[2] Something of a *Fürstenspiegel* (a didactic text for princes), this unpublished fantasy depicts an intellectually gifted Arab nationalist (considered by some to be a "dangerous man") bringing an upright British colonial civil servant to self-consciousness regarding the gap between the *forms* of imperial government and its stated ends: the improvement of other peoples. After establishing that both of these men are exceptional in their refusal to pursue material gain as an end in itself—for the author this is the precondition of righteousness—Richmond has Abdullah (the Arab) prod Dinsdale (the English official) into recognition of the paradox between colonial "law and order" on one hand, and the "cause of virtue" on the other. To adhere to the forms of imperial government that assign a moral "shell" to the abrogated "kernel" of a civilizing mission, is to become a man who is "virtuous outwardly but not inwardly." To thwart it—in the sense of being a pure nationalist motivated only by his opposition to imperialism—is to became an "honest rogue," who, in attempting to do away with the *forms* of present rule, simultaneously abrogates his people's ability to give expression to virtue. "Both [types] are alike in lacking the inner conviction of anything better."[3] Revealing that he is in no sense a classic, cut-throat, oppositional nationalist of the sort Dinsdale/Richmond fears, Richmond's Abdullah points the way toward the sublation of the dialectic of form and virtue in a remarkable process whereby empire, through its very *forms* of governance, fosters the outward expressions of virtue an indigenous people lack, and in doing so inaugurates a process that culminates in a natural dissolution of dominion;[4] empire *gains* in that loss, recuperating from the subject people a virtue the occupier once possessed but lost to greed.

> Abdullah: "The form of Government suitable to a people is an organism of slow growth, and not a machine like a clock, to be made, wound up and started."
>
> Dinsdale: "Then before the evil of foreign dominion can be removed, the impossible must be achieved."

Abdullah: "No, that is not the alternative; because foreign dominion can gradually give place to native rule. The power of natives can gradually be increased and the power of foreigners gradually decreased."[5]

In Richmond's subsequent thinking, architecture would emerge as the privileged implement of this historical transformation. Soon after the British conquest of Jerusalem in December 1917, Lord Allenby asked Richmond to "go to Palestine to examine and report upon the structural condition of the Moslem shrines in the Haram ash-Sharif at Jerusalem," and particularly the Dome of the Rock.[6] Arriving in the spring of 1918, Richmond remained in Jerusalem for approximately one year, preparing his report in two stages, along with an assessment of the capacity of the native population of Palestine to effect the necessary work.[7] In his initial findings of September 1918, Richmond reported: "The bones of the building are sound. Its *outer skin*, however, is in need of extensive renewal and repair."[8] As he began to prepare a detailed survey of this "skin"—"an examination tile by tile of the existing facing"—Richmond began to take cognizance of a stratigraphy of previous "renewals and repairs," eventually leading him to the conclusion that this "patchwork of effort extending over many generations" in itself *defined* the monument.[9] It is out of this observation that Richmond would begin to fashion a theory of history—later abstracted in his crucifixion pamphlet—according to which an immutable idea only presents itself immanently, in the successive refashioning of its mutable, architectural vestment. Commenting upon the "tendency of the building to adapt itself to new conditions," in his final report on the Dome of the Rock Richmond suggests:

> This tendency still continues, as it has continued for twelve centuries and more. And though, through this process of change and adaptation much have been lost that might in other circumstances have been preserved—and though, to that extent, it is to be regretted—yet it may, on the other hand, be welcomed by many as an *unmistakable sign* of a determination to maintain the building, if not altogether in its original, at least in some form, and as a proof of continued vitality in the ideas and the beliefs that the building has, except for the short period of the Frank occupation, symbolized without interruption from the seventh century to the present day. For change has been a condition of the building's existence and of its continued power to represent those ideas. Had there been no change the building would have disappeared.[10]

The pressing question, then, was: "Who would repair the skin by replacing the missing tiles?" Richmond took the remarkable step of relating the regeneration of the "shell" of Palestinian Islam—the institutional and formal expressions of a faith long suppressed by foreign dominion—to the "shell" of the structure itself. In his view, the resurgence of the former necessarily coincided with the restoration of the latter, in a process that implied something like the realization of the fictional Abdullah's vision of an East incrementally refashioning the carapace of its own Spirit—as an "unmistakable sign." By assuming responsibility for the reclothing of its own shrine, Richmond believed, Palestinian Islam and the Orient as a whole would simultaneously begin to renew the formal traditions (political and religious) that constitute the incarnation of Spirit. This accounts for Richmond's dispute, early in 1919, with David George Hogarth (the noted archaeologist of Hittite capitals, keeper of the Ashmolean Museum, and director of the Arab Bureau in Cairo between 1916 and 1918) over the manufacture of replacement tiles.[11] Hogarth had suggested (or so Richmond thought) that examples of fallen or removed tiles should be sent to Europe as models for substitutes to be made there—perhaps as a temporary solution until a better plan could be fashioned.[12] Richmond disagreed, arguing that even if it might result in failure, it was necessary to "give the East a chance."[13] He offered two reasons for this suggested course, in the process introducing a dichotomy between the shabby industrialism infecting Western culture and a romantic Ruskinian faith in the surviving crafts of the East, however degraded they might appear. First, Richmond suggested that it was possible that research "might bring to light the continued existence of knowledge and traditions upon which may be based at least a hope for reviving this art."[14] Secondly, Richmond pointed to previous replacement tiles of German manufacture installed on the Dome in 1912, and—with no small degree of sarcasm—indicated that "these melancholy specimens afford Muslims very encouraging advertisement of European skill."[15] In his final report, Richmond took matters even further. He suggested that even if tiles of superior Western manufacture could be found, these replacements—lacking in *historical* purpose—would never be preferable to an honorable decay of the monument; at least dilapidation still conveyed an important historical meaning.[16]

I think that Richmond, the polemicist of Spirit, only takes this extreme position in order to expose a false dichotomy. Substituting tiles for the political actors of his dialogue on foreign dominion, he establishes a paradox between "outwardly virtuous but inwardly corrupt" foreign tiles and "honest rogues" of local provenance in order to suggest a *Mittelglied*, or resolution to the paradox: by sponsoring the craft traditions that were the very mark of a surviving idea in the East, the West could recognize and regain in these the very instrument of its own salvation—in other words, it could cut the same remarkable deal worked out by Abdullah and Dinsdale in the dialogue on foreign dominion.

Realpolitik, and not idealism, prompted the British government to arrive at much the same conclusion as Richmond in the matter of the monument's restoration. But it arrived there by a circuitous route, in itself illustrative for the way in which it presents the monument as a monad for contemporary political circumstances. Shortly after he left Palestine in April 1919, Richmond began to lobby the British government for funds to publish his report, in order to publicize the urgent need for the £E80,000 which, in his estimation, would be required to effect repairs to the Haram as a whole.[17] In these appeals, Richmond resorted to a line of argument that he would repeat in almost all of his subsequent exhortations to Britons concerning the restoration of Islamic shrines. As the source of an uncanny animism— Richmond called it the "material symbol of a mighty Religion" and the "living symbol of a living faith"—the monument commanded so great a reverence among the world's Muslim population that England's investment in its preservation would "cement friendship and disarm enemies."[18] (Richmond either appeared not to realize that his own suggestion implied something he would later deny with vehemence—that is, that as a magnet of reverence the monument could be "used" for political ends—or, thinking that the interests of Islam and those of the British Empire were one [in the model of his fictive dialogue], he believed he could entice England to rediscover its own *ethical* self-interest in the concerns of the mosque's devotees.)

In the Foreign Office, the political opportunities afforded by Richmond's argument about the "material symbol" were soon understood, and his proposal achieved a measure of support.[19] Moreover, the minuted—or annotated—correspondence on Richmond's proposal indicates that by the summer of 1920, the newly appointed high commissioner for Palestine, Herbert Samuel, was taking part in the British government's deliberations on the matter. In fact, even though he had committed the Palestine government to contributing to the publication of the report, within a month and a half of the establishment of a civil administration there, the high commissioner seems to have shifted the focus of official discussions from the recruitment of funds for the publication to the question of the £E80,000 needed to carry out the repairs themselves. Arguing that "the condition of these famous buildings" was quickly "going from bad to worse," Samuel suggested that a broad subscription for funds should be undertaken under the patronage of King George V.[20]

In Whitehall, initial reactions to Samuel's recommendation were positive, but soon reached a stalemate that wedged the question of the sanctuary between imperial interests in Egypt to the west, and India to the east. Believing that Islam in general was, at the time, "bent on political issues," and that Muslim agitators in Palestine had successfully linked the fate of the country with the fate of holy sites during the so-called Nabi Musa disturbances the previous spring, in early September some Foreign Office officials endorsed Samuel's scheme. Their general sentiment, as expressed by G. H. Fitzmaurice, was that it "would be a tangible *démenti* of the rumour put abroad that the Zionist Jews contemplate interfering with the Moslem Sacred Places in Jerusalem with a view to rebuilding the Temple on its ancient site."[21] Responses from the colonies were not so sanguine, however. In Cairo, Baghdad, and Simla (the summer capital of the British government in India), Samuel's proposition became the unwitting occasion for a referendum on the future administration of Islamic affairs in a postcaliphate, post-Ottoman era. In Cairo, British colonial officials seemed concerned about the Egyptian Muslim establishment's sense of its priority in the region (and perhaps, by extension of their own) when they responded that best results would not be achieved by recourse to a public subscription under the aegis of the British crown, but by "a local appeal initiated by the Sheikh of [the] Mosque at Jerusalem through the Sheikh ul-Islam [Shaykh al-Islam] at al-Azhar [in Egypt]."[22] "This method," a communication of 15 October suggests, "would be less likely to arouse suspicions of any political motive."[23] The telegramed response from India was even more negative:

We hesitate to endorse the proposal made by the HC [High Commissioner] for Palestine. Khilafat Agitators in India, finding it impossible to maintain fiction that British forces are in occupation of Holy Places of Hedjaz, are now apparently concentrating on our occupation of Jerusalem, and to minor degree of Baghdad. We cannot but think that the proposal for restoration of Mosque at Jerusalem according to plan of Christian Englishman, the mere fact of whose preparing the plans would imply that he had penetrated into every part of the building, and enclosure would be used to excite Moslem public sentiments throughout the world. . . . Sultan of Turkey is still Khalifa until Moslem world otherwise decide, and it would undoubtedly appeal to Moslem imagination if, in recognition of this fact, we were to invite Sultan himself to issue an appeal.[24]

By late November 1920, Samuel and the policy makers in Whitehall were unanimous in their opinion that while the caliphate question should be avoided at all costs—in other words, that while nothing should be done by Great Britain to encourage or reaffirm the authority of a caliphate rendered null by the dissolution of the Ottoman Empire—an appeal originating from Muslim authorities in Jerusalem should be attempted, more or less on the lines originally suggested by officials in Cairo. To this end, Samuel notified the foreign secretary that the grand mufti (Kamil al-Husayni) was prepared to launch such a campaign, adding: "It is suggested that a local Moslem committee might be formed to organise the distribution of this appeal to all portions of the Moslem World . . . in which a favourable reception would be expected."[25] Surprisingly, the source of this "suggestion" was probably the Samuel administration's newly appointed assistant secretary for political affairs, Ernest Tatham Richmond himself.[26] Having been recruited by Samuel two months earlier, Richmond abandoned an unsuccessful architectural partnership with Sir Herbert Baker in London to become the principal "liaison between the government and the Muslim community . . . in effect, to be the high commissioner's chief adviser on Muslim Affairs."[27] In that position, Richmond would soon play a decisive role in political events that would influence the fate of the Dome of the Rock, even as those same events would have significant repercussions upon his belief that the renewal of the building's form could actuate history.

In late March 1921—barely four months after these deliberations—the grand mufti died. Paradoxically, this bound the British administration to conduct a new election in accordance with Ottoman law, while at the same time it had to modify the procedure to take into account the end of Turkish sovereignty in local religious affairs. The high commissioner would have to assume the role formerly occupied by the Shaykh al-Islam (the highest authority in the Ottoman religious bureaucracy) in Istanbul, by selecting the replacement from a list of three candidates provided by an electoral college comprised of local ulama (Muslim scholars or religious functionaries) and officials. The elections, held on 12 April 1921, yielded three nominees, but the candidate of the late grand mufti's family, who was, according to some representations, "the people's choice," was not among them. This candidate was Muhammad Hajj Amin al-Husayni, the younger half-brother of the deceased mufti, and, until his pardon the previous August, a fugitive from the

British for his role in the Jerusalem disturbances of 1920.[28] While Samuel was inclined to delay any appointment on the grounds that the election was "technically imperfect," Richmond and the governor of the Jerusalem district, Ronald Storrs, attempted to persuade Samuel to appoint al-Husayni nevertheless.[29] Samuel never recorded his reasons for doing so, but in May 1921 he offered the appointment to al-Husayni. (The appointment was never officially confirmed in writing, or gazetted.)[30]

In the period between the first ballot of these elections and the appointment of Hajj Amin al-Husayni, his supporters in Jerusalem posted a proclamation stating that the "Jews were interfering in the election of the Mufti." Exhorting Muslims to "awake and prevent danger before it occurs," the communiqué suggested that a series of "accursed traitors" had conspired with Jews to catapult the lead candidate (a cleric named Husam al-Din Jarallah) to the position of mufti for the following reasons:

[1] To assist the Jews in the exchange of Moslem Wakfs and their sale to them specially the Wakf Abu Midien near the Wailing Place [sic]. [2] To assist the Jews in killing the national spirit in the country. [3] To agree to all Jewish Zionist claims and accept them on behalf of the Moslems. [4] *To help in handing over the Jews the Haram Esh-Sherif, the Dome of the Kock [sic] and El Aksa that they might pull them down and build in their place the Temple and the place of sacrifice as stated by Alfred Mond* [a noted Anglo-Zionist] *and the president of the Zionist Commission Dr. Eder.* Moslems you must know what you have been brought to in your own country in the Jews mock your religious feelings and public opinion.[31]

Pointing to such Muslim criticisms of the election, Richmond's detractors, such as the Zionist Organization's Frederick Kisch, suggested that the elections were indeed "technically imperfect" in that they abrogated the ulama's consensus; to Kisch (and later observers) claims of Jewish plans to rebuild the Temple in the place of the Aqsa constituted a piece of demagoguery fashioned by Arab nationalists in concert with Richmond, for the purpose of corrupting a purely religious affair.[32] According to this view, Muhammad Hajj Amin al-Husayni and his allies simply sought to motivate the masses into opposing the election results by preying upon their concerns for holy sites. Conversely, Richmond believed that his influence in the affair was no greater than that of the pro-Zionist officials who were resolutely "against Amin's candidacy."[33] In his understanding of events (as I will presently indicate), it clearly followed that the proclamation, in expressing concern for an endangered patrimony, actually put forward the legitimate "sense of the people."[34]

Historians and contemporary observers alike have focused almost exclusively on the truth content of this proclamation, attempting to assess whether and to what extent its claims could be substantiated. Far more significant than the proclamation's validity, however, is its representational schema: in the way it relates the *sensus communis* to the fate of architecture, the poster represents a decisive turn in the history of how this conflict came to represent itself to itself. Two moments—two paths actually evident in subsequent representations of Palestine's politics—introduce themselves in this decree. The first approaches a reflexive register: with the words "as stated by Alfred Mond" there is already the embryo of an argument that the truth of a political situation might now present itself to view, without mediation, in the way *others* invoke the adequacy of architecture to history. Emerging out of the corresponding (failure of) claims that history reveals itself transparently in the way people use monuments to instigate change, this is a vision of historical adequation that would be elaborated in the subsequent speech acts of the new grand mufti during the remainder of the decade, and it is also a claim that would enter into general currency after the disturbances of 1929. (Then, as I indicate in part 3 of this study, political actors' claims for the instigation of mass violence necessarily relied upon representations of others' representations of monuments, that is, citations and even pictures.) The second moment—already implicit in the emergence of the first—betrays itself as the persistent claims for architecture's "uses" in the face of a normalized *incapacity* on the part of political actors to establish architecture's adequacy to history in the monument's function at all; in other words, in a continuing but irreducible debate concerning what, or who, instigates the architecture that is presumably "used" to instigate others to action.

Richmond is the intellectual representative of the fate of this second potentiality. In his presentation of the Haram/Temple Mount's historical function, an operative theory of adequation fulfills itself (in the sense of becoming unselfconsciously contradictory) only in the attendant paradoxes of a theory of motivation: forced to admit a contingent relation between form and meaning where he would otherwise assert only a relation of necessity, Richmond moves inexorably toward representations of agency that negate his own concept of the monument's "uses." That is, they contradict the very norm of adequacy to which the monument putatively gives rise. In the long run, in fact, he will find himself resorting to a materialist theory of architecture's uses in order to preserve an idealist one.

This happens in three stages, in which one may witness Richmond's progressive "submission to Necessity" as consciousness of an "alien fate" (in Hegel's language) gradually intrudes into his vision of Palestinian Islam's remanifestation via the care of its architecture.[35] At first, during the time of the election of the mufti in 1921, Richmond finds himself incapable of arguing for such remanifestation without according a role to Jewish adjuncts in this process. Later, as he begins to champion emerging Muslim institutions in Palestine, between 1922 and 1924, Richmond finds that in order to conceptualize the dialectical relation between Islam and its monuments in an "Arab awakening," he needs to accord an active and greater role to a Jewish/Zionist opposition. Finally, in order to protect the new mufti and his faction from charges that they incited the violence of August 1929, Richmond resorts to the suggestion that in the Buraq/Wailing Wall disturbances, the Jews themselves provoked the Muslim masses to action, in this fashion annulling his theory of architecture's relation to history, reducing it to a mere instrument of secular politics, a materialist weapon.

In 1921, following the crisis that led to al-Husayni's appointment, Richmond became convinced of the fact that in Palestinian Muslims' popular rejection of the government-run elections for mufti, he had begun to witness history in the process of assuming its correlate form: Spirit forming its shell. Looking to the collective "mazbatas" (colonial vernacular for the Arabic maẓābiṭ, meaning protocols, petitions, minutes) sent to the government by al-Husayni's supporters as the spontaneous and organic formation of historical will, Richmond seems to have believed that the sensus communis simply confirmed al-Husayni, just as al-Husayni, in articulating the "threat" to monuments by Jews, gave voice to the same sensus communis. (By contrast, since the argument that the original, formal elections had been "legal" and proper emanated from the Jewish legal secretary of the Palestine government, Norman de Mattos Bentwich, "and his entourage," Richmond implied that in the eyes of the Muslim people these findings were themselves "illegal" and could only confirm the Husayni camp's original claims concerning Zionist intentions to begin with.)[36] In the abrogation of the formal elections, then, the authenticity of a popular election was actually confirmed. Writing to Palestine's high commissioner, Sir Herbert Samuel, in June 1921 with the aim of finalizing what had to date only been an oral confirmation of al-Husayni's appointment, Richmond summarized

55

what he considered to be the features of contemporary Palestinian public opinion:

> I submit that briefly the position as it presents itself to a very large number of people is as follows:
>
> 1. That the Jews do not want Hajj Amin to be Mufti.
>
> 2. It is believed that the elections have been arranged under Jewish influence so that Hajj Amin should not be elected.
>
> 3. The vast majority of the people desire the appointment of Hajj Amin.[37]

Even as he locates the sense of the people in the rumors and suspicions that fuel collective coherence at the time of the election of the mufti in 1921, Richmond's vision of history takes a decisive turn. Because, now, he argues that the Spirit of the East—in its historical refiguration—can only organize itself in relation to an alterity that the same Spirit, in the process of its own exteriorization, negates; by advancing a *false* imago of history (Richmond's "humbug"), the Jew assumes a *necessary* role in Islam's remanifestation.[38] More specifically, the Jew and the Zionist are dealt the role of a "naïve consciousness," whose very insufficiency both drives and confirms a phenomenology of Spirit—since in this display, Islam sees confirmation of a "supersensible world."[39] Because it is unable to abandon the fantasy of pragmatic sense-certainty (of vulgar immediacy) as it encounters virtue's assumption into historical form, Jewish nationalism confirms Palestine Islam's organic agglomeration and, as the elections themselves proved, in doing so it actually *propels* the (mass) "historical self-consciousness" of the East. In this way, Judaism simply gives to an idealized Islam ever greater capacities for representing itself to itself, that is, for giving form to its historical self-consciousness.

But at the very moment in which the Jew is accorded this historical role, Richmond's theory of representation begins to compromise itself, and in ways that will derail his concept of agency as well. If, for example, one works through Richmond's understanding of the Husayni camp's claims about the Jews' imminent takeover of the Haram—that is, Richmond's implicit belief that a regulative ideal presented itself in the form of a rumor—this crisis becomes readily apparent. To assign Jewry's false consciousness this kind of role in Muslim self-consciousness and cohesion is to admit, first of all, a contingency of meaning into a place where only an immanence of meaning (a meaning arising from an existing meaning) is both presumed to hold sway and to instigate history. In other words, the paradox, here, is that the same Haram that the Husaynis say the Jews wish to take over (the Haram that is the mark of a political imperative beyond its own developing significance, and hence a Haram contingent upon externals for its meaning) is the same monument that, in its function as a concrete symbol of its own purposes, is supposed to be used by Palestinians to instigate virtue into a correlate historical form.[40]

With this paradox, "politics" (in Richmond's parlance) simultaneously presents itself in the *agency* of an intrusive and false consciousness that is intent upon reducing a legitimate manifestation of Spirit—the rise of a collective consciousness to self-consciousness in representation—to little more than a system of agitation, a gerrymandering of significances by the few to instigate the many. In short, Richmond will now argue that the Jew and his agents in the administration actually *participate* in the auto-emancipation of the East by attempting to *deny* it. This is not a position that Richmond fashions in the abstract. It can be found in the record of his struggles with other officials in the Palestine government over the proper interpretation of the pan-Islamic movement as a whole and, more specifically, over the characteristics of the same movement in Palestine. Since at least October 1920, Criminal Investigations Division (CID) reports and communications from Palestine's high commissioner to Whitehall related local tensions concerning the management of Shari'a courts (Muslim religious tribunals) and the management of *awqaf* (that is, Muslim religious trusts) to what they considered "a wider and extremely dangerous movement."[41] "Press agitation," the CID reports continued, was "conducted with the object of arousing the fanaticism of Moslems, of creating a feeling of diffidence and hatred against the constituted Government and thus preparing the ground for a future general insurrection."[42] In the examples cited by the CID reports, these tensions arose when the legal secretary, Norman Bentwich—a Jew—attempted to make Muslim religious courts subject to greater governmental oversight. But also at stake in the official interpretation of those tensions was a vision of history according to which Arab masses, presumed to have no collective volition of their own, must be aroused (like so many excitable molecules) by the "nationalist, pan-Islamic and anti-foreign" propaganda conducted by "a score of leading agitators."[43]

Richmond's marginalia on these reports call into question this normative presentation of events in order to dissociate the mufti from such aspersions of incitement. He asks for "proofs" of the allegations of agitation, and turning to the matter of the mass phenomenon as a whole, he asks point blank: "But what does one mean by the pan-Islamic movement?"[44] Against the charge that individuals "arouse" the "fanaticism" of Muslims to material ends (the incitement theory of agency) Richmond counters with assertions of a collective agency that is only mistaken for incitement, arguing: "No—Whatever its effect, I believe it [i.e., the movement prompted in part by concerns over non-Muslim intrusion into Muslim affairs] to have owed its Causes to the desire of men, or of a people to advertise themselves."[45] Richmond elaborates upon this notion of a collective "advertisement" during a subsequent phase of the same dispute, and it is precisely then that he (first) finds himself incapable of establishing any conception of Arab mass agency without according to Jewish opposition a necessary role in its formation. The controversy (in Richmond's representation of events) centered on the legal secretary's ongoing efforts to ensure "that the Government should retain administrative control of the Shariʿa courts."[46] During the continuing debate on this issue, in March 1922, Richmond suggested that Norman Bentwich's plan to appoint as Shariʿa courts' inspector the same man who had won the original election for mufti in 1921 was simply an example of "Jewish interference" in the workings of the newly established Supreme Muslim Council (SMC), the new administrative body for the management of Muslim affairs, headed by the grand mufti, Hajj Amin al-Husayni.[47] Arguing that the nominee—Husam al-Din Jarallah—was merely a puppet of his Jewish bosses, Richmond asked in his official communication to the chief secretary of the Palestine government, Wyndham Deedes, on this affair: "Who can tell what a man of his ability [Jarallah] might not be able to do by all manner of intrigue carefully planned and thought out by his temporary, it is hoped—masters the Zionists, led of course by that arch-Zionist, the legal Secretary, to wreck the unity of the Moslem Community, a unity which all good Moslems are so persistently working to establish, and which all evil minded persons are trying to destroy?"[48]

When Richmond speaks of a "people's desire to advertise themselves," then, he seems to be defining Muslim unity as a collective externalization of self-consciousness (in Hegel's language, a "kenosis") via the monuments whose substance "is in itself self-consciousness."[49] But it is exactly this collective singularity of a revealed religion that the enemies of Islam seek to misrepresent and discredit in the eyes of those in the British administration who should most actively encourage it. Writing in his diaries directly after this battle with Bentwich, Richmond makes it clear that he was fighting "to counteract the anti-native virus with which the Jews seconded by Deedes' own ignorance and prejudice have filled his being."[50] Richmond consequently attempted to "inoculate" Deedes against this virus by making it plain to him that leaders like the grand mufti had not taken opportunities "to appeal to the people's passions and to rouse them to violence on a great scale."[51] Rather, al-Husayni himself was part of something far larger. Richmond tried to impress upon Deedes that any "pan-Arab," Islamic or "pan-Islamic" imperative could not be reduced to a vehicle of political "agitation," as others had suggested, but actually represented a legitimate manifestation of a historical will.[52] In April 1922, after Deedes solicited Richmond's opinion on the Syrian Union, the latter seized the opportunity to reaffirm this position:

> The "Pan-Arab" movement . . . is a rather inadequate description of a general stirring among the peoples of the East. It has been growing for many decades, and now becomes with each year more noticeable. The War helped it forward greatly. Its direction is towards renaissance and independence. Its symptoms are an increased consciousness of national, racial, religious, historic and social ties. It includes folk who are not Moslems. Its results will, it is hoped, be the establishment of a new relationship with Europe, a relationship involving equality in place of subjection. In Palestine as elsewhere the movement is progressing. *"Zionism" is helping it, for it is providing a useful cement.* It is a positive movement and is no more artificially "engineered by agitators" than are any other great human movements. It is incomparably more important than the negative movement against Zionism. This movement is only a symptom, perhaps even a minor one, of a really big thing that is going on. Asia had a past when Europe was a forest inhabited by savages. As the successors of these savages gradually poison themselves with a feverish industrialism etc. Asia is recovering from a long rest-cure, is beginning to look about, to move and to recognise that she is still alive, to remember what she has been and to move towards new achievement. . . . The western people who can recognise this will have a great opportunity.[53]

In the first stage of Richmond's drive to paradox, then, an originary invocation of the monument's utility (Richmond's reading of the mufti's claims about Zionism and the Temple) necessarily coincides with the intrusion of the Jew into any possible conception of Muslim collective agency, that is, as its "useful cement." In the next stage, the actual restoration of monuments appears to correspond with a Jewish threat to (any conception of) collective agency. And in a very precise way: now Zionism will present itself as the force of instigation that threatens to reduce the "great stirring" Richmond described to Deedes to little more than the "negative movement"—a reaction formation—against that threat.

The specific issue of concern here was the status of the newly formed Supreme Muslim Shari'a Council (SMC), and its campaign to recondition the shrines of the Haram al-Sharif. Richmond believed that by undertaking the task of restoring these monuments—and particularly the reclothing of the Dome of the Rock's vestment of tiles—this newly formed institution for the autonomous administration of Palestinian Islam corroborated its own identity as the corresponding clothing of Spirit. In this way, the formation of council simply confirmed the vision of history that he had elaborated in the dialogue on foreign dominion of 1912 and in his exchanges with colonial officials over the Dome of the Rock's condition in 1919: in a sequence of remanifestations, form instructs virtue to assume its own correlate societal form. Describing a tour of the Haram that he took with the grand mufti and president of the SMC in 1922, Richmond believes himself to have witnessed this principle first hand:

> We visited the new offices of the Moslem Council now being constructed by adapting some of the existing rooms in the buildings on the West side of the Haram area. Hajj Amin is very interested in the work. He also showed me the new Moslem Orphanage housed in the old Sarai. He is justly proud of this Institution. . . . These interests and this active work are drawing out all that is best in Hajj Amin. He is keen to get on with the work of repair in the Haram area and will have £8000 available. We are to make a special visit to decide how the money can be distributed among all the buildings.[54]

However, as Richmond continues to develop a vision of events according to which the Haram *itself* confirms a relation of necessity between the ideals of a people and its emerging institutions (a "philosophy of right," by virtue of his equation of its inevitability with ethical fulfillment), this same vision begins to be contested from within the ranks of Palestinian Islam.[55] Shortly after the SMC was established by an order in council on 20 December 1921, it instituted a technical commission—which included Richmond among its members—to prioritize the repairs on the Haram. In addition, following the template of the high commissioner's original proposal of 1920 (and according to Richmond, at his own urging), the president of the SMC "sent delegations to the Islamic world to collect the very considerable sums of money needed for the restoration."[56] (Traveling as far as India, the delegation's successful fund-raising techniques became the focus of political concern to the British, who debated whether the delegation was more involved in solicitation for money or political agitation.)[57] In August 1922 the SMC also engaged the services of Mimar Kemalettin, the man who had been the chief architect of the Department of Awqaf in Istanbul prior to the fall of the Ottoman Empire, and a principal ideologist of national romanticism in Turkish architecture.[58]

Priority was given to the Aqsa Mosque, which was suffering from significant structural degradation, and to the tile program of the Dome of the Rock. The former was shored up and restored by 1927.[59] Work on the latter would eventually be deferred, but not before figuring as the cause of a political dispute. In 1919, when Richmond had argued with Commander D. G. Hogarth that in the matter of the tiles it was necessary to "give the East a chance," he was relying on the fact that, thanks to the British Foreign Office's Sir Mark Sykes, a representative of the same Anatolian tile-making tradition responsible for the sixteenth-century ("Kishani" ceramic) covering on the Dome of the Rock had found his way to Jerusalem. Named David Ohanessian, this refugee from the Armenian genocide was seen by both C. R. Ashbee (civic adviser to the Jerusalem municipality) and Richmond as indispensable to their efforts to "reclothe" the monument.[60] And so, as early as January 1920—prior to the formation of the SMC—waqf authorities seem to have entered into a contract with Ohanessian to produce tiles for the Dome of the Rock.[61] With the creation of the council and the formation of its technical committee, however, this agreement seems to have been abrogated in favor of a decision to import tiles directly from Turkey, under Kemalettin's supervision.

In the eyes of some, at least, this irregularity (among others) suggested that the tile of the Dome of the Rock did not confirm a relation of necessity between form and meaning—that is, a "remanifestation," in Richmond's language—but an arbitrary and contingent one, since the reglazing now presented itself as the mark of the SMC's political and temporal ends. (The monument emerges as a materialist weapon.) On 5 November 1923, two former employees of the SMC sent a secret memorandum to the Palestine government outlining how, in their view, the council and its president had behaved in a manner "contrary to the Spirit of the Order constituting it [the SMC]."[62] In direct contradiction to Richmond's "philosophy of right" in matters concerning the SMC, ʿAbdallah Mukhlis (the institution's former chief accountant) and Yaʿqub Abu al-Huda (former maʾmur awqaf of Jerusalem, the district manager of religious trusts) argued that "in approving the establishment of this Council, the government had in view public policy but the Council has been transformed into a private institution" for the consolidation of Husayni family power.[63] Describing the workings of the "Technical Committee" charged with the repair of the shrines, Mukhlis and Abu al-Huda alleged the payment of immense advances to Kemalettin and a corresponding series of de facto kickbacks so that Husayni family members would be appointed to technical posts associated with the restoration.[64] Moreover, in their narrative the tiles themselves emerged as emblems of corruption, not regeneration. Recounting how Kemalettin at first approved Ohanessian's work and then rejected it in order to import tiles from Kütahia (the traditional center of tile making in Anatolia, from which Ohanessian himself came), Mukhlis and Abu al-Huda stated:

> In spite of all this and the fact that the Council should encourage the Eastern industry in an Eastern city which is a tourists resource and near the Dome of the Rock which needs always the services of the Manufacturer to do the necessary repairs, the Council has sent Kamal Bey [sic] [that is, Mimar Kemalettin himself] to Constantinople where he has spent over 4–5 months away from his work and then sent a member of the Council to Constantinople and Angora to make agreement with the manufacturers at those places, and in fact there exist no tile factories there at present. Kamal Bey may be excused for his doings in which he aimed at strengthening his power in Constantinople and encouraging the industry there, but what excuse could the Council have for not encouraging and developing this useful industry in Palestine and economise the expenses of the repairs of the Haram al-Sharif which are collected through delegations from different parts of the world.[65]

Richmond's response to accusations of this kind were complex, and they need to be understood in light of larger battles he was waging within the administration. In the first place, it is important to note that these kinds of allegations were not new, only newly specific. By 1922, in tandem with the activities of the delegation sent by the SMC to solicit funds for repairs of the Haram, Zionist leaders and elements within the British administration protested that the grand mufti was "using" the Haram to "instigate" Muslim support for his own political agenda.[66] As I have already pointed out, in Richmond's mind this "materialist" argument was itself the suspect symptom of a Jewish conspiracy to derail a "great stirring."[67] And so, soon after Mukhlis and Abu al-Huda's memorandum reached his desk, Richmond seems to have considered these claims more of the same. In a letter to his wife written only a few weeks later, he states somewhat triumphantly: "I have taken the edge and the point off efforts to hinder the Moslem reconstruction work."[68]

In his official capacity Richmond tried to block government response to the memorandum on procedural grounds. His minuted comments of 29 January 1924 state: "Presumably the complaint was sent confidentially, we are therefore precluded from . . . [sending] it to the council for their observations."[69] This argument seemed to have met with little sympathy among his colleagues, some of whom treated the allegations as an occasion to revisit the matter of government jurisdiction over the SMC.[70] Ronald Storrs, the governor of Jerusalem, refused to sanction Richmond's attempt to deflect attention from Mukhlis and Abu al-Huda's charges of corruption in the SMC, and toward a Jewish conspiracy of rumor and innuendo against Islam in Palestine.[71] To Storrs, Richmond's charges were disturbingly familiar, being the continuation of an ongoing dispute that had erupted between them only a few weeks before.[72] Five days after Mukhlis and Abu al-Huda submitted their memorandum, Storrs communicated with Brigadier Gilbert Clayton—Wyndham Deedes's successor in the post of chief secretary of the Palestine government—pointing out that intelligence summaries confirmed that the delegation sent by the SMC to the Arab world and India for the purpose of raising funds for the restoration of the Haram was involved in political agitation.[73] (To Storrs, in short, Mukhlis and Abu al-Huda's charges of politicking were redundant, and confirmed concerns emanating from other quarters that were even more grave.) On 13 December 1923 Richmond wrote to the chief secretary in an attempt to rebut the governor's communiqué; he suggested that as the intelligence summaries on which Storrs's arguments were based relied upon information provided by paid "informers," they were themselves suspect. In his own mind, this observation permitted Richmond to sustain the SMC's position as the necessary institutional shell to the kernel of Muslim virtue (and not as a body of insurgency), but only by augmenting the putative power of the "paymasters" of the alleged stool pigeons. He alludes to a cabal, an unacknowledged force and menacing agency "that would desire nothing more than the discrediting of . . . the entire delegation that has gone to India."[74] "It is not out of the question," Richmond continues, "that one of these [paymasters] would invent the information of the kind desired and get it put before those in authority in an apparently regular manner."[75]

"Those in authority" were equally suspect. At the time when Richmond penned this response, he had already committed himself officially to the view that Storrs, and the administration as a whole, were part of the same conspiracy.[76] In fact, in a shocking memorandum on the activities of his office that seems to have been quashed by his superiors Richmond suggested that the Palestine government had simply become a mask for Zionism, and that as such its role was simply to criminalize Arab nationalism.[77] Among the darkest of its tendencies, he suggested, was the fact that the "officers of the administration should take part in politics and play the part of Zionist propaganda agents," and that "the Administration should give its countenance and support to an attempt to undermine with the object of destroying the Supreme Muslim Council, the aim being to replace its president and members by individuals representing themselves as 'loyal' to the British policy in Palestine."[78] Consequently, Richmond maintained that his own role in the administration had necessarily been to work against this trend of draping Jewish interests in British clothing,[79] and, more important, "to encourage the direction of Moslem energies towards constructive work, such as the proper administration of their Wakf affairs, the proper maintenance of their sacred buildings. . . . rather than allowing these energies to waste themselves upon political agitation that might not only be harmful but of less positive result in bringing about the attainment of their desires."[80]

Believing the SMC to be the victim of malicious Jewish and pro-Jewish misrepresentations of Arab self-representation, Richmond necessarily refashioned the architectural emblem of the East's historical regeneration into a figure of this same crisis, with striking results for his own theory of adequation. In the fall of 1923, concurrent with Storrs's first communications to the chief secretary concerning the political activities of the SMC, Richmond ceased to represent the restoration of the Dome of the Rock's skin of tiles as an end in itself, that is, as the immanent remanifestation, or materialization, of Geist. Instead he presented it as an apotropaic principle: it had *another* end beyond its own immanent logic, to serve as the foil to the intentions of the Other. In this way, the monument begins to pay tribute to the contingency that Richmond attempts to hold at bay—that is, to a vulgar theory of utility, according to which political actors are presumed to make use of monuments to achieve their own ends. The Haram now presents itself as an instrument for warding off misrepresentations of an authentic vision of representation, an "unmistakable sign," in Richmond's words, of a people's determination to stop that which would overcome them. As he finished his own monograph on the Dome of the Rock in October 1923, Richmond cautioned:

> In the preservation of the Dome of the Rock all civilized humanity must be interested. In this connexion it may be worth while to add that, astonishing as it may seem, there are those who, for reasons best known to themselves, would wish to see the Dome of the Rock discredited in the

eyes of the world and regarded as a building that has been so ill treated by time, so neglected by its guardians, as to have lost any value it may once have possessed: a building that might well be left to a natural and rapid decay, culminating in its early demolition and replacement by a worthier shrine built perhaps to the honour of some other Faith. This conclusion might be sound if the premises upon which it is based were true. That they are not true, and that the building is worth every effort that can be made to preserve it, will be obvious to any who impartially examine it.[81]

Zionism can no longer appear in Richmond's understanding of events as the *adjunct* of a historical "stirring" marked, materially, by the dialectical relation between communal forms adequate to the remanifestation of shrines, and shrines adequate to a reemergent sensus communis—a historical Idea. It is now the inherent correlative menace to any conception of Arab identity: on one hand, indispensable to any conception of Arab agency *as* a great stirring, and on the other, threatening to reduce the self-representation of Palestinian collective sentiment to little more than a tendency of opposition motivated by a force outside itself. In the next and final stage in Richmond's drive to self-contradiction, however, any expression of Arab aggregate agency will dissolve into little more than the "negative movement" he once feared it would become, simply a consequence of the Other's instigation-by-misrepresentation. While this last step is inexorable, Richmond will only reach it five years after writing his memorandum on paid informers; that is, following the mass violence of August 1929, in response to accusations that the Arab leadership (with Richmond as the "man of mystery" "pulling the strings" behind them) manipulated the masses' relation to shrines in order to incite them to violence.

Richmond's experiences in the interval between his two periods of service in Palestine (1924–1927) are crucial to any understanding of this last and final movement toward a paradoxical conception of architecture's adequacy to history. In January 1924, approximately one month after he sparred with Storrs on the matter of the SMC's delegation to India, Richmond notified the high commissioner, Herbert Samuel, of his intention to quit the administration and return to private life.[82] He resigned effective 1 April, after informing the high commissioner that he had come to the conclusion that the government was inspired by a "spirit" he could only regard as "evil."[83] Upon his return to England in May 1924 Richmond began to publish articles hostile to the Palestine Mandate, some anonymously.[84] It is in these essays that Richmond begins to fashion a broader theory of "humbug," or historical duplicity, maintaining that Zionism in Palestine was little more than the thinly veiled vanguard for a global imperative, that is, a metastasizing materialism that encompassed both capitalism and Bolshevism and threatened Christian civilization as a whole.[85] During this interregnum between his two periods in Palestine, Richmond also converted to the Catholic faith (in February 1926), in this way ending what he described as a long period of "wandering" in a spiritual "wilderness." In the Catholic Church, he also seems to have found a well-established language for his own untutored, but heartfelt, idealist philosophical world view. (Even prior to his conversion, Richmond had suggested that "if these Anglo-Catholics are really on a path of Reason, Tradition, Beauty and real sincerity, it would be almost too good to be true.")[86]

Richmond's conception of architecture's historical mission in the East did not remain unaffected by his meditations on both Mammonism and Christianity. During the interregnum, Richmond authored a book entitled *Moslem Architecture, 623 to 1516: Some Causes and Consequences* (1926). In it he suggests that at the time of its founding Islam found only "the rudest expression" of its religious needs, but that it moved toward self-consciousness of "a desire that the splendour of its invisible spirit should be expressed materially by an appropriately splendid body."[87] Looking to Jerusalem, Richmond suggested that this trajectory fundamentally united Christian architectural expression with Muslim construction in an idealist project that had, historically, been misinterpreted by historians as little more than an aggressive counterphobic mimeticism. Acknowledging Muhammad ibn 'Ahmad al-Muqaddasi's oft-cited suggestion that ʿAbd al-Malik Ibn Marwan built the Dome of the Rock as a political response to the Church of the Holy Sepulchre, Richmond engages in a formal analysis of the Dome of the Rock to make the claim that the "architect was not imitating the Holy Sepulchre or any other building."[88] Rather, in doing what was "structurally necessary" to give formal expression to a privileged holy site, the labors of the architect of the Dome of the Rock actually represented Islam's internalization of the same principles that had motivated Byzantine architectural expression— that is, it assimilated the very specific knowledge for rendering Spirit incarnate that had been developed in "Christian art."[89] (To Richmond this was even attested to by the fact that "before being clothed in its Persian dress [of mosaic tile] in the fifteenth century, its appearance externally, covered as it was in marble and mosaic, must have been as Byzantine in character as its internal appearances still is to a large extent.")[90] In his introduction to *Mos-*

lem *Architecture*, Richmond elaborates upon the precise nature of Islam's tutoring to the materialization of Spirit: "Islam not only came into possession of many already standing and many partially ruined buildings produced by the civilizations which had been overrun, but also acquired, for the service of the new faith, what was far more precious and essential, the living knowledge and skill possessed by the conquered races and inherited by them from a remote past. It was this knowledge and this skill which, when incorporated by Islam, were to re-express themselves in forms of a new character."[91]

The implications of this new position are remarkable because here the very history of the Dome of the Rock suddenly appears as a corrective to Richmond's own earlier misprision. In other words, the aporia at which Richmond himself had arrived in 1923 when he reduced the monument to an apotropaic principle (an implement of politics which was, at the same time, supposed to be the instantiation of history) had repeatedly been shown to be false by the monument itself. Insofar as its "remanifestations" were based on the subsumption of other civilizations' forms of devotion as art, the changing significance of the Dome of the Rock—its immanent historical development—coincided with (and was indistinguishable from) a drive to ever greater forms of universality: it embodied a synthesis of Hellenistic, Byzantine, and Persian forms. And it is this reality that was misinterpreted as "mimeticism" or apotropaism of a political sort, even by Richmond in a moment of weakness.

Meanwhile, back in Palestine, Herbert Samuel had already been replaced as high commissioner by Viscount Field Marshal Sir Herbert Plumer, the famed "Plumer of Messines" of First World War fame. During the first year of Plumer's administration, John Garstang, the director of Palestine's fledgling Department of Antiquities, informed the administration of his intention to resign effective 21 December 1926. Unwilling to promote P. L. O. Guy, the Chief Inspector of Antiquities in Palestine (whom he considered "undisciplined," according to Colonial Office sources), Plumer requested Leo Amery, the colonial secretary, to begin to search for a suitable candidate.[92] Consequently, an ad hoc search committee was formed under Sir Frederick Kenyon of the British Museum. With some ambivalence, Richmond applied for the post, having been urged to do so by his elder brother, H. W. Richmond (who also wrote on his behalf to acquaintances in the Colonial Office and to select members of the search committee).[93] Richmond was not included in the committee's short list, but as several of the favored applicants removed themselves from consideration, a sentiment expressed by Sir Gilbert Clayton (still civil secretary in the Palestine Government) appears to have prevailed. Writing to Amery on 7 March 1927, Clayton argued: "It is true that he [Richmond] is not a professional archaeologist, but I do not think you would get a first class man for this pay which Palestine can afford to give."[94] The committee finally endorsed Richmond in mid-May 1927, but the recommendation met with immediate opposition among several Colonial Office officials—among them Sir John Shuckbrugh—who argued that the colonial secretary would personally have to warn Richmond against interfering in political matters. Shuckbrugh opined: "Nothing that I myself or my department could say to him would carry any weight, as he has always looked upon us as entirely wrong-headed (if nothing worse) in our Policy in Palestine."[95] In June 1927 High Commissioner Plumer notified the Colonial Office of his intention to appoint Richmond but to hold him to a pledge not to take part in politics. Richmond willingly acceded to Plumer's request, informing the high commissioner that he had "no desire to have, in Palestine, any further contact with politics and with a policy" he "heartily disliked."[96]

Returning to Palestine in the fall of 1927 to assume the directorship of its Department of Antiquities, Richmond arrived with a somewhat modified understanding of history. He now saw in the restoration of the Dome of the Rock not only the salvation of empire according to the model of his dialogue on foreign dominion, but also, no less importantly (and following the argument of his book on Muslim architecture), the continuation of the Hellenistic and Byzantine Idea implanted within the structure thirteen centuries before. The monument, in short, merged Arab and Latin peoples in a common "Mediterranean culture" that was, in his view, "still very much alive" and vital, precisely because it showed them both to be marked by common "spirit of devotion . . . to things unseen."[97] This was in direct contrast to the "new 'civilization' presented by the Anglo-Saxon-Judaic world" seeking to "make the lost provinces of the Eastern Mediterranean a new Semitic block."[98] Writing to his brother shortly before a ceremony organized by the grand mufti and the SMC to celebrate the completion of structural repairs to the Aqsa Mosque in August 1928, Richmond reiterates the operative vision of adequation he had developed long before, but in the manner of a catechism spoken by a man who has now discovered a relation between another's worship and his own "really-believed religion":

> I have at least this satisfaction, that it was in those days that I laid some stones upon which has been built a structure, which promises to be as lasting as can be expected in this world of change and decay. *A structure that is spirit incarnate.* If you, as I hope, come to Jerusalem I will show

you the outward, visible and material manifestations of that spirit in the great work of preservation and reconstruction that is being carried out in one of the most splendid sanctuaries in the whole world. I refer to the consolidation and reconditioning of the great Aqsa Mosque—a job which I started and, by the Grace of God made administratively, technically and financially possible. The final phase of this work was the reconditioning of the place of congregational prayer at the southern end of the Haram esh-Sharîf [sic]. It is nearly finished and the Moslems are going to have a great ceremony at the opening. As this may be looked on as horrid boasting, "I ask," as the Moslems say, "for the forgiveness of Allah." I shall go to the opening and shall say a prayer of thanks that those hard and sad days of unsupported fight against Faginism in the Holy Land were not altogether without something I can contemplate with immense pleasure, for the Moslems have come up to the scratch in a wonderful manner and their work is one of marvellous solidity and beauty. It has been inspired, *as our own work was once upon a time*, by a devotion that derives its intensity and its resultant beauty of expression from a really-believed religion.[99]

The same structural repairs to the Aqsa that Richmond celebrates as the exteriorization of an Idea (the "outward," "visible" manifestation of Geist) also inaugurate the final "self-sundering" (*Erinnerung*) of architecture's adequacy to history in his version of a phenomenology of Spirit.[100] As Richmond recuperates a sense of architecture's noble "uses" that is conspicuously opposed to a vulgar theory of the monument's "utility," the political actors involved in a looming crisis over the Buraq / Wailing Wall explicitly invoke the same restoration of the Aqsa in an utterly contradictory way. Refusing to treat the Aqsa, or the Haram, as a materialization of the devotion to things "unseen," political enemies in Palestine do not only agree to treat architecture as the reflection of *choses vues*, but take this position even further. Palestinian Arab political elites and the Zionist establishment both begin to suggest that in their opponents' *representations* of the monument's commensurability with history, the truth of the contemporary situation presented itself directly to intuition. (In the way one's opponents represented the Wall, the reality of their political position was disclosed.) In this atmosphere, Richmond's thinking is driven to a crisis it cannot overcome, and can only rehearse over and over again.

The situation in which these representations were made is well known, and remarkably well documented to boot.[101] On 24 September 1928, on the

Jewish day of atonement, Yom Kipur, a Jewish beadle attempted to erect a screen in front of the Buraq/Wailing Wall in order to separate women from men in prayer.[102] Immediately after the partition was set in place, the SMC vigorously protested the action as an infraction of the "Status Quo"; that is, the policy concerning holy sites according to which, under Article 13 of the Mandate, Great Britain nominally froze religious rights and practices in the conditions that existed at the end of Ottoman rule.[103] As Bernard Wasserstein puts it, this "illegal construction" was then "forcibly removed" by the police.[104] The British government was compelled to conduct an inquiry, culminating in both a report on the incident, and in December 1928, an official statement of policy regarding the wall. The latter affirmed the proprietary right of the Muslim religious trust within which the wall stood (the Waqf Abu Madyan) to bar any partitions and exceptional appurtenances of prayers from the site. At the same time, the finding confirmed the customary rights of Jews to continue praying there. Viewing the impasse over the Wall as the "appropriate catalyst" to fury, contemporary observers and subsequent historians describe the months following this incident as a period in which the escalation of sentiments surrounding the monument—whether manufactured or real, incited or organic and spontaneous—led inexorably to the mass violence that finally rocked Jerusalem and Palestine in late August 1929:[105] "Palestine began to simmer and boil again. In September [1928] a couple of incidents occurred, petty things, the second of them sprung from the unauthorized bringing of a screen to the Wailing Wall by some of the Jewish worshippers. As a result of these incidents feelings mounted gradually higher during nine months, supported by all manners of paper and verbal incitements, and ended unsurprisingly in an outbreak."[106]

In expressing the surprising sentiment that the relation between representation and mass violence is "unsurprising," the theory of causality presented here betrays itself as the historiographic perpetuation of the phenomenon it documents; inasmuch as this explanation of the origins of the crisis unselfconsciously points to *representations* of architecture's "uses" in order to posit an unproblematic fit between a historical truth and its manifestation, it is a surviving representative of the kind of claim that superseded Richmond's own claims concerning architecture's adequacy to history. In November 1928, for example, the newly formed Lajnat al-Difa' 'an al-Buraq al-Sharif, or "Defense Committee for the Noble Buraq," published a communiqué in which it suggested that if the SMC had not undertaken the restoration of the Aqsa Mosque, the dilapidation of the structure would have encouraged Jewish designs upon it. Rehearsing much the same apotropaic logic that Richmond presented in his Dome of the Rock monograph of 1923 (and then abandoned in order to recuperate his theory of pure utility—a utility of devotion), this proclamation linked Muslim frustration of Zionist aims upon the Aqsa to the redirection of Jewish intentions on the Buraq/Wailing Wall:

> Their souls longed that it might not be able to stand any tremble or earthquake, but it should fall down and crumble and remain only an optical memory when it will become easy to realise their hopes thereon. But their hopes in that respect were also soon disappointed for the SMC was in a position, thanks be to Allah and to the munificence of the Moslems and to their generous help, to remove the danger from it and to repair it thoroughly and properly. And this was what caused the Jews to return to their first method of hoping for an exchange of the Wakf and an acquisition of the Wall of the Aqsa Mosque for themselves.[107]

Jewish and Zionist countercharges to such claims were swift. More importantly, they suggested that the truth of the contemporary political situation presented itself transparently, in the untruth of Muslims' claims concerning Jewish intentions at the Wall.[108] In an open letter to the Muslim community of Palestine dated November 1928 (shortly in advance of the release of Great Britain's White Paper), the Va'ad Hale'umi, or Jewish National Council, argued that "Following upon this incident [at the Wall] . . . legends, distortions of fact and calumnies which have been denied years ago, were resuscitated and circulated among the public, in order to represent and describe the conflict relative to the Wailing Wall as a general attack of the Jews on Moslem Holy Places."[109]

71

Seemingly incapable of moving into this reflexive accusative framework, that is, the one in which the claims for architecture's "uses" are superseded by claims concerning the Other's *representations* of architecture's uses, Richmond shows himself similarly unable to contend with the inclusion of his own persona within this new political dramaturgy. Reviewing the journalist Itamar Ben-Avi's accusations that "Richmondism" (Richmond's behind-the-scenes manipulation of the Arab leaders, who in turn manipulated masses) was to blame for the fury unleashed during the Buraq/Wailing Wall crisis, the alleged "puppet master" appears to recognize no performance here, except perhaps the performance of Jewish duplicity that would ratify the specific content of Arab claims. Stated differently, Richmond can only sustain the notion that Arab collective agency is not a performance—but a legitimate manifestation of Spirit—by shifting the properties of "Richmond-ism" onto Zionism:

> The Zionists needed a new cry to stimulate enthusiasm. The wail-ing wall incident gave them their opportunity. This provocation again roused the Arabs. Hence the war again took an active though unpre-meditated form. Now we are to have the same mandate, the same methods backed by troops, renewed immigration due to an enthusiasm which has been worked up by advertisements and emotional appeals. The animosity of the Arabs will increase in proportion as we proceed "manu militari." That, in these circumstances, there will be another outbreak in a few years is as certain as that the sun will rise tomorrow.[110]

In that instant, Zionism no longer helps the great stirring of the East "materially, by providing a most useful cement," as Richmond had once ar-gued, but now instigates Arab reactions at will and for its own material ends. (Jewish premeditation triggers an "unpremeditated" Arab response.) More-over, Eastern peoples' transitivity with monuments now presents itself as the fetishistic "string" by means of which the new puppeteer makes history. Richmond has inadvertently arrived at a materialist vision of adequation. And even more remarkably, by 1929 he has unwittingly conducted an imma-nent critique of his own prior theory. As Hullot-Kentor puts it, "the devel-opment of idea" (here, Richmond's failed phenomenology of Spirit) betrays itself as the "object's self-dissatisfaction" with the conceptual home devised for it as it "at every point moves towards what is not idea."[111] Each time architecture is asked to stand for its own immanent significance, it per-forms that immanence by contradicting Richmond's demands of it outright. If Richmond's phenomenology does not point, then, directly toward a uto-pia in which architecture gains identity with an Idea by virtue of its proper uses, his critical project—like that of Idealism as a whole—nevertheless "has its truth"; in it, "no one is capable of stepping out of the world consti-tuted by labor into another and unmediated one."[112] The promise of a "ful-filled" time survives in Spirit's broken promise.

4. CATACLYSM AND POGROM: AN EXERGUE ON THE NAME OF VIOLENCE

At Easter, 1920, anti-Jew riots occurred in Jerusalem. Religious ceremonies took on a political aspect. I had ample warning that these riots might occur and I warned General Bols and Waters-Taylor. I also had ample evidence that Haj al-Amin (who later became the Mufti of Jerusalem) was stirring up the Arab element in Jerusalem. . . . I considered that these events were an exact replica in miniature of a *pogrom*.
—Richard Meinertzhagen, *Middle East Diary*

How and by whom the first blow was struck is not accurately known; but in such instances the smallest incident would naturally suffice to cause a *conflagration*.
—Zionist Executive, "Memoranda Circulated by the Zionist Executive . . . Concerning the Riots in Jerusalem"

THE HISTORY OF BRITAIN'S MANDATE over Palestine was marked by periodic mobilizations of mass violence. These upheavals were identified by contemporary observers as decisive moments of historical change.[1] The significance accorded to each riot, strike, or revolt was in part due to the perceived influence exerted by popular outbreaks on British policy regarding both the project of Zionism and the independent national aspirations of Palestinians. Consequently, most of the Mandate era's major acts of violence were interpreted in contemporary documents as attempts to influence a reticent colonial administration to implement a given policy, or to rescind the findings—called White Papers—of Britain's imperial machine.

More often glossed over is the fact that the struggle to assign a name to that violence has also been a significant part of the history of the same violence. The bloody confrontations between British colonial authorities and rioters, Zionists and Palestinians, that were enacted in disturbances and general strikes appear to have been perpetuated within a simultaneously contested, yet collusive communicative framework. All sides embraced a common way of speaking about the historical enigma of violence—in reality, the enigma of agency—that simultaneously allowed opposing political interpreters to speak as if they were invoking history's proper name. One may look, for example, to the flurry of despatches to London issued by Zionist leaders following the so-called Easter, Nabi Musa, or Jerusalem riots of April 1920—and even more important to the representations made by Chaim Weizmann (of the Zionist Commission) before General Allenby, then high commissioner of Egypt—and recognize that the name *pogrom* was consistently invoked: (telegram) "Three days pogroms against Jerusalem Jews direct outcome agitation fostered in press assemblies demonstration many months without opposition from administration by well known agitators. Stop."[2]

In contrast with this understanding of violence as something instigated by elites who instigate masses (the pogrom), a more or less unified array of designations employed by British officials in the wake of Palestine's riots consistently present an image of violence that is organic and cataclysmic. For example, the Palin Commission's report on the violence of April 1920 concludes that "it seems to have been evident to everybody that [the riot was] a *storm beating up and* [that it] *might burst at any moment.*"[3] Even more common was the term "conflagration":

> [Question] 946. Have you not collected from any of these reports information to this effect, that there were meetings being held in Mosques

at these various places in the week before the outbreak? —Certainly there were meetings.

[Question] 947. But I mean meetings at which inflammatory speeches were delivered? —Certainly, that was part of the working up of the *conflagration* which was bound to occur, unless the atmosphere was changed.[4]

An exchange between Major Alan Saunders, Acting Superintendent of Police, and Sir Boyd Merriman, the chief counsel of the Zionist Executive, during a session of the parliamentary commission of inquiry on the causes of the Wailing Wall or Buraq riots of August 1929 attests to what was at stake—tactically—for opposing political players in obtaining a general acceptance for their respective names for violence. To name the mobilization of violence a pogrom is to directly transcode the riot from a sign of resistance against an active Zionist program in Palestine directly into a signifier for European ethnic and religious persecution against a passive Jewish populace. The shift from "riot" to "pogrom" necessarily imposes upon the Palestine disturbances the principal characteristics of the European model: incitement and maneuvering of the masses by an elite, and a passive acquiescence or complicity by the state to the subsequent slaughter of the persecuted minority.[5] It is for this reason that Merriman, for example, attempted to make Major Saunders acknowledge the primary importance, as well as his previous knowledge, of apparent acts of incitement by religious nationalist "personages" at mosques during the week prior to the "pogrom."

Like Molière's Monsieur Jourdain, who never realized that he had always been speaking in prose, Saunders was probably unaware of the fact that he was perpetuating the standard rhetoric of imperial policing in his reply to Merriman's query. By referring to riots as "conflagrations," the colonial official absolved the empire of the responsibility to anticipate or subdue what was, in essence, a force of nature. Moreover, the tactical function of Saunders's "prose of counter-insurgency"—to cite the historian Ranajit Guha's groundbreaking study of such pronouncements—is not only to free the state from the burden of responsibility for disturbances but to represent their violence as a spontaneous event elicited by tensions, such as "racial hatred," that would in any event have run high on a periodic basis, and which would, more importantly, have existed quite apart from the gross fact of British imperialism.[6] Contained within the word "conflagration" is an entire ecology of violence: "They break like thunder storms, heave like earthquakes, spread like wildfires, infect like epidemics. In other words, where the proverbial clod of earth turns, this is a matter to be explained in terms of natural history."[7]

Although the examples I have just presented constitute the most recognizable and enduring uses of the opposing models of violence—the "pogrom" as the mark of an incitement theory of historical change, and the "conflagration" as the sign of a theory of spontaneous historical transformation in atmospheric violence or turbulence—these same examples are not in any sense fixed as the exclusive property of the Zionist political establishment or the British colonial administration. Being part of a "movable host of metaphors, metonymies, and anthropomorphisms"[8] in which history has been problematically identified with mere causality, the "conflagration" and the "pogrom" have appeared as fungible moments in the contest over the naming of violence that was entered into by the three principal national-political constellations during the Mandate era itself. Just as one may find, for example, Zionist invocations of a conflagration (see the second epigraph at the beginning of this chapter), there were also Palestinian memoranda to the British government that appear as direct reversals of the Zionist figure of the pogrom, charging that acts of incitement by "a certain number of Jews," and attempts "to injure religious feelings" of a native populace served as the principal causes of the violence of 1920, ultimately "leading to the massacre of a number of innocent Moslems and Christians, among whom were women and children."[9]

Constrained by the same "assimilative" perspective—that reduces history to causes and effects—the historiography of Palestine and Israel repeats this conflict over the name of violence.[10] As critics, scholars, and present observers of the conflict unselfconsciously privilege instances of mass violence as the pivotal moments of historical change, they perpetuate the figuration of that violence invented during the Mandate: especially in the images of the cataclysm and the pogrom.[11] Yehoshua Porath's *The Emergence of the Palestinian-Arab National Movement, 1918–1929*, which remains one of the principal accounts of the era and one of the most exhaustively researched texts on the subject of the Arab political leadership in Mandate-era Palestine, describes the "disturbances" of 1929 as "*pogroms* in which 100 orthodox Jews of the 'old community' were murdered" and relies on the memoirs of a Palestinian nationalist to support his reading of the mass violence as a necessarily *incited* phenomenon: "'Izzat Darwaza, who served for years as a member of the AE [Arab Executive] and was in the 'thirties employed by the SMC [Supreme Muslim Council] . . . stated that the national movement was overcome by weakness but it renewed its activity for some time after the al-Buraq uprising, and it was this [reactivation of the movement] that those who caused the uprising from behind the scenes had hoped for." [12]

Conversely, Philip Mattar's biography of al-Hajj Amin al-Husayni, *The Mufti of Jerusalem: Al-Hajj Amin al-Husayni and the Palestinian National Movement*, maneuvers between the "cataclysm" and the "pogrom" in order to refute what he calls "the predominant view in the historiography of Palestine . . . that the Mufti transformed this minor religious and legal dispute [over the Wall] into a political struggle." [13] What emerges in this account, then, is an apparent challenge to the norm of an accusative historiography —a certain metahistorical awareness—which, through its own charges, preserves an accusative historiographic norm intact. Predictably, in Mattar's account, the accusation of incitement is itself turned back upon the Zionist movement, and particularly upon the revisionist Zionist camp's press during the months prior to the disturbances of 1929. Mattar notes, for example, that "*Do'ar Hayom* implied that the Muslims were worse than the hooligans of the Russian pogroms. Most of the articles called for the 'redemption' or the 'expropriation' of the Wall." [14]

At the same time, in his examination of the critical relations between the grand mufti and the Palestinian masses during the collective violence of 1929, Mattar also draws upon something much like the organicism of the "cataclysm" (insofar as violence is represented as a force of nature) in order to disengage the grand mufti from the arena of violence. Al-Hajj Amin al-Husayni, like Saunders, appears as a figure who was incapable of stopping the spontaneous mobilization of an organic body. Describing the events of 23 August 1929, the first day of a week of violence, Mattar notes: "Soon after the Friday prayers, the crowds gathered outside the mosque. . . . The Mufti and some Arab and British policemen went from group to group in an attempt to disperse them, but failed. Soon the Moslems began pouring out of the Haram . . . the violence spread through Jerusalem." [15]

If the "pogrom" and the "cataclysm" have persistently hovered between the two most discernible opponents of the present—between Israeli-Zionist nationalism and Palestinian emancipatory nationalism—the interchangeability of the "pogrom" and the "cataclysm" (their relational reciprocity) has guaranteed their inclusion within a series of other recognizable geopolitical oppositions. In the history of Palestine and Israel, the "cataclysm" and the "pogrom" may appear, and have appeared, as the refractions (as Fredric Jameson would describe them) of larger confrontations between metropole and periphery, colonizer and colonized, and between East and West—in short, between identities that are themselves allegorical, structurally interdependent, and driven to contrariety.[16] For example, in his *Seat of Pilate: An Account of the Palestine Mandate*, John Marlowe relies on the opposition between these tacit theories of spontaneous and incited violence in order to represent his history of the era as "one of the three last attempts on the part of western Europe to re-integrate the Levant into the civilization of the Mediterranean."[17]

But this same positional instability—the fact that Mandate historiography is itself *defined* by the alternating displacements of the names it gives to the violence it privileges—also attests to a strange contiguity between "cataclysm" and "pogrom." The names for violence bear witness to an insuperable relation between the cogency and play of meaning, derailing the very separability of these designations in their presumed deployment. The designations of violence inaugurate a dialectic that presents itself to cognition obliquely, each time a putatively immediate history appears to sanction the name of violence, only to introduce its own mediation sub rosa, as if it were a menacing alterity at the heart of a politics of nomination.

The problematic contiguity between the cataclysm and the pogrom can be discerned in the political examples I have already presented. For instance, Major Alan Saunders, the acting superintendent of police during the August riots of 1929 (the man who speaks for all those who have a stake in depicting violence as a conflagration), unwittingly resurrected the "pogrom" under cross-examination by the Zionist Commission's lawyer. As the proper name for a privileged violence, his "conflagration" also shows itself to be heterogeneous and nonconceptual in normative political terms, insofar as it is driven by its own lack to include that heterogeneity as a negation of its own premises: the policeman cannot successfully evoke the image of the conflagration without also privileging the function of an elite corps of inciters whose "inflammatory" speeches at mosques necessarily "spark" the fire. Thus, immanent within the "conflagration" is an inevitable pogrom.[18] Conversely, the concept of the pogrom invoked by Zionist leaders and historians in the examples already cited always already accommodated a "cataclysm" that assumed violence as a force of nature. In its etymology, the term itself is rooted in a Russian expression meaning "like thunder," emerging from, and referring continuously to nature.[19] Beyond that, conflagration emerges out of pogrom: in Zionism's counterphobic inclusion of the enemy's name for the instigation of history, "nonidentity [emerges] under the aspect of identity."[20] In a proclamation issued by the Va'ad Hale'umi [Jewish National Council] prior to the August 1929 riots, the Jewish leadership articulated a perpetual, though paradoxical, concern over imminent and spontaneous outbreaks of pogroms. Unwittingly ratifying the agency of an organic mass whose potential for violence precedes an elite's incitement, the council called upon its "Arab brethren [to] disperse the poisonous clouds of false rumours" which could—one may suppose—precipitate a brewing "cataclysm."[21]

These examples of a violence whose proper name goes astray suggest that the intrusion of the nonconceptual into history's own names for the motivation of history coincides with the intrusion of the Other.[22] From this standpoint, the historiography of violence would itself be inseparable from a history of domination: a "success-in-failure," as Gayatri Chakravorty Spivak refers to it.[23] Perennially and unwittingly summoned into priority, a subaltern identity (an identity that can only be identified by its difference) emerges in the form of a contrariety that history cannot expunge from explanations of its own instigation.

Within the logic of this subaltern paradigm, the very name that this struggle accords to violence furthers a natural history of causality that is simultaneously menacing and homeopathic to a "bourgeois-nationalist elite." In that name the same elite sustains the motivation of history as a privilege of its own ranks, even as it appears to give priority to the mass violence of an entire category of people that it excludes from the realm of agency altogether. From this perspective, the "cataclysm" and the "pogrom" are not only problematically opposed names; they also normalize, in a collusive fashion, the basic contradictions of a history that is chronically equated with a concatenation of means and ends, triggers and explosions. When either of these names is, to all appearances, deployed, historiography privileges mass violence as the vehicle of a historical transformation. However, the participant in these outbreaks—the rioter, the member of the mob—is denied by historiography any status as self-proximate architect of change. Historiography either objectifies the insurgent into an implement of a nationalist elite through the figure of a pogrom, or successfully transforms the same insurgent into a cataclysm through a fetishism of language that reduces history to nature. In its own immanent logic of expression, the historiography of Israel and Palestine's violence effaces what it represents and annuls what it privileges.

"A given alternative," however, "is already a piece of heteronomy."[24] To see the intrusion of the nonidentical as the mark of subaltern agency may itself be to sustain an "assimilative perspective" in the course of an *Ideologiekritik*. This conclusion reaffirms the argument presented by Spivak in her compelling reading of the subaltern historiography's political project, as she suggests that to posit/conflate errancy with agency may itself be to risk "insidiously objectifying the subaltern."[25] Spivak describes this as a "metalepsis," or substitution of cause for effect, in which a subaltern historiography of "assimilative perspectives" itself "describe[s] the clandestine operation of supplementarity as the inexorable speculative logic of the dialectic."[26]

Spivak implies that the inexorable fate of language—errancy—is itself erroneously identified/reified. I do not interpret this to be a polite dismissal of subaltern historiography on her part, as much as a critique of the positive negation they practice in attempting to extrapolate a subaltern consciousness from the "negative" consciousness of an elite. Keeping faith with the notion that the subaltern can only be identified by its difference, Spivak suggests that the subaltern is not to be intuited directly, as the imputed negation of a negation. In this sense, she correctly points out subaltern historiography's reliance upon the "speculative logic" of an idealist dialectic: by tacitly sustaining Hegel's assertion that the "whole is the true," subaltern historiography's negation of the negation "would be another identity, a new delusion."[27]

The suspicion of *all* identity (the broken promise of Hegel's dialectic) necessarily extends to dialectics itself in Spivak's analysis. This is the promise she keeps, as she explains the "necessary," or irreducible, failures of a historiographic project that equates the "clandestine operation of supplementarity" with history's own immanent logic, posited as a logic of contradiction. However, this is also a positing. Within this argument, play in language assumes the role of the nonidentical per se. And with that premise, an identity thesis is exhumed: the "is" of semantic *différance* (its certainty) hypostatizes the "what is not as yet" of all actuality, which has always been that abstract actuality's promise of something better.[28] Maintaining the logic of historical causality—that is, of instrumentality—within its critique, the "metalepsis" described by Spivak resolves itself into a chiasmus instead, pointing toward a dialectic after all, but one that is utterly negative. Negative, not only because the nonidentical would remain other to its positing (here, other to the withdrawal of Being marked in language as "supplementarity" or "différance"), but because the promise of another, reconciled existence survives even in our failure to articulate the impossibility of reconciliation in this one.

III. PAPER

The Zionist body which is trying to create a Jewish kingdom in Palestine, dreams of taking from us the al-Aksa Mosque, built upon the ruins of Solomon's temple, and of reconstructing their temple. . . . Weizmann has declared that Palestine must be Jewish just as England is English. Zangwill, the author, says that the Moslems must vacate Palestine. Sir Alfred Mond, one of their leaders, swears that he will devote his latter days to the building of a Temple on the site of the al Aksa Mosque. Dr. Bentwich, Secretary of Justice in the Palestine Government, in his book *Jewish Palestine* writes that the frontiers of Palestine must be the Sinai desert to beyond the Tigris and Euphrates. The Zionists have gone so far as to publish pictures of the Jerusalem showing Zionist flags on its walls, and the crescent on the dome replaced by a Zionist crown. They distribute such illustrations to their followers.

—Shaykh ʿAbd al-Qadir al-Muzaffar, *Public Call to the Muslim People from your Brethren, the Muslims of Jerusalem and the Rest of Palestine* (1922)

The Arab is an extraordinary being. He is easily raised to
a pitch of excitable enthusiasm, which fortunately dimin-
ishes with equal speed. The method of communication
through the Mosque, where religious and national aspirations are combined with great facility, makes combined
action easy to organize, and during the summer of 1929
agitation was developed to a dangerous pitch in the traditional manner, until the temperature of the Arab population was raised to a flash point. The stories that were told
may seem incredible to reasonable people, but were implicitly believed by the Arab peasants. They were told that the
Jews had stormed the Mosque of Omar and had desecrated
the holy Moslem places.

—Lord Melchett (Henry Ludwig Mond), *Thy Neighbor*

ON 6 DECEMBER 1931, Muhammad al-Hajj Amin al-Husayni, the grand
mufti of Palestine and president of the Supreme Muslim Council of Palestine
(SMC), convened in Jerusalem an International Congress for the Defense of
Islamic Holy Places.[1] In late November 1931, shortly in advance of this same
congress, Dr. Chaim Arlozorov, the head of the Jewish Agency's Political Bureau, had published a pamphlet in Arabic entitled *Zionism and the Islamic Holy
Places of Palestine (al-Sahyuniyya wa'l-Amakin al-Islamiyya al-Muqaddass fi Falastin)*. The tract was essentially the translation of a press conference Arlozorov held on 18 November of the same year, during which he attempted
systematically to refute "all claims by Muslims that the Jewish Agency is set
to occupy, supersede [take over], and ultimately destroy Islamic monuments
in Palestine."[2] *Al-Sahyuniyya* was, according to the Arab Bureau of the Jewish Agency, "distributed in thousands of copies in Eretz Israel and in neigh-
boring countries."[3]

This booklet was soon countered by another, a refutation of Arlozorov's
refutation of Arab claims published by the Society for the Protection of the
Aqsa Mosque and the Islamic Holy Places in Jerusalem (Jam'iyyat Hirasat

al-Masjid al-Aqsa wa'l-Amakin al-Islamiyya al-Muqaddasa bi'l-Quds), in which the authors argued that while Jews had been offered other sites to colonize, "their interest in Palestine was driven by a religious conviction to reclaim the Temple, which was around the Aqsa, and to establish a Jewish government [kingdom] in Palestine."[4] The unnamed authors of these *bayan*, or proclamations, who were part of the political apparatus of the grand mufti (as president of the Supreme Muslim Council), drew extensively upon a series of previously printed pamphlets, proclamations, and representations made by the Defense Committee for the Noble Buraq [Lajnat al-Difaʿ ʿan al-Buraq al-Sharif] and other Arab sources during the tense period leading up to the Buraq, or Wailing Wall, riots of 1929.[5] Chief among these was a small gazette called *Bayan ila Ikhwanina al-Muslimin ʿAmmatan*, or *Proclamation to our Muslim Brethren Generally*, which in turn incorporated and catalogued a series of Jewish and Zionist representations of Islamic monuments in Jerusalem—I am referring to actual pictures—which were given as much attention as written sources, and treated as manifest signs of Zionism's latent imperative to build a temple in place of the Aqsa.

Arlozorov's political bureau was well aware of the previous Arab pamphlets and proclamations, as well as of many of the contemporary statements in the Arabic press that drew upon them, and perpetuated their type of accusation. In fact, this entire style of argumentation had been closely monitored by the Zionist establishment since the early 1920s, and on some occasions, the Zionist Executive (the precursor to the Jewish Agency) even warned the government of Palestine about the dangers of such presentations in the Arabic press, accompanied with cautions that such assertions and rumors regarding a threat to monuments could incite the Palestinian masses to violence.[6] In *al-Sahyuniyya* Arlozorov not only cites contemporary reports of this kind appearing in Arabic newspapers, but also refers to their precedents, arguing that what was then taking place was a reprisal of the situation that had transpired in 1929, when, in his view, the Supreme Muslim Council attempted to deflect internal Muslim criticism by "creating a rumour about Jewish intentions to occupy the Aqsa Mosque."[7] Attempting to break out of this political dramaturgy, or performative "frame" (as Erving Goffman would refer to it),[8] Arlozorov challenges what he presents—or appears to present—as his opponents' engrossment with the furniture of politics (threatened monuments), adding: "The same tactics are used now."[9] Similarly, the Palestinians' refutation of Arlozorov's refutations reveal a tacit familiarity with the history and conventions of this style of exchange, but display important differences. In reiterating arguments already familiar from the past—the proclamations and pamphlets from 1929 and before—the Society for the Protection of the Aqsa Mosque and the Islamic Holy Places in Jerusalem did not only disclose the operative dimension of their enterprise, their instrumental treatment of previous charges. In returning to familiar roles and scripts, the political actors tacitly acknowledged the dramaturgy itself.[10] And they did so precisely through their categorical refusal to "break out of frame," or in other words, by their unwillingness to abandon their participation in the definition of the same situation that Arlozorov calls into question (in this way, effectively making his effort to estrange a situation itself appear strange).[11]

In short, despited Arlozorov's point-by-point refutation of the Palestinian accusations, the Society for the Protection of the Aqsa Mosque's repetition of these same accusations became, in the language of J. L. Austin, "performative utterances" in their own right; as statements that were simultaneously deeds, they necessarily "keyed," or reaffirmed, the conflict's existing performative framework.[12]

In what may be the most revealing aspect of the exchange between Arlozorov and the Society for the Protection of the Aqsa Mosque, each of these opponents turns to a "role-character formula": a way of defining events so that "the individual, in the guise of the character he is performing, comments on himself as a performer or upon his fellow performers."[13] Thus, in *Bayan Jam'iyyat Hirasat al-Masjid al-Aqsa*, the Society for the Protection of the Aqsa Mosque concludes its own refutation of Arlozorov's pamphlet by contrasting the Jews' "belittling tone" with the Muslims' refusal to "debase themselves to the same level."[14] Here, a Muslim performance of high-minded awareness of how things sound is opposed to a Jewish lack of self-consciousness about the vulgarity of its own claims. Conversely, referring specifically to the recirculation of the same old hearsay about the imminent takeover of the Dome of the Rock by Jews, Arlozorov can offer in *al-Sahyuniyya wa'l-Amakin al-Islamiyya al-Muqaddasa fi Filastin* only two possible characterizations of his opponents' performances: in their talk of monuments the instigators of such rumors are "either fanatics, steeped in darkness, and promoters of obscurantism . . . , [who are therefore] unfit to be considered leaders capable of dealing with high issues such as the relations between peoples and different religions; or they are liars in pursuit of individual gain."[15]

Like Goffman, I am interested in the "special possibilities that result from this mutually assessed mutual assessment."[16] Immanent within such dramaturgies—inherent in their form—is a tension between contingency and play, so that the performance of the "role-character formula" can either constitute a "reflexive" breaking of frame (the subject's momentary passage to enlightenment regarding the demands that the staging of a political reality makes on their own presentation of events) and thus, of a certain agency, or its inverse: a "frame trap" within which the role of the players now itself constitutes a structure, or "self-sealing interpretive vocabulary."[17] As the very performance of false consciousness, a "frame trap" would appear to be the projective recognition of the dramaturgy, but only in part, as the unmasking of the performative strategy of the "other side," a task that explains the need for the "role character formula" to begin with.[18]

With the appearance of a politics of monuments that can only be accounted for in the putative passage from the irresponsible play of "fanatics steeped in darkness" to the agency of self-interested "liars," the performance of a certain self-consciousness of the dramaturgy itself becomes that which sustains, as it also refigures, actors' claims for the immediacy of their own circumstances. In other words, with the passage of Arlozorov and the Society for the Protection of the Aqsa Mosque to these critical and reflexive assertions about one's opponent's representations of one's own relation to monuments, this struggle approaches the understanding of architecture's adequacy to history that would dominate its subsequent phases; the conflict advances toward a moment when its antagonists would finally argue that an immediately intuited political reality could find confirmation in architecture's representation, and not simply in its use.

The passage from what I have called an "operative" model of adequation of the kind presented by Ernest Richmond, to this "critical" or "reflexive" or "self-conscious" one disclosed in the Society for the Protection of the Aqsa Mosque and Arlozorov's "role-character formulae," necessarily involves something like the superimposition of a concern over the appearance or significance of an architectural figure, like that of the Dome of the Rock, onto the already familiar political argument about its deployment. In other words, if in Richmond's work the project of immediacy was obsessively and anthropomorphically figured in terms of an animistic relation between the Dome of the Rock's "tissues and sinews" of tile, and a steadfast "soul" of stone within it that had to be restored and sustained in order for the nation itself to be sustained,[19] then here, with the reflexive model, no such actual architectural investment is necessarily required. No restorations, no demolitions. Instead, the bayan and their stylistic precursors constitute the emergence of an effort to analyze precisely those kinds of deployments of the monument to unmediated instrumentality; a passage from tiles and stone to papers and leaflets and speech acts that drive politics ineluctably toward a kind of art criticism. This "art criticism" normalizes—it doesn't resolve—the stereotomy of the figure, in the sense that it routinizes and renders transparent the nonconceptual element built into the figures nominally impressed into politics.[20]

In its modern form, the impetus toward this new reflexive concern, or debate, over the significance of the deployment of figures roughly coincides with the rise of what I have called the operative vision of adequation, as its corollary. As I suggested in chapter 4, it already insinuates itself immediately following the death of the mufti of Jerusalem, Kamil al-Husayni, in March 1921, when Richmond witnessed the elections for the position of the new mufti, and then helped to maneuver the government of Palestine to nullify the election and nominate Muhammad Hajj Amin al-Husayni (the younger half-brother of the deceased mufti) to the post.[21] In this election of 1921 al-Husayni gained fewer votes than a cleric named Husam al-Din Jarallah on April 12, 1921.[22] Consequently, the Husayni faction initiated a smear campaign against Jarallah, posting leaflets in Jerusalem on the eve of 19 April accusing the latter of being a Jewish Zionist mufti, who, if appointed, would "assist the Jews in killing the national spirit of the country" and who would help "in handing over [to] the Jews the Haram Esh-Sherif, the Dome of the Kock [sic] and el Aksa that they might pull them down [and] build in their place the Temple and the place of sacrifice as stated by Alfred Mond and the president of the Zionist Commission Dr. Eder."[23]

Beyond the clever rhetoric that transposed al-Husayni's opponent into a Zionist functionary, what emerges as a clearly discernible topos in this election propaganda is the same operative formula already encountered in Richmond's defenses of the Dome of the Rock from the same period. In this message, the coherence, or unity, of the Palestinian "national spirit" is, once again, simultaneously affirmed and threatened by virtue of its relation to a monument that perpetually stands in place of that same cohesion, and which for that reason (because of its inadequacy to the vision of adequacy it names) repeatedly has to be deployed as such. But at that moment, and in the same leaflet, the very invocation of the threatened monument as an exhortative "tool" begins to be subsumed by its corollary—a deployed figure—when, in the form of a citation of Sir Alfred Mond's statements regarding the rebuilding of the Temple, this operative model of adequation necessarily occasions its own impossibility. The political "use" of the citation itself hinges upon the ability of those who invoke the danger posed by the "Temple" to the mosque to effect a complete distinction—a stereotomy—between figural and denotative meaning. For Mond's rhetoric to be used as "evidence" in the proclamation, it has to denote a real intent, rather than function solely as a trope of regeneration. Yet it is precisely this stereotomy that will be called into question by the "Temple" itself. On 1 July, following a query by a member of parliament named C. W. Bellairs regarding Mond's statement, the high commissioner for Palestine, Sir Herbert Samuel, cabled the Colonial Office asking: "Grand Mufti and other Moslems have represented that uneasiness has been caused by Mond's reference to rebuilding of the temple. . . . What precisely was the language used? Can you send me a reassuring explanation from Mond?" [24]

The Colonial Office's response, which was delayed for two weeks owing to a difficulty in getting a copy of Mond's speech, relayed the language of the original statement (as paraphrased in the Daily Telegraph) and added: "As was pointed out in reply to Bellairs' question Mond was speaking figuratively of the future of Palestine and had no idea of suggesting any interference with the actual site of Solomon's temple." [25] This same point was recorded more forcefully by the secretary of state for the colonies, Winston Churchill, who asserted in the Colonial Office file on this matter: "The whole thing is a ridiculous misunderstanding, arising out of some perfectly legitimate after-dinner eloquence on Sir Alfred's part." [26]

However, even as the Colonial Office's responses implied that the reaction to the Mond incident could be traced to a confusion, back in Palestine, of figural language for denotative speech, in Palestine itself those same clarifications would be incorporated within further Arab clarifications, thereby denying any validity to England's tacit aspiration to a "metapolitical"—one is tempted to say, semiotic—analysis of Mond's speech. In this way, Palestinian Arab sources not only continued to cite Mond's proclamation, they also cited the secretary of state for the colonies' own telegrams of explanation regarding Mond's statements as evidence of England's ratification of the plan to rebuild the Hebrew Temple. During the 1920s, and after, in the Defense Committee for the Noble Buraq's Bayan ila Ikhwanina (1928), the Society for the Protection of the Aqsa Mosque's Bayan Jamʿiyyat Hirasat al-Masjid al-Aqsa (1932), and even in the grand mufti's own work, Haqaʾiq ʿan Qadhiyyat Filastin (Truths Concerning the Question of Palestine, 1954), the statements of both Mond and the Colonial Office were cited—without context, and often inaccurately—in such a way as to negate any assertion that Mond's announcement was a legitimate piece of "after-dinner eloquence." In Haqaʾiq (which also quotes the pamphlets of 1928 and 1932 without citing them), for example, Mond's proclamation is translated to read that he was inclined to dedicate his remaining days to rebuilding the Temple (as cited in the *Daily Telegraph* and quoted by the Colonial Office reports), and that he intended to rebuild it "in place of the Aqsa."²⁷ The Colonial Office's official response to the mufti of 1921 appeared in *Haqa'iq* as follows: "Sir Mond explained that his inclination is to rebuild a great and perfect building on the site where Solomon's Temple previously stood (the Aqsa Mosque)."²⁸ In the bayan as well as in al-Husayni's recapitulation of these events in *Haqa'iq* these citations are also underlined, as if in emphasis of the very problem of representation they themselves raise: that the immediacy of the situation confirmed by the "Temple" is only the immediacy of a mediation.²⁹

Given their continued assertion after the Colonial Office's clarifications, these series of "citations"—of Mond, in particular—do not merely represent a repetition of the position held before the telegram from Whitehall was sent. With the grand mufti's inclusion of the Colonial Office memoranda and Mond's speech into his own hermeneutic of the monument, a kind of dramaturgic refusal to "break frame," similar to that later exhibited by the Society for the Protection of the Aqsa Mosque, first presents itself as an inchoate development in the "erection" of the political frame itself. In other words, the negation of the metaphoric and, in their minds, therefore, metapolitical interpretation of Mond's words, can only be sustained performatively, in the emergence of a kind of "dramaturgical discipline" on the part of those who would refuse such a link.³⁰ However, this same performative rebuff of the trope—or, in this instance of one's opponents' "expressive overtones"—bears failure in its own form, and specifically in the form of emphases and lies, eventually rendering it apotropaic. In each instance in the bayan and in *Haqa'iq*, where Mond's proclamations about the Temple are held to disclose themselves as "concrete symbols" of Zionism's intentions, the Arabic texts *themselves* underline and so emphasize those citations with which they have tampered in order to "secure" the immediacy of the architectural figure. But that is the point. It remains a figure whose reliance on performances, emphases, modifications, and additional paraphernalia of certainty tacitly confirm the very irreducibility of that which these actors feel called upon to cancel: the abstraction that dominates their political circumstances.

This is consequently the juncture at which both truth and lies have to be considered in their "extramoral" or "nonmoral" sense.³¹ There is little doubt that the Majlissiyyun (or, members of the SMC's faction) invent quotes, and that (at the same time) those same inventions bring to crisis the illusion that the originary "truth" of the metaphor is itself not a covering lie of some sort—since "to be truthful [in the normative sense] means to employ the usual metaphors . . . to lie according to a fixed convention."[32] At the same time, there is also little doubt that the "lie" of metaphor (i.e., the new "lie" imposed upon metaphor by virtue of its refiguration in the bayan) is itself only confirmed as metonymy, and not as a pure ideograph, since to be self-evident (and for that reason effective) for the Majlissiyyun it must necessarily also appear as a figure of displacement. The historical truth of the Mond "citation," then, is not simply the truth of propaganda, or of "misrepresenting the utterances of well-known Jewish personalities," as is implied by the historians Uri Kupferschmidt and Zvi Elpeleg, but the truth of a series of accretions, appendages, and added "evidence" that of necessity attach themselves to the quote between 1921 and 1932, and again in 1954, as it is cited and recited and contorted in the effort to render it identical with those elements that it summons to self-certainty.[33] In other words, if the story of the career of the repetitive appearances of the Mond citation is in some sense the story of the failure of these efforts to attain a scission between history and its own instigating gesture, it is also, simultaneously, the story of the successful normalization of that abortive effort, ensuring the ongoing precipitation of the apotropaic figure into the "properly" political.

This passage required the introduction of figures—actual pictures—into the contest of proclamations and pamphlets. (I analyze these images extensively in the following chapter, but here I wish to present the way their *existence* was debated in the contestations over the significance of the Mond quote.) In July 1922, soon after the Colonial Office officially responded to the mufti concerning Sir Alfred's bit of "after-dinner eloquence," a Palestinian delegation led by Shaykh ʿAbd al-Qadir al-Muzaffar departed for Mecca to attend a pilgrimage congress.[34] There, according to Martin Seth Kramer, the delegation worked to "garner support for Palestinian resistance both to Zionism and the recently imposed League of Nations mandate for Palestine."[35] In this project, which Kramer calls the first Palestinian effort to mobilize specifically Muslim (as opposed to simply Arab) support for the Palestinian cause, al-Muzaffar and the delegation disseminated variations of a leaflet entitled *Nidaʾ ʿAmm ila al-ʿAmmat al-Islamiyya, min Ikhwahihum Muslima Bayt al-Maqdis wa Saʾir Filastin* (*Public Call to the Muslim People from your Brethren, the Muslims of Jerusalem and the Rest of Palestine* [1922]).[36] In fact, al-Muzaffar, who appears to have been the author of the proclamations in question, was equally adept at articulating the appeal on both Islamic and Arabist grounds, addressing one variant of the "General Call" to the "Dignified Iraqi Nation," and another to the "Islamic Nation" as a whole.[37] One can only speculate that it is due to al-Muzaffar's capacity to negotiate between these (not altogether) distinct discursive consituencies that Ronald Storrs, the governor of Jerusalem, described him as an "Arab intriguer." According to Storrs, the shaykh "perorated [only] . . . when assured of no cold light of fact upon his invective."[38] Anticipating Arlozorov's conclusions by a decade, Storrs's "prose of counter-insurgency" condemned al-Muzaffar to a no-man's land of agency somewhere between fanatics and liars, noting: "Every statement is either an *expressio* or a *suggestio falsi.*"[39]

In the proclamation itself al-Muzaffar "perorates" as if from the declamatory position of the "Palestinian Muslim" people, who in their role as "the guardians of the Aqsa Mosque" attempt to warn the Islamic world that their sacred sites in Jerusalem are "under immense and deplorable danger from the Zionists."[40] He then cites Chaim Weizmann, the head of the Zionist Organization; Israel Zangwill, the Anglo-Jewish writer; Norman Bentwich, the attorney general of Palestine; and of course, Sir Alfred Mond, to disclose the nature of Jewish designs on Islamic monuments.[41] This style of argument is already familiar. But what is new here is what follows this regular concatenation of citations that collectively fail to sustain the immediacy of the Dome of the Rock in a split between rhetoric and telegraphy: in the distinction between a temple of "after-dinner eloquence" and a temple-in-the-planning, al-Muzaffar continues: "These peoples' self-confidence and aspirations [have] reached the point of depicting the sacred house of God with Zionist flags flying on top of it, and [with] the Crown of Zion placed on the honored stone instead of the crescent. These images are distributed among their people."[42] Reminding Muslims that this danger would be intensified by the imminent ratification of Britain's mandate over Palestine, he then adds: "We call upon the Muslim world to be prepared for the solemn day to denounce this violation which is against [our] rights and justice."[43]

The delegation's activities did not pass unnoticed. According to the Meccan newspaper *al-Qibla*, the Palestinian delegation's efforts were met with "spontaneous" demonstrations in defense of the Aqsa and against the British Mandate for Palestine. At one of these events, Prince Zayed "gave a speech at which he pointed to a picture representing the Dome of the Rock on which the Zionist crown was placed. At that moment the crowd shouted for the destruction of the crown of Zion and the abolition of the Zionist national home [policy]."[44] Similarly, the British consul in Aleppo recorded the publication of al-Muzaffar's proclamation in the Syrian newspaper *al-Nahda* on 13 July, and forwarded its translation to Whitehall.[45] A British military officer in the Middle East named John Thomas Woolwrych Perowne reported directly to Lord Balfour—the former secretary of state for foreign affairs, author of the Balfour Declaration, and at the time the lord president of the Council (the minister responsible for the king's Privy Council)—that he had received intelligence to the effect that the Palestinian delegation to the pilgrimage congress had gone to Mecca "to stir up trouble in the focus of Islam."[46] According to Ronald Storrs, it is as a consequence of the success of these efforts that the Palestine gendarmerie's CID (Criminal Investigation Division) received reports that after the pilgrimage congress, "rumours were circulating, to the effect that the Jews tried to stop Sheikh 'Abdel Kader al Muzghr' [sic] from entering Palestine."[47]

What is so striking about al-Muzaffar's declaration concerning the picture is that at the very moment when the apotropaic, in the conventional sense of the term (i.e., as a menacing figure), actually intervenes in the scene of history, it simultaneously disappears in the reporting of that appearance. As that which could be summoned to give proof to the series of citations that had already been summoned as proof of political intentions, the picture vanishes: it presents itself only as a transparent window into a political elite's cynical imperatives, or as the immediate reflection of organic forces, a *volunté generale.*

For example, within a year of al-Muzaffar's declaration in April 1923, Frederick Kisch, the Zionist Executive's political officer in Jerusalem, met with Musa Kazim al-Husayni, the former mayor of Jerusalem and head of the Palestinian Arab Executive.[48] This interview took place shortly after the return of a Palestinian delegation to London, the completion of legislative council elections, and the installment of a conservative government in England—in short, at a time when Anglo-Arab-Zionist relations were particularly strained. In his political diaries, Kisch records that after passing through a series of political topics, their conversation turned to the same picture described by al-Muzaffar. He then records the argument that ensued in the following way:

93

> [Kisch]—". . . Vous exagérez . . . vous parliez d'eux tout à l'heure en disant qu'il faut songer à ce qui rapproche et non pas ce qui divise. On a eu tort d'inculquer dans l'esprit de la masse simpliste l'idée que les juifs veulent s'emparer de la Mosquée d'Omar."
>
> [Musa Kazim al-Husayni]—"Ce n'est pas nous, ce sont les juifs eux-mêmes qui ont fait photographier la Mosquée d'Omar avec le drapeau sioniste flottant au sommet de la coupôle."
>
> [Kisch]—"Dites plutôt que c'est là l'oeuvre d'ennemis imbéciles

aussi bien des juifs que des musulmans. Je puis vous certifier, moi, que les juifs respecterons toujours la Mosquée d'Omar et tous les Lieux Saints Musulmans et Chrétiens. Les Musulmans n'ont ils pas la garde des tombeaux des prophètes juifs, des rois juifs, et même du grand législateur, Moise?"

[Mosa Kazim al-Husayni]—"Parfaitement, les Musulmans reconnaissent tous les prophètes et les respectent. De tous temps ils ont gardé tous les Lieux Saints aussi bien des Chrétiens que des Israelites." [49]

Although it may not look like it at first glance, in this charged debate over "who"—exactly—is using "what," Kisch and Musa Kazim al-Husayni are trying to define the exact relation between a motivating figure and (historical) agency. First, competing efforts to explain the "uses" or "tactics" of imagery are themselves disclosed to be tactical, in the familiar [Goffmanian] sense of attempting either to establish or to break "frame." But they are in no way familiar in their specific historical context, insofar as the ripostes between these two opponents inaugurate the same dramaturgical conventions that would become second nature by the time of Arlozorov's exchanges with the Society for the Protection of the Aqsa Mosque, and inaugurate them precisely in the context of each side's disenchantment with the other's explanations concerning the (evidentiary) uses of a picture of the Dome of the Rock. And the formal characteristics of this "interaction ritual" are critical. Implying that both he and his Arab counterpart are part of the same "performance team" of rational politicians who stand opposed to all the "imbeciles" and "enemies" who widen the religious divide, Kisch clearly attempts to entice Musa Kazim al-Husayni from (what Goffman would characterize as) his "frontstage" position, and toward a collusive "backstage" communication, away from politics' formalized, codified speech acts to another framework that is putatively free of the restrictive etiquette of such posturing. [50] As the aim of such communication would be to acknowledge the "uses" of risky, inflammatory devices by the Palestinian's side, in a sense Kisch actually invites him to accept a theory of figuration that sees the apotropaic image as something utterly contingent upon the agency of those who display it, something standing behind politics and already backstage. ["On a eu tort d'inculquer dans l'esprit de la masse simpliste l'idée que les juifs veulent s'emparer de la Mosquée d'Omar."] For his part, Musa Kazim al-Husayni appears to perform the role of someone who does not think there is a 'backstage' zone to which one could possibly retreat in this collusive communicative framework. And, in so doing, he effectively invites Kisch to accept a theory of figuration according to which the picture's meaning precedes any political body's cynical manipulation. Insofar as Musa Kazim's "ce n'est pas nous" stance concedes no orchestration on the Arab side—and denies a "backstage" locus of agency to which it would be possible to repair—then, by default, all that is left is something like a Jewish fetishism of images that fails to recognize itself as an inflammatory practice, even though it actually takes center stage, both in the conflict and in any viable interpretation of its instigation. ["Ce n'est pas nous, ce sont les juifs eux-mêmes qui ont fait photographier la Mosquée d'Omar avec la drapeau sioniste flottant au sommet de la coupôle."]

As they debate whether pictures motivate people or people motivate (the meaning) of pictures, these political operatives confirm the dialectical aspect of the very device they attempt to introduce into evidence: the picture of the Dome of the Rock. Their arguments founder in the attempt to locate the political "utility" of images in the distinction between photographs and their mimetic architectural referent. There is a direct correspondence between Kisch's play for Musa Kazim's admission of a "backstage" interpretation of agency, and the Zionist representative's understanding of the "uses" of monuments themselves, their apotropaic power. (Here, the monument itself is the "backstage" of representation, or the referent of mimesis: "On a eu tort d'inculquer . . . l'idée que les juifs veulent s'emparer de la Mosquée.") This position disavows, even as it privileges under the theory of "inculcation" underlying Kisch's vision of agency, the device putatively deployed by an elite to mobilize a "simple mass": a picture produced by Jews that is quite front-stage in the matter. Inversely, the Palestinian's refusal to break frame —his steadfast reliance on a "front-stage" position that lays the project of apotropaism on those who would pretend that he is operating "backstage"— similarly founders on the distinction between the referent and the referend of menace at the moment when he says: "Ce n'est pas nous." Because in Musa Kazim al-Husayni's theory of agency, no Jewish leaflet could be counted upon to menace Arabs if it didn't attempt to disrupt the transitivity between simple masses and architecture that he presumed to be in place already, "backstage," as the referend of that representation. In laying the claim for a Jewish figural provocation, Musa Kazim al-Husayni confirms a theory of Muslim Arab fetishism of monuments—or of architecture.

Clearly, this interview solved nothing. The picture's evidentiary status as a political implement could not be accounted for.[51] So what could be the goal of so fruitless a discussion about the ends of figures? Kisch may have offered an unwitting reply when, paraphrasing Musa Kazim, he noted: "Il faut songer à ce qui rapproche et non pas ce qui divise." One possible "end" to this exchange may well have been to regularize an ideological "frame" according to which everyone agrees to act as if figures actually have ends. At the same time, it is important to recognize that this conversation already anticipated the price of "frame." Just when the claims regarding the uses of images passed over into mutual interpretations regarding the claims for those uses, this debate also presaged a point at which opponents would be driven to anticipate their counterparts' interpretations of figures, thus driving this political history inexorably toward a completely reflexive theory of adequation, that is, toward a moment when the interpretation of figures themselves would be indistinguishable from the interpretation of the conflict.

This fully reflexive politics of adequation is palpably imminent in the subsequent tactics of both Kisch himself and his opponents. By 1927, the head of the political department of the Zionist Executive in Jerusalem could review a press clipping in the local Arabic newspaper most closely associated with the grand mufti and the SMC, and, without questioning whether representations of architecture actually "have" ends, already envision the ends to which the interpretation of those figurations of architecture would be put by his opponents. In December 1927, Kisch was made aware of an article in an Arab-American newspaper called al-Hurriya that was subsequently reprinted in the Palestinian al-Jami'a al-'Arabiyya under the heading "Misleading Zionist Propaganda." This article claimed that Zionism itself—and not Palestinian Islam—viewed an American model of the Second Temple as a prefabrication of the real thing:

> Jewish propaganda announces that the Zionists are endeavouring to rebuild Solomon's Temple on the ruins of the Moslem Mosque, second to that of Mecca and Medina. It is even alleged by that propaganda that the various parts of the Temple made of stone, and iron have been completed in Europe and America and will shortly be gathered in Palestine for the final erection of the building. . . . Those who have raised this Jewish question are quite aware that the fact of announcing the project constitutes a menace to peace in Palestine.[52]

This is familiar. Al-Jami'a al-'Arabiyya clearly is stretching the type of declamatory "ce n'est pas nous" position articulated by Musa Kazim further, laying the charge of an inflammatory (mis)interpretation of the model at the feet of Zionism. In doing so, it anticipates the customary argument of Zionism—itself already familiar from the history of this contest over citations and their adjuncts—that such claims constituted an Arab misrecognition of the figural for the denotative, and of the referent for the referend. Consequently, the only "metacritical" position open to Kisch is the one he was advised to assume by Gershon Agron [Agronsky], the editor of the *Palestine Post*. Agron notified Kisch: "I am suggesting to all Hebrew papers to ridicule the 'Alhuria' [sic] libel regarding the rebuilding of the Temple. I believe, however, that this is such a monstrous charge that the Government should be called on to say something very strong on the subject. . . . I very much fear that unless strongest measures are adopted we shall never hear the end of this."[53] Consequently, Kisch contacted the chief secretary of the Palestine government on 30 December 1927 and suggested that when al-Jami'a al-'Arabiyya had presented the story of the model as if it emanated from Zionist propaganda sources callous toward Muslim sensitivities, the Arabic newspaper itself had mischievously engaged in a potentially dangerous arousal of the same sensitivities:

> It would appear that these reports—in so far as they are honest in their origin—refer to an American non-Jewish project for building in the United States a model of Solomon's Temple to be set in artificial scenery representing the former site of the Temple. . . . [T]he Executive are not in a position to say whether the publication of these reports in the 'Uljamea Ul Arabia' [sic] is creating any excitement among the Moslem population of Palestine, but I think it right to bring the matter to your notice so that—in case such excitement has been occasioned—the Government should itself make some announcement to these most mischievous and dangerous rumours.[54]

With this "scary model," a specific political seme is introduced, never again to be abandoned. That seme is one according to which political opponents self-consciously relate the representations of architecture to the possibility of the subaltern's violence through interpretations of the other's interpretive ideological frame. In the contest of recrimination about the models, both sides in this conflict appear to agree that a certain domain of figuration is ineluctably linked with a potentially explosive and historically transformative violence—because of the other's (mis)representation of one's own relation to objects, figures, and models. And still, even as politics approaches this reflexive thinking about architecture's adequacy to history, a fundamental question emerges with even greater urgency: who exactly is "using" the architecture that confirms the immediacy of political circumstances by virtue of its utility? Stated differently, who is the subject of apotropaism and what is its object? In the tense period between the first skirmishes of the Buraq/Wailing Wall crisis in September 1928 and the International Muslim Congress of 1931, this very question forms the pivot around which all the debates of the Defense Committee for the Noble Buraq, of Chaim Arlozorov and the Jewish Agency, and of the Society for the Protection of the Aqsa Mosque and the Islamic Holy Places would turn, without resolution. In these disputes, politics finally lapses into a contest over the proper interpretation of political representations—quite simply, lapses into a kind of art criticism—and in so doing, it unwittingly discloses that the dialectical relation between figuration and agency that had emerged in earlier debates surrounding the proper "uses" of architectural images was also a constitutive feature of the images themselves.

Mr. Hopkin Morris: "Is it suggested that this picture has affected the Arab mind in any way?"

Mr. Silley: "Most decidedly, most emphatically. It is the sort of thing that would create trouble more than anything else."

—Examination of ʿAbd al-Qadir Rashid by Reginald Silley before the Shaw Commission

"You do not think the Jews have designs upon our Sacred Places?" he asked. "Very well. I will produce evidence." He left the room for a few moments and reappeared with a file of papers. Opening these he produced maps of Jerusalem showing all the well-known monuments described in Hebraic writing as Hebraic shrines. The Mosque of Omar, crowned with a Jewish crown and with the verse from the Koran that is inscribed round the façade transposed into a Jewish religious quotation etc.

—*Egyptian Gazette*, 14 November 1931

A CRITICAL QUESTION—an art-historical question—was debated in the political culture of Mandate-era Palestine between 1928 and 1936. It has never been resolved in the years since, as it centers upon the adequacy of images to the historical actuality of which they are a part. While political elites were led to argue that social reality "appeared" in figures, "with polemical truth, as well as ideologically," they nonetheless found themselves called upon to explain how the reduction of pictures to historically contingent, ideological *faits socials*, simultaneously opened an irreducible gulf between the same figures and the reality they named.[1] Conversely, as political elites were led to argue that such a position was itself a kind of "philosophical mystification" guaranteed to confuse the fact that semantically autonomous figures simply appeared in social reality—as if parthenogenically—and were simply there to be "used," elites found themselves called upon to explain how such putatively autonomous figures could so successfully name a reality that they did not equal . . . or were not a part of.[2] From the perspective offered by the figures that would actually be debated in this fashion, it is clear that as the political culture of Mandatory Palestine began to pose these art-historical questions, it also found itself compelled to elaborate those same inquiries along a series of three related indices of representation that were, from long experience, already familiar to art history itself: the iconic or symbolic, the performative, and the allegorical.[3] I am referring, respectively, to interpretations of an image as something ontologically indistinct from, or isomorphically contiguous with, what it represents (as with an idol);[4] to interpretations of an image as something that enacts what it discloses (in the way that a flap in the drawing of a door in a greeting card might actually open);[5] and lastly, to interpretations that see figures as a cipher language of history.

In October 1928, shortly after the first of the major crises surrounding the Wailing Wall/Buraq in Jerusalem, the Defense Committee for the Noble Buraq (Lajnat al-Difaʿ ʿan al-Buraq al-Sharif) published a pamphlet entitled *Proclamation to Our Muslim Brethren Generally (Bayan ila Ikhwanina al-Muslimin ʿAmattan)*.[6] In an effort to establish the trail of political citations that characterized the history of such publications, I began the previous chapter by noting that this pamphlet was a kind of template for that of the Society for the Protection of the Aqsa Mosque and the Islamic Holy Places in Jerusalem (Jamʿiyyat Hirasat al-Masjid al-Aqsa Waʾl-Amakin al-Islamiyya al-Muqaddasa biʾl Quds), which in turn was responding to Chaim Arlozorov's *Zionism and the Islamic Holy Places [al-Sahyuniyya waʾl-Amakin al-Islamiyya al-Muqaddassa fi Falastin]*. However, it appears that the *Bayan Ila Ikhwanina al-*

Muslimin 'Amattan was itself loosely modeled on the shorter proclamations taken by the delegation of Shaykh 'Abd al-Qadir al-Muzaffar to the Hejaz in 1922. Like those earlier proclamations, this pamphlet begins by establishing Palestinian Islam's custodianship of the sacred sites and then enumerates what it presents as the arrogant ambitions of Zionism through a series of citations. Predictably, after arguing that Zionists/Jews (the sentence is not clear on this point) "did not take into account at all their offending four hundred million Moslems in the matter of their first Kibla and their third Mosque,"[7] it cited Alfred Mond's bit of "after-dinner eloquence" as proof of this insensitivity, and followed that observation with a familiar compilation of other references to the writings of Israel Zangwill and Norman Bentwich. Following these, in a direct paraphrase of al-Muzaffar's proclamation, the *bayan* spoke of pictures, arguing that the Jews' "plots and their ambitions have reached such a degree that they have started publishing and broadcasting pictures of the sacred House of Allah and the Zionist flags are hoisted on the walls thereof, and the Jewish crown is established on the dome of the noble Rock of Allah instead of the crescent."[8]

What differentiates this pamphlet from those that follow the formula of references upon references to the Mond quote is the insertion of an actual figure—apparently the same one displayed by Prince Zayed at the rally in Mecca—now accompanied by an explanatory legend "giving in Arabic the equivalent of the Hebrew inscriptions" in the original (figure 4).[9] (The figure presents the Dome of the Rock in the center of an architectural frame, along with a series of other sites in Jerusalem holy to Jews. Known as a "mizrah," it was intended to be placed on a wall to indicate the direction of prayer in a Jewish household.) The significance of this figure's appearance in the pamphlet is attested by the intensive investment in its interpretation that would follow. For example, in 1932, as the Arab Bureau of the Political Department of the Jewish Agency for Palestine attempted to provide a complete Hebrew translation of the response of the Society for the Protection of the Aqsa Mosque to Arlozorov's pamphlet, it reviewed all of its intelligence on the history of this and other pictures in order to formulate future responses to its possible reappearance in the Arab press.[10] Moreover, the illustration was reproduced in various versions of the same pamphlet by the Society for the Protection of the Aqsa Mosque in 1931 and 1932. It also appeared later, in accounts relating to what historians refer to as the *Nakba* (the catastrophe) of the Palestinian diaspora following 1948. For example, in Mahmud al-Abidi's *Mihnat Bayt al-Maqdis*, this strange figure appears as retroactive evidence of the imminence of the catastrophe.[11]

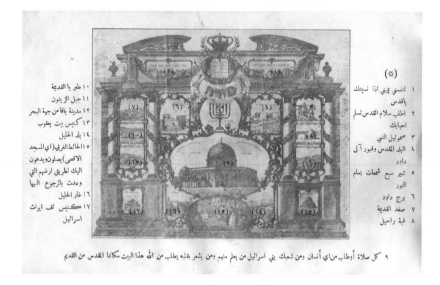

FIG. 4   The Shaw Commission's Exhibit No. 86. The "Vinograd Picture," as reproduced with an accompanying index in the booklet Bayan ila Ikhwanina al-Muslimin ʿAmmatan (1928–29). (The exhibit number refers to the pamphlet from which the picture is taken.)

Note: Colonial No. 48, the Shaw Commission's voluminous record of its meetings, identifies every exhibit by number, but it does not reproduce the pictorial evidence debated before it in 1929–1930. In order to identify these, it is necessary to triangulate between at least three sources. The Bayan Jamʿiyyat Hirasat al-Masjid al-Aqsa waʾl-Amakin al-Islamiyya al-Muqaddasa biʾl Quds (1931) reproduces many of the same pictures, but it does not identify their exhibit numbers. The Arab Bureau of the Jewish Agency's review of this pamphlet (CZA/S25/2976) outlines the history of each of the reproduced images and refers to the statements made before the Shaw Commission about some of them. By connecting these sources with the descriptions of the images that emerged during the many sittings of the commission itself, it is possible to identify each of the pictures, even though several of them are variants of an original.

However, the normative dramaturgical and discursive template for most interpretations of this and other figures would be elaborated in the disputations between the respective representatives for the Arab and Zionist Executives in their appearance before the Shaw Commission on the causes of the violence associated with the Buraq, or Wailing Wall, in August 1929 (the so-called Buraq, or Wailing Wall, riots).[12] For these men, there was no question that in the very aspect of this figure's appearance, one necessarily had to be able to discern either the malicious and cynical agency of "liars" or the passion of "fanatics." For example, following the paradigm already familiar from the Kisch–Musa Kazim al-Husayni debate, Sir Boyd Merriman, the chief counsel for the Zionist Executive, repeatedly attempted to speak about the picture published by the Defense Committee for the Noble Buraq in a way that would distinguish between an autonomous "front stage" of depiction and a politically contingent "backstage" (i.e., a real, Machiavellian history) of the picture's reproduction. For him, the very self-evidence of this figure required one to move beyond its manifest appearance to the putatively real issues that lay beyond the confines of its frame. And so, in his summary Merriman stood before the commissioners and stated: "I am not going to treat that thing seriously. What I ask you to consider seriously is the use that has been made of it."[13] By contrast, in an extension of Musa Kazim's "ce n'est pas nous" argument, the chief legal counsel of the Arab Executive, W. H. Stoker, would resist Merriman's dramaturgical effort to break out of what he considered to be the picture's ideological "frame," essentially arguing that the political sentiments manifest in both the figure's form and its execution were themselves already part of a long-standing pattern of intemperate expressions—by Jews. In his interpretation of the figure, the image fit into a pattern of Jewish figuration that preceded the Arab pamphlet of 1928, and which originated, predictably, with Alfred Mond's infamous bit of after-dinner eloquence, as recorded by Stoker:

> I [Stoker] cannot for the life of me see what there is wrong in starting a society with the object of looking after their holy places, but there is a good deal more than that behind it because there appear to have been made speeches in the House of Commons, among others by Lord Melchett [Sir Alfred Mond] which, although they were called figurative statements, were very significant; there were also pictures which could be bought in Jewish places showing representations of the Mosque of Aqsa and other places like that and other matters of that sort which were genuinely exciting the suspicions or re-arousing the suspicions of

the Moslems as to what the intentions of the Jews were as regards the Holy Places generally.[14]

Still and all, after all this posturing, the meaning of the picture remains elusive. As Stoker and Merriman found themselves debating the self-certainty of figures—in this way confirming the inverse, their ambiguity—these opponents were necessarily forced to confront—and more, to corroborate—the dialectical character of the same images. Elaborating a problematic that persists into the present, in their engagement with these architectural figures Stoker and Merriman were enticed into rehearsing what Adorno has called the "coercive state of [a] reality" of representation, as if it were only the "antagonistic entirety" of this particular conflict.[15] For them, and for those who would follow, the very question posed by their *own* presentation of the actuality of the figures was as concrete as it was abstract: was what was being depicted here "taking place" in the figure, or objectively, beyond its confines? Each time the politics of priority has posed this question about the figure in precisely these terms, it has unwittingly confronted the fact that in posing the question it rehearses a dance of adequation (or an "aesthetic occupation"). It necessarily relies upon and summons into existence something beyond the architectonic figure, something that is not itself the (political self-evidence of the) architectonic figure—in this way inaugurating yet another promise of adequacy to be both extended and revoked *en abîme*.

I cannot, then, turn directly to a reading of the infamous image printed in the *Bayan ila Ikhwanina al-Muslimin 'Amattan*. Instead, I necessarily choose to read the interpretations of figures performed by the participants in this conflict as if they themselves disclosed "the Achilles' heel of an entire system" of which they are a part; in other words, to paraphrase Paul de Man's paraphrase of Adorno's reading of Hegel's *Aesthetics*, as if they "would be the place where the inadequacy of [this conflict's] theory of language [of meaning] would be revealed."[16]

That sublime inadequacy discloses itself most clearly, first, in the image of a man looking at a city. This new picture was introduced into evidence by the Arab Executive's attorney, W. H. Stoker, during his first examination of the grand mufti al-Hajj Amin al-Husayni before the Shaw Commission on 2 December 1929. Having invited the grand mufti to review all the things that caused Muslims to feel an increased apprehension "as regards the intentions of the Jews in the future," Stoker was told that "those apprehensions were increased by statements, by pictures, by declarations and by scientific

FIG. 5 The Shaw Commission's Exhibit No. 48. Published in *Dos Yiddishe Folk*, 30 April 1920, and reproduced in *Bayan Jam'iyyat Hirasat al-Masjid al-Aqsa wa'l-Amakin al-Islamiyya al-Muqaddasa bi'l Quds* (1931).

or literary books."[17] Among these, the grand mufti singled out an image that the commission would log as "Exhibit No. 48" (figure 5), explaining:

> This shows Dr. Herzl looking at crowds of people entering the Dome of the Rock upon which there is a Zionist flag. The impression that this gave to the Moslems is this, that they were more convinced of their belief that the Jews intend to come in great numbers to take and enter the Temple and put upon it their Zionist Flags. . . . [Then, working through the figure itself, the mufti states:] It was evident that this dome here referred to the Dome of the Rock in Haram area, because next to it in the picture there is this round minaret and the only round minaret in Jerusalem is this one right there in the precincts of the Haram area, and therefore it could not be interpreted as anything except referring to the Dome of the Rock.[18]

Sir Boyd Merriman, the attorney for the Zionist Executive, dismissed this claim, arguing, in effect, that the meaning of the figure could not be inferred from what was depicted within its confines. He and subsequent Zionist interpreters raised the following points: that the figure originated in a Yiddish language newspaper in New York; that it had been published in 1922, long before the Buraq/Wailing Wall crisis; and that it apparently was meant to exhort Jews to support the then imminent approval of Great Britain's Mandate over Palestine.[19] For Merriman, then, the autonomy of the figure (insofar as in his eyes its origins proved that it was not in any sense part of Jewish "designs" on Muslim holy places) confirmed the political contingency of its use by the grand mufti himself. Here we begin to witness the strategic interaction built into the reflexive turn. Merriman consequently stated that the real question posed by this picture boiled down to "how many Arabs in Palestine read the New York Jewish paper," and "how many would be aware of that [picture] if somebody had not thought it necessary either to make or to import a pictorial representation of that cover in leaflet form?"[20]

At this juncture, it is worth noting that even though neither Merriman nor the Arab Executive's counsel appear to have been aware of it, this kind of image—a picture depicting Herzl looking toward Jerusalem, with a stream of Jews approaching or passing the city—had been a well-established topos of Zionist pictorial representation since before World War I. The picture in the New York newspaper derived from a series of postcards and postage stamps that superimposed a famous photographic portrait of Herzl (actually standing on a hotel balcony in Basel) upon a landscape of pioneers approaching the city of Jerusalem.[21] Bypassing the significance of a political history of figuration sedimented in the image itself, W. H. Stoker nevertheless countered Merriman with the same conclusion that he would necessarily have reached had he known of the picture's antecedents, or previous layers. At the hearings' conclusion, the counsel for the Arab Executive actually cited Merriman's own reading of "Exhibit No. 48"—more specifically, his argument that the picture was only an old Jewish propaganda figure calling for the ratification of the Mandate—as evidence of the fact that what Merriman had designated a simple exteriority was actually an elementary trait of the figure itself, always already found within its frame. Translating the ambiguity/dialectic of the figure into the agency of the Other, Stoker unwittingly articulates the very problematic that is the subject of this book: "Either this was a representation of Jewish aspirations and desires of the possible fulfillment of them, or it was not, but if it was intended to be a campaign to appeal for the acceptation [sic] of the principle of the Mandate, it seems to me quite clear it is an admission that this picture means what it is purported to mean."[22] Undermining his own position, Stoker then reads the picture retroactively—as seen from the perspective of an anticipated future—to disclose the fact that in order for the "picture to mean what it purported to mean" it has to refer to—it has to be contingent for its meaning upon—

something else (beyond the "acceptation of the Mandate"). Deducing that the necessary aim of Zionism was the reconstruction of Solomon's Temple, Stoker adds: "I do not suppose anybody can think that the Jews, an ambitious race as they are, with their aspirations as regards the National Home, are likely to be content to wail at the Wailing Wall for ever." [23]

It is clear, then, that even as they attempt to answer the riddle of the apotropaic figure, Merriman and Stoker only perpetuate the mystery of its figuration; this time, in an abortive stereotomy between one's enemies' vulgar, iconic interpretations of the figure and the inverse: one's own aniconic refusal to succumb to coarse theories of (magical-operative) figural adequation. The problem, however, is that each of these tactical readings of the other side's iconographic "fallacy" necessarily depends upon one's own belief in the iconographic adequacy of something else. Strangely, everything here hinges upon the putative self-evidence of a representation showing a domed structure with Zionist flags or symbols upon it. From the position of Stoker's constituents, if such a figure were necessarily the reconstruction of Solomon's Temple—as Stoker, following the grand mufti himself, alleged—then one could only conclude that no matter how many denials were offered, for Jews themselves Exhibit No. 48 assumed the status of an icon. Subsequent interpretations of the image confirm this. In the Society for the Protection of the Aqsa Mosque's bayan of 1931–1932, the same picture of Herzl opposite Jerusalem was reproduced with a new caption that relied upon the self-evidence of that iconic interpretation of the buildings in order to attempt, once again, a retroactive explanation of the figure's own anticipatory status vis-à-vis the disputes of 1929. Foregrounding the relation between Herzl and the structure with the flags atop, the inscription reads: "Herzl, the Zionist leader, in front of [or opposite] the Buraq, and [already] opened from it [wa-futiḥa minhū], a road into the Aqsa Mosque." [24] From the perspective of Merriman's constituents, a refusal to break the dramaturgical frame of an aniconic reading of this figure would necessarily appear as the very mark of their opponents' own status as either "liars" about such idolatry or "fanatics" (to paraphrase Arlozorov) who could not discern the distinction between figures and truth. It is not surprising, then, to find that in its assessment of the same bayan of the Society for the Protection of the Aqsa Mosque, the Jewish Agency's Arab Bureau refuses to identify the structure with the Zionist flag as the precinct of the Aqsa, the Dome of the Rock, or the planned temple, describing it only as "Jerusalem built dome upon dome, and embedded upon one of them is the Zionist flag." [25]

But it does not end there. The same detail of the mounted flag that tacitly sustains the premises of adequation in a larger context of its reciprocal disavowal (i.e., in the picture of Herzl as a whole) is itself dependent upon the possibility of establishing a distinction between one's opponents' vulgar conflation of representation with reality, and one's own refusal to lapse into political ideographies of this sort. In other words, the tacit redemption of adequation that the detail discloses is itself dependent upon the familiar presupposition/argument that one's opponent cannot distinguish between figuration and objectivity in the detail itself. The positions taken in 1932 by the Society for the Protection of the Aqsa Mosque and the Arab Bureau of the Jewish Agency are echoes of past arguments in multiple senses: they not only repeat the problem of immediacy that they presumed themselves to have bypassed in their dismissals of the figure of Herzl as a vulgar icon, but also rehearse positions taken in debates before the commission of 1929 with respect to a series of other figures—which explicitly foreground architecture as apotropaiaea of political priority. These other images show the Dome of the Rock with a series of Zionist and Jewish adjuncts (emblems, inscriptions, and symbols) whose "proper" iconography was critical to each side's claims for the others' mischievous iconolatry.

As with the Herzl image, these claims were principally discussed during the grand mufti's review of the pictorial and literary evidence for Zionist "designs" on Muslim monuments and in the cross-examinations that followed. As he works through an exemplar of this kind of image—one apparently introduced into evidence and reproduced later in the *bayan* of the Society for the Protection of the Aqsa Mosque (figure 6)—al-Husayni describes the features of the entire typology of images in the following way: "On the top of it [are] two Zionist flags, and the two flags have on each of them two seals of Solomon, and one has heard, particularly the Moslems, that in the picture which shows the Dome of the Rock, in the place of the verses of the Koran you have some verse in Hebrew. This is particularly referring to the Mosque." [26]

Much of the debate that ensued revolved around a variant of this image that was logged into evidence as Exhibit No. 78. First, the grand mufti was asked by friendly counsel to explain the meaning of this picture in greater detail. Consequently, al-Husayni once again focused upon the relation of the Hebrew inscriptions to the represented monuments. After dismissing the idea that the relation between image and text could be accounted for because of the historical, rather than national/religious significance of the represented monuments, the grand mufti continued: "They could have put other historical sites than the Mosque, such as the Holy Sepulchre, which is

FIG. 6 The Shaw Commission's Exhibit No. 69B. "Mizrah" image by Moshe Ben-Itzhak Mizrahi (n.d., but presumed to be from the early 1920s). Reproduced in the *Bayan Jam'iyyat Hirasat al-Masjid al-Aqsa wa'l-Amakin al-Islamiyya al-Muqaddasa bi'l Quds* (1931).

extremely historical, but because of what we know of the designs of the Jews *there is a meaning towards the Dome of the Rock here.*" [27]

Sir Boyd Merriman, the counsel for the Zionist Executive, attempted to uncover a conspiracy of "liars" in the mufti's claim for Jewish "fanaticism." He consequently asked the grand mufti to confirm that he was aware of an explanation of the picture's purpose, as well as of a translation of the Hebrew inscriptions that had been written on the back of the figure by the grand mufti's own cousin, Jamal al-Husayni; these described the exhibit as an old Austrian greeting card for the Jewish New Year, and dismissed it as irrelevant. [28] As with the previous interpretation of the Herzl figure, for Merriman, the function/use of the figure constitutes its meaning, as if from "outside" its own confines. Merriman consequently attempts to establish a direct relation between his interpretation of the significance of the inscription on the back of the figure and his corresponding interpretation of a "backstage" of politics, which would confirm the mufti's "front-stage" position as nothing more than a ruse, an act. In that way, the entire exhibit, front and back, would be exposed as an index of Arab tactics. But the grand mufti's response is equally familiar, though no less significant for the theory of figuration it presents. Al-Husayni simply argues that it is the meaning of the picture that confirms its use, that is, that the ends of the piece of paper are subordinate to the ends of the depiction printed upon it; ends that are in some sense already "within" the frame. The mufti asks of Merriman: "What is the meaning of reproducing pictures of three Moslem shrines on this picture on this page and sending it in connection with New Year's greetings? Why not other picturesque views of Palestine?" [29]

This was only an opening gambit for both the opponents. Turning to the front of the picture, the stalemate repeats itself, but in a way that discloses— again, as with the Herzl image—that the argument for the fetishism of the Other actually presupposes one's own problematic reliance on the iconographic adequacy—one's own belief in the self-proximate status of something else: the supplement to the building, and more specifically, the writing on the Dome of the Rock. Quite remarkably, as they looked at the inscriptions on the picture of the Dome of the Rock, the fundamental questions that each of the opposing bodies needed to pose, and to answer, was: "In what way does the writing signify? Does it 'mean' in its transitive transparency, or in its objective form?" At the same time, it is equally clear that all involved in the debates before the commission of 1929 were as baffled as they were impatient with the concrete intrusion of so abstract and seemingly trivial a question into their own political discussion. After Merriman exhibited some frustration in his attempts to clarify exactly what could be at issue in pictures that contained Hebrew text on the Dome of the Rock, in a prophylactic move the Arab Executive's own counsel asked the grand mufti and president of the SMC: "What is the objection, is it to what is in the Hebrew verses, or that they are Hebrew verses put against Moslem holy places?" [30]

Even though the mufti replied that both "showed the designs of the Jews on Moslem Holy Places," [31] it is apparent that this could only be a momentary hedge. In keeping with long-standing positions of their own clients, in the subsequent line of argumentation assumed by the advocates for the opposing national camps, the two theories of representation just posed were presumed to be mutually exclusive. Motivated by their belief in the uncontested ubiquity of this figural convention in Jewish history, the protagonists of the Zionist position necessarily interpreted the inscription of the Dome as a transitive, immaterial kind of textuality (in vulgar terms: all message, no medium). Its significance lay in what it actually "said," and not in the apparition of the message, that is, the shape or the position or the context of writing. In its autonomy, then, the inscription confirmed the status of the Dome of the Rock to be that of a reusable scaffold for more direct representation. And in so doing, the text ratified the subordinate status of depiction to inscription in a way that not only exonerated Zionism, but also relegated the Arabs' "reading" of such "writing" to the status of a rude iconolatry. This was—I believe—the reasoning behind the last arguments of the Zionist Executive's representatives, as they recalled a witness named Mordechai Eliash, who in turn presented the commission with an engraving from 1546— published in Italy—that appeared to conform to the same typology of the inscription on the Dome, even though it preceded both Palestinian Arab nationalism and Zionism by centuries. [32] In his conversation with Eliash, Lord Erleigh, one of Merriman's colleagues, also highlighted the fact that since this genre of images preceded Zionism, the meaning of the writing in the debated figures could not be reduced to the form of its immediate appearance in the contemporary scene: "You, I think, called attention to one of the coloured pictures which was put in by the other side and drew attention to the fact that it depicted the Dome of the Rock and that, where the Koran legend appears, there was a Hebrew legend. Dr. Eliash happened to find these books [i.e., the historical precedents]. All I want to show is that there is no significance, that it is not a proof of Zionist aspirations. It has been done for years." [33]

The Arab Executive's position necessarily presupposed another theory of inscription altogether. In the leaflets of 1922, in testimony before the commission, and in the bayan themselves, they foregrounded the fact that the Hebrew texts in these pictures displaced Qurʾanic verses on the original building. The claim, then, was that a Zionist iconolatry disclosed itself in its *own* reliance upon the formal self-evidence of writing, that is, in the prior significance of its *aspect*, or shape, over the significance of "what it said." (Prior to the grand mufti's arguments about such inscriptions, this point had already been made quite clearly during the testimony of ʿAbd al-Qadir Rashid, former editor of *al-Jamiʿa al-ʿArabiyya* and thus responsible for the duplication of several of the images in the pages of the newspaper. Focusing upon inscriptions on the Dome of the Rock in his cross-examination of Rashid, Sir Boyd Merriman asked: "Do I understand you to say the Hebrew inscription is an offence?" Rashid's response: "Any Arab who will see this and who is not familiar with the Hebrew language will see the Mosque of Omar in the middle and will no doubt believe that the Jews have a certain covetousness in regard to the Mosque.")[34] From the standpoint of the Arab's distrust, then, Zionism's inclination to give priority to the denotative dimension of images (i.e., to the ideal of pure depiction), marks the Hebrew writing as something akin to a hieroglyph: a decoration or supplement to the structure that alters its significance, transforms the monument objectively. In this way, the very presence of textual figuration itself becomes the guilty mark of Jewish iconic practices.

This argument presents itself—albeit negatively, because of the strictures of the interrogatory process—in Reginald Silley's cross-examination of Mordechai Eliash. Silley, who was another lawyer for the Arab Executive, asked Eliash to examine the very first exemplar of this kind of drawing (inscription and dome), which had been discussed by the grand mufti, submitted into evidence as Exhibit No. 69B and later reproduced in the *Bayan Jamʿi-yyat Hirasat al-Masjid al-Aqsa waʾl-Amakin al-Islamiyya al-Muqaddasa biʾl Quds*; this is precisely the same figure described as "a coloured picture" by Erleigh (figure 6). Silley then forces Eliash to make a comparison between it and the Italian baroque engravings that—in Eliash's view—would undermine the Palestinian Arab argument for Zionist iconism. He first asks Eliash if he is aware of the fact that there are inscriptions on the Dome of the Rock itself, and that "these Koranic inscriptions have been replaced by Hebrew inscriptions" in the picture.[35] Eschewing the kind of voodoo theory of inscription with which he is being indirectly charged, Eliash responds: "I would not say replaced."[36] Silley retorts: "The place occupied by the Koranic inscriptions *on the original*—in this picture those inscriptions are replaced by Hebrew inscriptions. Can you point to anything of that sort in any of the things you have shown to the Commission?"[37] Eliash explains that there are similarities to such depictions in his historical examples, but he is forced to concede that his collection contains no illustrations in which Hebrew inscriptions occupy the place on the Dome of the Rock where Qur'anic inscriptions normally reside. Silley points once again to the contemporary figures that had been discussed by the grand mufti, and repeats, in précis, the theory of inscription that is damning to Eliash's own, precisely because it subsumes the writing, as a pictorial detail, within a project of mimesis. Silley rejoins: "This is on the building itself."[38]

The lawyer is playing his witness like a violin. Indeed, within seconds Silley will force Eliash to concede that the truth of the thing hinges on the mimetic likeness of the illustrations to the original, in that way repeatedly restaging the referent of interpretation as the dome, not the text. After making Eliash acknowledge one last time that in the Italian example from the sixteenth century there were no Hebrew inscriptions "in replacement of Koranic inscriptions," Silley is presented with Eliash's last line of defense; namely, that as the contemporary pictures under review were produced by an elderly, Sephardic rabbi, they necessarily constituted something both beyond the purview of Zionist ideology, and, as forms of art naïf, were clearly beyond the interpretive boundaries of Silley's Ideologiekritik: "I have asked the artist who drew this picture; he is a man of about 65, a Sephardic Rabbi, who besides being a reverend gentleman, also dabbles in artistry; I asked him for the reason for this. He said that he had done it for 30 years and that there is a good sale for them on the Feast of the Tabernacles [Sukkot]."[39] But even this was no defense. Silley immediately subsumed this argument within a logic of mimesis as well, forcing Eliash to concede that the putatively naïve art of the "reverend gentleman" bore an even greater resemblance to the actual monument than the baroque exemplar. According to this logic, the autonomy of the text, its transitivity, could not be sustained in the face of its overwhelming formal consistency—the overdetermination of its position and shape—in relation to the "real thing." The moral: when correspondence is itself a presumption of guilt, the greater the likeness of the figure to its object, the more damning the evidence.

All was not lost, however, for the Zionist interpretation. On the following day, Sir Boyd Merriman staged a neat metacritical coup. After reminding the commission that the matter of figuration was not marginal to the conflict but central to it (because the Arab Executive perceived the picture to be proof for "Jewish designs that this campaign [of the grand mufti et al.] was intended to combat"),[40] he stated that it would be ludicrous to attach a particular significance to the fact that "Jews have written, in one form or another, Hebrew texts expressing their hopes round pictures of what at present represents the perfect architectural expression of the holy site on the top of Mount Moria common to both religions."[41] He then explains: "Do not forget that: the Dome of the Rock, the Rock itself . . . the sanctity of the rock itself is one which is common to the history of both religions."[42] With this argument, Merriman now appears to transform the architectural referend (or signified) that had been thrust into priority by Silley, into nothing more than a referent (or signifier) for something else. The damning inscriptions only "express" hopes in their status as adjuncts to other signs that are themselves nothing more than "perfect architectural expressions" of an absent presence. Here, mimesis suddenly exonerates, in the degree to which it discloses itself to be just the most perfect referent of the most perfect referent.

But now, the picture, not to mention the inscription, are even more concrete in their abstraction than ever before. Silley, the grand mufti, Stoker, and the Arab Executive subsumed an inscription, or text, within a language of figures. In so doing, they necessarily assumed the identity of referend and referent, to outline a theory of the artwork's political contingency. Leaving aside, for the moment, the remarkable paradoxes of a theory of semantic contingency that presupposes the formal autonomy of the object, what is even more remarkable is the fact that as the custodians of the Arab political narrative of priority stage a kind of coup de grâce for the figural—and subsume even the exemplars of Eliash within a lexicon of pictorial depictions of displacement—they also disclose the necessarily transitive dimension of the same inscription. A crisis presents itself to view in this exchange: if the figure with the Qur'anic inscription were adequate to its own norm of adequacy, no displacement of its meaning could ever be possible, no matter how many centuries of Jewish inscription had taken place. "If the space for a change (necessarily also an addition) had not been there in the prior function of the sign-system, the crisis could not have made the change happen."[43]

Merriman and the Zionist Executive subsume the picture within a framework of textuality that is premised upon the necessary difference between referend and referent; they think they witness a condensation of signifiers inaugurated by a lack on the part of the signified. This accounts for their regular refrain that the picture does not signify, that "it doesn't mean anything." In this way, the custodians of the Zionist political narrative of priority—even Eliash, who almost blows their case vis-à-vis pictures—argue not only for the materiality of language in the immateriality or transitivity of its grammes, but also for the autonomy of the artwork. Paradoxically, however, at the very moment in Merriman's rendering when the picture performs its semantic autonomy by disclosing the referential dimension of its referend, it inaugurates the moment of its own contingency by summoning into being an arch-signifier, a literal bedrock of figuration. Here, the metonymic transitivity of architecture is founded upon the putative figural immutability of stone upon which it seems to rest. The ghost of General Gordon—the concept of magical adequation—begins to resurrect itself here.

With the exhaustion of these theories of inscription, one discovers another working knowledge of the pictures' self-evidence during the hearings. Another elaboration of the reflexive theory of adequation will present itself: one that relies less upon the self-evidence of the contents than on the certainty of the code that relates things to one another in the debated representations. Nothing is resolved, nor are prior contradictions or incongruities overcome. Instead, they are only normalized into oblivion, in a practice that privileges the self-certainty of the syntagmatic arrangement of particulars over the self-evidence of the particulars themselves. Immanent within the insufficiency of a theory of iconic, or symbolic, inscription is the presumed sufficiency of a working theory of allegory.

Why does this happen? Having failed to establish absolute distinctions between the "representative and the semantic functions of language,"[44] Silley and Merriman unwittingly guarantee the pictures' ongoing success as ciphers of a historical condition, precisely by virtue of the question of a picture's temporality that has entered into their arguments about what replaces or superimposes itself upon what. Once that debate is framed in such terms, they approach the idea of allegory as a form of adequation proper to a historical experience of inadequation (i.e., of an experience of the inevitability of replacement upon replacement). But they sustain within that idea a belief in the self-evidence of the concrete symbol sub rosa, in the presumed immediacy of an axiomatic code that organizes any possible concatenation of imagery into a relation of identity with the politics that imagery stands for. In simpler terms, this is, in the first instance, a performative theory of the artwork, since the picture is now presumed to inaugurate the very sequence of its own political transcription. And the sequence itself is allegory, not because it is something like the orderly genome to the proper sequences of reading, but on the contrary, because it performs a "conflict between a conception of the self in its authentically temporal predicament and a defensive strategy that tries to hide from this self-knowledge."[45]

Considered, first, as this "performative" theory of the picture, the allegorical imperative disclosed itself to have been the principal, and conspicuous, preoccupation of debates surrounding another figure, the penultimate object of discussion during the hearings of the commission of inquiry. A Jewish flag originally sold to children for the feast of Simchat Torah or Sukkot (accounts vary) was introduced by the Arab Executive to the commissioners as a cipher for Jewish intentions as a whole. It was called Exhibit No. 76 (figure 7). Stoker described this unusual image to the grand mufti as a figure containing an actual portal from its front to back, a "movable flap" leading from a depiction of the Wailing Wall "into the picture on the other side."[46] The grand mufti concurred, and explained its significance in this way:

> The Moslems interpret this as follows: That this is the Wailing Wall, if you lift it up it will show a gate and the gate leads to the Temple, and in fact behind the Western Wall of the Mosque, which is called the Wailing Wall, is the Haram esh-Sherif. I am now translating this. It is written in Hebrew here. "The Burak, which is the Western Wall, is the only thing that remains of our Holy Temple." This idea of the Jews to obtain the Wailing Wall and from there to obtain the Mosque as can be explained from this picture and way it is put [together] is the cause of the anxiety of the Moslems and also explains why the Moslems are not prepared to give way to anything with regard to the Burak other than what has been the custom up to now.[47]

During his cross-examination of the grand mufti, Sir Boyd Merriman did not immediately focus on either the uses of the figure or the correctness of al-Husayni's translation of the inscription, as he had attempted to do with the other images. Instead, he tried to make the grand mufti appear to be the fabricator of a phantom sequence, an allegorist of the worst order, a peeler of fake flaps. He prodded al-Husayni with choreographed incredulity, asking: "Do you seriously suggest that these are supposed to be doors into the Temple?" Refusing to break frame, the mufti then elaborated upon his reading and described the succession of associations that had to take place in order to understand the latent meaning of the flag: "What people understood from this picture and seeing the picture of the Burak on the other side, you take up that piece of paper and open the door, the people who saw this and myself believed it was a provocation by the Jews, if you can take the Burak you can get what is behind the Burak, that is the Temple."[48]

Merriman did not dwell upon whether it would actually be possible to arrive at a proper allegorical reading of the figure(s). Instead, he raised the thorny problem of intention. In other words, he attempted to question

FIG. 7 The Shaw Commission's Exhibit No. 76. The "Simʿhat Torah" flag or the "flap picture," both sides. Reproduced in the *Bayan Jamʿiyyat Hirasat al-Masjid al-Aqsa waʾl-Amakin al-Islamiyya al-Muqaddasa biʾl Quds* (1931).

whether the sequence that the grand mufti described was actually present "within" the work, or whether it had been contrived to appear there. And, contrived in two senses: literally, through a manipulation of the original representation, and phenomenally, either as the projection of the interpreter's false consciousness or of his duplicity. Raising the first possibility, Merriman implied that the figure's "code" necessarily demanded that one understand the grand mufti's own reading to be nothing less than the elaboration of a counterfeit sequence inaugurated by al-Husayni's, or his colleagues', own tampering with the image. So he repeatedly asked the mufti to look at the banner and to acknowledge that the flap the grand mufti had referred to was not original and that it therefore could not be the key sequencing device of an allegorical image: "If you will look at it, is it not plain that as it was sold it was stuck down?"[49] To this, the mufti quickly responded by incorporating the possibility of a closed flap within his original reading of the figure as allegory. Speaking as if from the position of the Jewish makers of the picture, the grand mufti explained: "This figure shows that the Burak is at present closed, when we [the Jews] get the Burak it will be easy for us to open this and go to the Temple."[50]

Merriman then attempted to raise what he clearly considered to be the second form of possible contrivance, or intention, by showing that no actual modification to the figure need have taken place at all in order for the mufti's interpretations to be exposed as the allegorical mischief of (again) either "fanatics" or "liars." Consequently, he walked the grand mufti through what he perceived to be the "proper" sequence of the image, pausing at each element in the figure to ask al-Husayni if he understood what was—from Merriman's position—its correct significance. Thus, Merriman inquired: "Do you recognize the Ark of the Covenant?" Attempting to make the point that if read properly, all of this figuration was internally coherent as a religious and not a political allegory, Merriman exclaimed: "Tell me if it does not look as though the scrolls of the law are inside?"[51] Predictably, the response was not an admission of misreading on the part of the grand mufti, but, once again, a subsumption of Merriman's own interpretive framework within his own, so that even the features explained by the Zionist Commission's attorney confirm the grand mufti's own reading of the performative displacements built into the very structure of Jewish figuration. Taking another step in the same sequence, al-Husayni responded that the element pointed out by Merriman "also shows the designs of the Jews. . . . Here is a minaret and underneath it a Mosque."[52]

Both men conceive of the flapped picture as something that necessarily bears in its operation the correct key/sequence to its own explication. But at the same time, it appears from the nature of their conversation that this train of dueling allegoremes could go on forever, effortlessly continuing into infinity quite apart from the existence of portals flapping in the wind, in other words, quite apart from the appearance of performative elements that actually open and shut certain spaces of interpretation only to open others unwittingly. The grand mufti and Merriman appear to be incapable of explaining the seamless fit between their conflicting interpretations, as if the actual index to the reading of the figure they each believe to be immanent within the very form of the picture weren't always already the one that inaugurates and is reprised in the insufficiency and contrariety of their opposing readings.

More important, Merriman and the grand mufti also appear to be incapable of addressing the fact that the same index is indivisible into isolated moments of pure cogency or sheer play that each requires in order to reify his political position in a concrete symbol. That privileged sequence is itself neither adequate to a reality of which it is a part, nor, conversely, reducible to the autonomy of its own form. In this way it is guaranteed that the *méconnaissance* that attends each example of the reflexive movement of adequation (via interpretations of others' interpretations) is itself the paradoxical historical precondition for the figuration of history as allegory, or at least of allegory when it is understood as the very performance of the self's "temporal predicament." [53] In short, in Palestine, politics was—and remains—a form of romanticism. It is in this exact sense of the performance of the self's "temporal predicament"—always recorded as the self-evidence of the figure to oneself and the simultaneous suspicion of the Other's misrepresentation of representation—that allegory shows itself to have been an irresolvable crisis at the heart of the image with which I began this analysis of the Mandate political culture's investment in art criticism. I am referring to the Shaw Commission's Exhibit No. 69A (figure 8): the same picture taken by the Palestinian delegation to the Hejaz in 1922, debated by Frederick Kisch and Musa Kazim al-Husayni in 1924, published in Al-Jamiʿa al-ʿArabiyya in December 1929, reprinted both in the Bayan ila Ikhwanina al-Muslimin ʿAmattan in 1929 and the Bayan Jamʿiyyat Hirasat al-Masjid al-Aqsa waʾl-Amakin al-Islamiyya al-Muqaddasa of 1931–32, analyzed by the grand mufti before the Commission of Inquiry of 1929 and finally included by Mahmud al-Abidi in his Mihnat Bayt al-Maqdis.

In the commission of inquiry, the nonidentical shows itself to be the overlooked allegorical substance of the image, the electricity that powers

FIG. 8 The Shaw Commission's Exhibit No. 69A, otherwise known as the "Vinograd picture." As reprinted in *Bayan Jam'iyyat Hirasat al-Masjid al-Aqsa wa'l-Amakin al-Islamiyya al-Muqaddasa bi'l Quds* (1931).

both its reproduction and hostile interpretations of its reproduction each time someone asserts that architecture bears a relation of identity with the reality it represents. In the first place, prior to questioning the grand mufti, Merriman had already run through a range of other interpretive strategies vis-à-vis the image during his examination of 'Abd al-Qadir Rashid, the newspaper man responsible for the reproduction of these various images in the Arabic press and the translation of their inscriptions into Arabic.[54] (The reports of the Arab Bureau of the Jewish Agency identify the actual source as Rashid's wife, a Jewish woman.)[55] In the exchanges with Rashid, Merriman treated 69A (fig. 8) and a derivative called 69B (already familiar from the debates on the inscriptions [fig. 6]) as paired palimpsests, rehearsing in them the familiar debates over utility, inscription, iconolatry, and performative figuration that marked the opposing counsels' arguments over the series as a whole. More importantly, it is apparent that Exhibit No. 69A was self-consciously debated in its allegorical dimension (even if no one named it as such) because of the tests that it was subjected to: Merriman repeatedly attempted to block the grand mufti from viewing the exhibit along with the legend to the figure that had been published with it in the *Bayan ila Ikhwanina* as Exhibit No. 69C (figure 9) (the figure 69A was reprinted with an index and superimposed key in the *Bayan ila Ikhwanina*; the booklet itself had been introduced into evidence as Exhibit No. 86 [fig. 4]). He simply didn't want the grand mufti to have recourse to either of the forms of contrivance that he feared to be at work in his presentations of the flapped, or performative, figure: the "literal" superposition of meanings performed by the legend and captions, or the "phenomenal" one that would dissimulate his internalization of the legend as if it were the allegorical figure's own syntagmatic code. Consequently, quite soon after Stoker invited al-Husayni to explain the figure, Merriman objected, arguing against the propriety of such testimony when it was not at all certain the grand mufti's explanation of the figure was independent of the Arabic language legend and captions appended to the picture.[56] Stoker appeared not to understand the objection, and the argument culminated with the following protest on the part of the Zionist Executive's counsel: "If the witness is giving evidence about what the picture conveys let him give it from the picture and not from a version of the picture in a printed book, or if he gives the latter let it be made plain he is giving the latter."[57]

Prior to this exchange, however, the grand mufti had already begun his explication of the figure with the observation that a series of Muslim holy sites were reproduced in it. Consequently, this constituted evidence of Jewish "designs in regard to all the Holy Places in general."[58] "My attention," he said, "is particularly drawn to the Zionist emblem, the candle-sticks, and also to the Ten Commandments and also the verses of the Torah which are typed in Hebrew next to each picture. My attention is also particularly drawn to a verse at the bottom of the picture."[59] At this point, the grand mufti, tellingly, is concentrating on the vertical axis of emblems at the center of the picture. Moreover, following Merriman's intervention concerning the book version and the pure version of the picture, when the grand mufti resumed his reading, he returned to the relation between monuments and emblems along the same vertical axis: "When we see the Holy Burak coming under the Dome of the Rock we understand it conveys the idea that the Burak is the entrance to the Dome of the Rock and when above that we see the candlesticks and the Ten Commandments and the crown and all the other pictures of the other Moslem places there is but one inference—that the Jews have designs on all our Holy Places."[60]

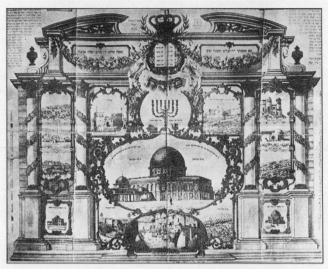

مطامع اليهود في المسجد الأقصى
والصخرة المشرفة.

الصخرة المشرفة وفوقها التاج اليهودي وشعار اليهود المبنى
كما تصورها لهم مطامعهم وإعمال صهيم
ظهر إلى الصورة كثيرا من الاماكن الاسلامية التي يطمع اليهود في امتلا

لمين في حيفا نشترك في المؤتمر

FIG. 9 The Shaw Commission's Exhibit No. 69C. The "Vinograd Picture,"
as published in the newspaper al-Jamiʿa al-ʿArabiyya, 15 August 1929. (The
exhibit number actually refers to the printer's block, not the newspaper
image.)

Quite obviously, Merriman rejected this interpretation during the course of his cross-examination of the grand mufti, as well as in his closing statements. But the nature of that rejection is as telling as the grand mufti's own reading, since in its mechanics it necessarily foregrounds what the Zionist Executive's theory of allegory had to be. His rebuttal boiled down to two related assertions: that the grand mufti cannot shake off the thorny problem of intention; and that, in that failure, the grand mufti exhumes language itself as a necessary supplement, whereas had it been *authentically* allegorical, it would require no such props.[61] By contrast, it is clear that to Merriman, "real" allegory would have to be autonomous in its coding and metaphoric in its organization; it would be a concentration of signs (in Jakobson's terms a system of "connections" dominated by relations of similarity) that would require no help from the outside for their corporate signification, and it would, inversely, effect no "actual" practice of displacement in the world — no damage beyond its own frame.[62]

For this reason, Merriman didn't need to speak about the pictures within the pictures, as the mufti had done. Instead, Merriman concentrated once again on actual and phenomenal contrivances—that is, insidiously "transparent," but alien features—that were imported into the figure, distorted its meaning, and guaranteed its false reading. Merriman's first critique—the same one he raised during his objection to the grand mufti's reference to a version of the figure that already had an Arabic legend and captions— was not only a kind of litmus test for allegory. It was also the precursor to his final indictment of the mufti as a member (really, the ringleader) of a conspiracy of false figuration. In his closing statements Merriman argued that al-Husayni could only present 69A as if it were the self-evident inventory of a general political displacement because "the Mufti, in going round the picture himself, used numbering on this little reproduction which enabled him to point out the texts he wanted to point out"[63] (i.e., the version in the bayan—Exhibit No. 69C). Here, then, "authentic" allegory is derailed by the introduction of an ulterior syntagmatic code—a code that is, quite literally, superimposed upon the image in a version printed in bad faith by people Merriman believed to be associates of al-Husayni. Only the displacement effected by this fake "assemblage of nonverbal signs" condones a reading of a political dispossession in the pictorial space where an originary combinatory system of metaphoric, mythical, and religious condensations once stood in collective self-evidence.[64]

Merriman also challenged what he perceived to be a second, less apparent, form of contrivance: the actual substitution of original elements in the picture with new ones guaranteed to effect a corruption of its inherent significance, symbol by symbol. These challenges focused on the replacement of Arabic captions for original elements, and on the mistranslation of scriptures cited in the original. In one instance, Merriman attempted to tease intention out of figuration by virtue of the differences between the original "mizrah" image—Exhibit No. 69A—and its reproduction in al-Jamiʿa al-ʿArabiyya, the newspaper most closely affiliated with the SMC (often simply described as the SMC's "organ"). Merriman directed the grand mufti's attention to the fact that in a version of the image printed in the newspaper on 15 August 1929—minuted as Exhibit No. 69C (fig. 9)—the margins had been cropped and a letter press omitted, so that the picture's prewar origins and its "self-evident" purposes were erased, leaving only a "misleading" Arabic caption in their place.[65] Having already grilled ʿAbd al-Qadir Rashid (the newspaper man) on the mechanics of that same cropping job during an earlier sitting of the commission, Merriman queried the mufti only about its significance: "Do you realise that the [original] inscription at the bottom shows that the picture is intended as a souvenir of that school to be given to the lady supporters or lady patrons?"[66]

Then, immediately after the exchange surrounding the letter press, the Zionist Executive's counsel directed the witness's attention to Bayan ila Ikhwanina al-Muslimin ʿAmmatan, the same "little grey book" the mufti had been looking at during his initial exposition on the significance of 69A. Working through the pamphlet more or less page by page, Merriman eventually raised a second and more egregious form of contrivance. He challenged the grand mufti about the verse at the bottom of the image as reproduced in "the little grey book"—the same passage that al-Husayni had referred to at the beginning of his exchange with Stoker (fig. 4): ("My attention is also particularly drawn to a verse at the bottom of the picture which reads as follows . . .") Merriman believed a second piece of textual contraband to be concealed there, this time in the form of a mistranslation of an original Hebrew verse from 1 Kings 38 into an Arabic version that implied the displacement of Islam. The Arabic translation stated: "Whoever of them knows and whoever feels in his heart shall demand from Allah this house our Holy Place old." The same biblical phrase, as translated by Merriman read: "What prayer and supplication soever be made by any man or by all thy people Israel which shall know every man the plague of his own heart and spread forth his hands towards this house."[67]

Here, more than anywhere else, Merriman appears to believe that the agency of intriguers could itself be exposed in the gratuity of their own intervention, that is, in the addition of extraneous language to a text (originally functioning as an image within a larger image) that would otherwise never have come to mean what the artificers were purporting to read into it as allegory. This, finally, accounts for the forcefulness of the lawyer's comments about this mistranslation in his closing arguments. In that address, he attempts to implicate the mufti and others in a figural conspiracy under the common heading of intention (effected by what he calls "invention"), so that the specific claims of Jewish "designs" would themselves be disclosed to be part of an even grander "design" to foment violence:

> Nothing whatever about demanding the house from Allah, pure invention, and invention designed to convey a particular impression that this shows that the Jews have designs to take physical possession of this house here represented and it cannot mean anything else in my submission, and I have no hesitation in making that assertion, not when you reflect at this very time, at the time when that book [Bayan ila Ikhwanina al-Muslimin 'Amattan] is put up, at the time when these conferences are meeting, at the time when orders are going out that branches shall be formed all over the country, of these precious societies [the Defense Committee for the Noble Buraq, etc.], at that time "al Jamia," [sic] not of course the official organ of the Supreme Moslem Council, was publishing week by week or fortnight by fortnight extracts from the Protocols of the Elders of Zion.[68]

See, finally, what happens here, with 69A: in 1929 the custodians of the Arab political figuration read the picture along what they clearly perceive to be a vertical axis of condensation/metaphor in an effort to effect a stereotomy between allegoremes of similarity and those of contiguity in its operative code. When one reads the figure top-down—as did the grand mufti— one reproduces a logic according to which similarity is suppressed and relations of contiguity are not only reinforced but privileged as the very self-evidence of the figure. Its allegoremes, now wholly metonymic, confirm the meaning of the figure as one of displacement. That performance, however, sustains its own dissolution to the degree that it indicates that the displacement is "not as yet." The very relation between elements that would serve as the precondition for the grand mufti's repeated "when we see this . . . we think" is one of nonidentity between all those bits and pieces of imagery that would convert the Dome of the Rock into the Temple. Immanent within the mufti's syntagmatic index of figural contingency is Merriman's register of semantic/mimetic autonomy; a register, however, that itself founders on the

125

distinction between the figure's position as a political fact and as an autonomous construction: between its "socially necessary appearance" and the inverse, a feigned appearance of social necessity that confirms not only the independence of the figure but also its manipulation at the hands of others.[69] In 1929, as so often before and since, the custodians of Zionist political figuration reprise metonymy as the very presence/agency of liars or fanatics. When one reads the figure laterally (in terms of the substitutions practiced within it), one consequently reproduces a logic according to which contiguities are disavowed and relations of similarity, combination, contextuality are not only reinforced but privileged as the very self-evidence of the figure. Its allegoremes, now wholly metaphoric and hierarchical, confirm the meaning of the figure as one of "homeopathic magic," to cite Frazer, and more importantly, to reproduce Merriman's "state of mind."[70] Here too, the abyssal character of the figure discloses itself in the immanence of its uncanny double, a metonymy that actually inaugurates the assembled figures within the figure into collective significance. Otherwise, how could Merriman account for the originary "fit" of what had been maliciously substituted by others?

■

To review the figure's logic in this way is to be driven close to despair over a future crisis—our own present—immanently projected in these anterior executions of the picture's reading. As future performers of an identity thesis equating architecture with politics, the current cult of the concrete symbol in Palestine and Israel's politics was actually created during the commission of inquiry of 1929; it was born in this picture. Because, surely, at that moment—when a figure was finally (though unwittingly) disclosed to be self-evident only in the irreducibility of its abstraction—the politics of the concrete symbol showed itself to be not only utterly reflexive in its vision of architecture's adequacy to history but irredeemably compromised by the "success" of that vision. At that same time, even as the politics of the material symbol occasioned a dialectic of recrimination that would become all too familiar to those of us who witness the present history of this conflict, it also inaugurated a recrimination of a negative dialectic—its ratification "in passing," in the very effort to get past the actuality of its own abstraction, as one commutes to the realm of putative political self-evidence, to the realm of realpolitik. Henceforth, politics—and that is all of us who even look at this place—brutally sustains an inadequate view of adequation as its preferred presentation of adequation. Henceforth, crisis will only recall crisis *en abîme*, as a prolonged aesthetic occupation.

IV. CELLULOID

CONCLUSION:

The morality of thought lies in a procedure that is neither   A TERRIBLE CARICATURE
entrenched nor detached, neither blind nor empty, neither
atomistic, nor consequential. . . . But how much more difficult has it become to conform to such morality now that it
is no longer possible to convince oneself of the identity of
subject and object. . . . Münchausen pulling himself out of
the bog by his pig-tail becomes the pattern of knowledge
which wishes to become more than either verification or
speculation.

—Theodor Adorno, *Minima Moralia*

THE REBUKE OF IDENTITY has always played a crucial role in the Israel-Palestine conflict's immanent progression, its logic of development. Declarations that symbols, however material, are inadequate to the norm of adequacy they sustain, have always ridden tandem with each new assertion that architecture confirms the immediacy of history. Despair tends toward determinate negation. In reviewing the Buraq/Wailing Wall crisis of 1929, the Jewish Agency's Chaim Arlozorov found in the actions of both revisionist Zionists and those he called "Arab radicals" only a "bloated programme of gestures" that amounted to nothing less than the triumph of reification. Stunned by the abstract logic encompassing the struggle, Arlozorov could only speak of "caricatures" and "illusions" supplanting the real, pushing Zionist politics into a dramaturgy over which it exercised no real control.[1] His anguish at this plight—matched, I believe, by Shaykh 'Izz al-Din al-Qassam's reported challenge to the grand mufti that he stop restoring mosques and start buying weapons instead—presented itself in the form of the following query:

> How did we allow ourselves to be pushed into a hopeless policy of prestige; how did it happen that around us a system of provocations should develop, built up and directed with cunning; that we make out of an issue which has never been the centre of our world [the Wailing Wall] a new idol; that we gave the Arab radicals a weapon which they can turn against us; . . . that we conduct a politics of bravura, which runs contrary to our main interests and which culminated in the bloody weeks we have experienced[?] . . . [I]f one burdens a powerless people, lacking external means of power and fighting for its very survival, with a bloated programme of gestures and illusions, totally devoid of reality—then a terrible caricature is being created.[2]

Cognizant of the fact that a gap between "illusion" and "reality" is inaugurated by the erection of this "new idol," Arlozorov nevertheless perpetuates it. As he tries to establish a new stereotomic distinction between the immediacy of material conditions of existence—for him this is always the mode of production—and the mediated nature of political representation, Arlozorov reverts to an identity thesis in his own rebuke of identity. In other words, by privileging the abstraction of truth (and in the process asserting the self-identity of "reality" in labor), he reasserts the truth of an abstraction. However, if this kind of undoing is the price paid by an immanent criticism, which can never escape taking part in what it portrays, then it is also the source of that criticism's ethical charge. The new semblance (of history's face) that Arlozorov creates is, in its very failure, the promise of non-semblance, just as the untruth of his assertion of immediacy is, in equal measure, the anticipation of truth, in the form of reification.[3]

This suggests that al-Qassam and Arlozorov do not only offer a rebuke of what I rebuke. They also offer a rebuke of *me*. To the degree that the fate of their critique is itself ideology, Arlozorov, al-Qassam, Richmond, the grand mufti, and the other historical players whose roles I have examined in this study do not only disclose that they were the keepers of a normative-yet-impossible vision of history (maintained, as I have persistently argued, under the aspect of its critique); rather, in so doing, they also reveal themselves to have always been the unlikely custodians of utopia, collectively keeping faith with the notion that things, as they stand at any moment in the history of this conflict, are neither conclusive nor tolerable.[4]

By contrast, in this study I have persistently privileged the nonidentity that pervades each claim for the identity of history and its designated instantiations, in the process working through this conflict's apotropaic logic. I have associated immediacy with failure, without privileging what that politically successful "failure" of inherences simultaneously signals: the refracted light of redemption. I have thought this a necessary expedient, given the present state of affairs in the Middle East, where Ariel Sharon's self-declared "visit of peace" to the Temple Mount/Haram al-Sharif in September 2000 and the *Intifadat al-Aqsa* that swiftly followed have together served to reaffirm the belief in the minds of many that an organic relation between monuments and violence explains this conflict and as such demands no explanation. (I remain convinced, in other words, that one of the normative answers to the quandary of this conflict's self-presentation actually perpetuates it.) However, to say (as I did at the outset of this work) that when others point to Jerusalem's monuments and speak of an intuited immediacy, they actually rehearse the struggle's long-standing inability to account for itself, is to give the impression—precisely by arresting things there—that "intransigence towards all reification" is in itself the model of freedom, when it is in fact only a token of its promise.[5] This is my own unfinished business: the rebuke of me I believe to be implicit in al-Qassam and Arlozorov's necessary failures, because they point to my own. A historiography of immediacy cannot culminate in transcendental perspective, as if in moving between the positions/accusations potentiated in monuments' inadequacy to the adequacy they represent, one is somehow deposited outside the conflict and above the fray.[6] Anyone who lives this struggle knows that to stand apart is already to be implicated, and that to presume a transcendental standpoint toward the culture of this conflict is to "speak the language of a false escape."[7] Even worse, a historiography of this conflict's logic of manifestations cannot offer anyone consolation in the certainty that language will always be the language of "false escapes" or, in other words, that when one points to the element of nonidentity that exerts itself from within claims for architecture's identity with history, one directly points to freedom in the play of language. Here, as indeterminacy takes solace in its own idea, it reverts to mere contingency. It begins to serve other ends.

In the course of writing this book I have been drawn toward a conclusion that is in some sense intolerable even to me, a conclusion expressed in the problematic relation between its first and last epigraphs: that the vision of Baron Münchausen pulling himself out of the bog by his own hair, once dismissed by Walter Benjamin as a synecdoche for the "bluff" of immediacy, now presents itself as the very emblem of any possible critique worthy of the name. If there is a promise embedded in An Aesthetic Occupation, if it maintains faith in a shabby, discredited, and anachronistic concept of utopia, it is precisely because of what is implicit in this, its own declarative dead end. In pointing to the failure of any claim for immediacy and showing that shorthand for a reconciled existence to be incomplete, one only begins to orient oneself toward redemption. Far more important would be to acknowledge (as I have only done once in this work) that the promise of another, reconciled existence survives in our failure to articulate the impossibility of reconciliation in this one.

132

Introduction: The Foundation Stone of Our National Existence

The epigraph to this chapter is from Walter Benjamin, "Critique of the New Objectivity," in *Walter Benjamin: Selected Writings*, vol. 2, 1927–1934, ed. Michael W. Jennings, Howard Eiland, and Gary Smith, trans. Rodney Livingstone et al. (Cambridge, Mass.: Harvard University Press, 1999), 417.

1 Aluf Ben, "Netanyahu Places the Responsibility for the Riots with Arafat," *Ha'aretz*, 26 September 1996, A4. The Israeli press records the events of the hours before the violence in the following way: "The guards of the Waqf heard the sound of the hammers and informed members of the Palestinian Authority in Jerusalem. These summoned Hassan Tahbub, who is the Authority's chargé d'affaires for holy places, who arrived at the time of the closing of the gate, saw what had taken place, was interviewed by the media, and then left. Inside the tunnel and next to the new opening . . . the mayor of Jerusalem, Ehud Olmert; a member of the religious nationalist organization Ateret Cohanim [named] Mati Dan; the director of the Western Wall Authority, Suli Eliav; and the director of the Authority for [the promotion of] Holy Places, Oded Viner, all embraced one another. Those present recited psalms

and sang 'If I Forget Thee O Jerusalem'; at 1:30 A.M. the alley was emptied and all was quiet. . . . In anticipation of a reaction, the police and border patrol received instructions from the prime minister's office to respond decisively to stone throwing." Sami Sokol and Nadav Shragai, "Tens of Palestinians Threw Stones; the Western Wall Square Was Cleared," *Ha'aretz*, 25 September 1996, A2. Unless otherwise noted, all translations from the Hebrew are my own. In translations from Arabic I have been greatly assisted by Mr. Hedi Ben-Aicha. However, I assume responsibility for any errors.

2 Dr. Abdul Qader Tash, "A Distortion of History and Truth," reprinted in *Arab View*, 20 October 1996, <http://www.arab.net/arabview/articles/tash4.html>.

3 Ibid. This is the way Jordan's Crown Prince Hassan is quoted in the Israeli press: "This step represents a provocation to the sensitivities of Arabs and Muslims in the entire world, in addition to a breach of the sanctity of the Holy City, and the national Arab Islamic sanctuary." Gai Behor and the *Sokhnuyot hayedi'ot* [News Services], "Arab League: The Aim of Israel Is to Undermine the Aqsa Mosque and to Build the Temple," *Ha'aretz*, 26 September 1996, A4.

4 Charles Krauthammer, "A Desecration of Truth: Israel Is Maligned While Palestinians Get a Free Pass," *Time* 148, no. 18, 14 October 1996, 104.

5 Georg Wilhelm Friedrich Hegel, *Phenomenology of Spirit*, trans. A. V. Miller, analysis and foreword by J. N. Findlay (Oxford: Oxford University Press, 1977), §20, 11. In Hegel's *Phenomenology of Spirit*, the movement of history coincides with the progression of Spirit to self-consciousness. This passage, beginning with the insufficiency of "sense-certainty" and ending with "absolute knowing," presupposes an immanent critique of identity per se (i.e., the assertion of a unity of concepts and things, as when we say: A = A). For Hegel, the immediacy of a "concrete shape in whose whole existence one determinateness predominates" proves to be an immediacy "whose mediation is not outside of it but which is this mediation itself" (§31, 19). Asserting that "the True is the whole" (§20, 11), Hegel suggests that the distance between "knowing" on one hand and "appearance" on the other drives a dialectic that finally completes itself (through progressive concretions) in Absolute Knowledge, or "Spirit that knows itself as Spirit" (§808, 493). In the same measure as "mediation is completely absent in the Absolute," Spirit's "free existence" in the Absolute reveals the "contingency of form"—even things like buildings—to be nothing other than History (§808, 493). Abandoning Hegel's critique of immediacy, subsequent generations of thinkers took the phenomenological imperative in quite a different direction; like Edmund Husserl, they sought to recuperate the notion of "immediacy" by propounding a distinction between the "pregiven world" we assume within culture and a "life world" of lived experience critically revealed by phenomenology. See Edmund Husserl, *Experience and Judgement*, trans. J. S. Churchill and K. Ameriks (Evanston, Ill.: Northwestern University Press, 1973), 50. In Maurice Merleau-Ponty's subsequent development of the concept, this life-world is "always 'already there' before reflection begins—as an inalienable presence," in turn marking phenomenology the practice that "puts essences back into existence." See

Maurice Merleau-Ponty, *The Phenomenology of Perception*, trans. Colin Smith (London: Routledge and Kegan Paul, 1962), vii. While an analysis of this philosophical tradition is beyond the scope of this study, I would like to point out that in my own history of the notion of the "immediacy" presupposed by political actors in their claims over the tunnel, I assume much the same skeptical stance taken by members of the Frankfurt school toward the later phenomenologists and toward Hegel as well. In a materialist turn, Theodor Adorno, in particular, understood philosophy's effort to arrive at a recuperation of ontological immediacy to be in itself the mark of a thoroughly historical phenomenon. Utterly affirmative, the phenomenological standpoint concerning an immediate life-world in reality signals the *irreducibility* of a mediation, that is, it reverts to ideology precisely because in it we encounter the "reduction to a concept of the negativity that makes the world the way it is." Theodor W. Adorno, *Negative Dialectics*, trans. E. B. Ashton (New York: Continuum, 1987), 167–170.

6 Tash, "A Distortion of History and Truth."

7 Krauthammer, "A Desecration of Truth," 104. For Olmert's accusation of Arafat's "insane incitement," see Nadav Shragai, "Olmert: The Behavior of the Palestinian Authority—'Maniacal Incitement,'" *Ha'aretz*, 26 September 1996, A3.

8 "The tradition of the oppressed teaches us that the 'state of emergency' in which we live is not the exception but the rule. We must attain to a conception of history that is in keeping with this insight." Walter Benjamin, "Theses on the Philosophy of History," in *Illuminations*, trans. Harry Zohn (New York: Schocken Books, 1969), 257.

9 Tash, "A Distortion of History and Truth" (emphasis added).

10 Edward Said, "In Search of Palestine," videocassette (London: BBC, 1998). In this film, Said refers to demolished Palestinian homes as the very "atoms" of this conflict.

11 The San Remo Conference, which took place at the close of World War I, allotted a de facto mandate over Palestine to Great Britain. The League of Nations conferred a mandate in July 1922, and it officially went into effect in September 1923. However, Great Britain conquered the country in a campaign lasting from late 1917 into the spring of 1918. It established a military administration over the country under the OETA (Overseas Enemy Territory Administration), which passed into civilian hands in 1920. Great Britain quit Palestine in May, 1948. For additional information on the British administration see Rachela Makover, *Shilton Uminhal Be'Eretz-Israel, 1917–1925* (Jerusalem: Yad Ben-Zvi, 1988); and Fannie Fern Andrews, *The Holy Land under Mandate* (Westport, Conn.: Hyperion Press, 1976). Also see Gidon Biger, *Moshevet Keter o Bayit Le'umi: Hashpa'at Hashilton Habriti al Eretz-Israel, 1917–1930* (Jerusalem: Yad Ben-Zvi, 1983).

12 Adorno, "Subject and Object," in *The Essential Frankfurt School Reader*, ed. Andrew Arato and Eike Gebhardt (New York: Continuum Books, 1988), 505.

13 Adorno, *Negative Dialectics*, 143.

14 If I have just raised the specter of a dramaturgy of conflict, I would like to make it

clear that in the performative dimension of a struggle, one encounters something far more problematic than the existence of a tacit (or even cynical) agreement or "interaction ritual" involving individuals in opposition. As Goffman has shown, this "interaction ritual" is in reality an entire syntagmatic code that frames "actors" qua actors and the "political" qua political. See "Where the Action Is," in Erving Goffman, *Interaction Ritual: Essays on Face-to-Face Behavior* (New York: Pantheon Books, 1967).

15 Karen Armstrong, *Jerusalem: One City, Three Faiths* (New York: Ballantine Books, 1996). By "hierophany" I am referring to a typology of the claims for the manifestation of the sacred in the profane. In this regard, see Mircea Eliade, *Traité d'histoire des religions*, preface by Georges Dumezil (Paris: Payot, 1949). Also see Paul Ricoeur, *Manifestation et Proclamation* (Paris : Aubier, 1974), 57–76; Jay Kim, "Hierophany and History," *Journal of the American Academy of Religion* 40 (September 1972): 334–348.

16 Benyamin Netanyahu, as quoted in Nadav Shragai, Sami Sokol, Gai Behor, Aluf Ben, and Sharon Sade, "Arafat Calls upon the Palestinians to Carry Out Protests and a Commercial Strike," *Ha'aretz*, 25 September 1996, A1.

17 Armstrong, *Jerusalem: One City, Three Faiths*, xvi–xxi.

18 Ibid., xviii.

19 Rashid Khalidi, *Palestinian Identity* (New York: Columbia University Press, 1997), 35. In its visitors' guide to the site, the Foundation for the Heritage of the Western Wall (Hakeren Lemoreshet hakotel hama'aravi) claims that as the stratigraphy of an earlier Jerusalem is redeemed in the space beneath the slopes of the Temple Mount (effectively bypassing a history of Islamic and Arab hegemony in construction in the zone directly adjoining the Haram al-Sharif), "the legacy of David and Solomon, Ezrah and Nehemiah, the Hasmoneans, Kings, Prophets, Princes and Tana'im [Mishnaic-era teachers] rises from the courses of stone." Misrad Le'inyanei datot, Reshut hamekomot hak'doshim—Hakeren Lemoreshet hakotel hama'aravi, *Minheret Hakotel Hama'aravi* (Jerusalem, n.p.).

20 Compare with Hegel, who describes the movement of knowing and appearance in architecture as follows: "This dwelling, the aspect of the universal element or inorganic nature of Spirit, now also includes within it a shape of individuality which brings nearer to actuality the Spirit that previously was separated from existence, and was external or internal to it, and thereby makes the work more in harmony with active self-consciousness." Hegel, "Natural Religion," in *Phenomenology of Spirit*, §695, 423.

21 Meron Benvenisti, *City of Stone: The Hidden History of Jerusalem*, trans. Maxine Kaufman Nunn (Berkeley: University of California Press, 1996), 4.

22 Ibid., 49.

23 With the exception of historiography's names for violence (which I examine in part 2), the relation between this history's "in passings" and broader historiography is beyond the scope of this work. However, it is important to note that formally, if not ideologically, Benvenisti and Khalidi display some affinities with the

projects of Eric Hobsbawm and Pierre Nora, respectively. See Eric Hobsbawm and Terence Ranger, eds., *The Invention of Tradition* (Cambridge: Cambridge University Press, 1983); and Pierre Nora, *Les Lieux de mémoire* (Paris: Gallimard, 1984). Rather than seeing the Palestinian and Israeli cases as particular representatives of those broader historiographic positions, however, I suspect that the broader historiographic traditions are, to some degree, called into question by the exemplars, which, in their own opposition reveal the problematic triumph of instrumental reason in the analysis of instrumental reason.

24 Khalidi's "touchstone" and Benvenisti's "quarry" seem to give one license to commute to the usual sites of interpretive labor, that is, to the "real conflict" and the "larger" taxonomies of religion, politics, the sign, national identity, that would either explain the history of this particular nightmare or solve it. In doing so, they identify time with causality, and the symbol with pure denotation. From the perspective of *time*, however, a telling of this conflict that considers the position of monuments in politics to be either implements of consciousness or fetishes necessarily inaugurates its own crisis of appearances. To think of Jerusalem as Rashid Khalidi appears to, for example, is to imbricate the historical subject—the source of the historical consciousness that he privileges—within a dialectic of "anticipation and retroaction": insofar as the figure that occasions identity is paradoxically already preformed as an exteriorization of the same identity, the figure, or city, or monument that is invoked is as unreliable a "reflection" of the history that it would account for politically, as it is its unavoidable "touchstone." In this connection, see Jane Gallop, "Lacan's 'Mirror Stage': Where to Begin," *SubStance* 37/38 (1983): 120–121. From the position of the *symbol*, the telling of Jerusalem's history inaugurates a crisis similar to the one that befalls the "time" of the monument. As that through which one putatively accounts for the immediacy of what has taken place, the monument can only appear either as a mute historical "given" (which, for that reason, cannot perform as an exhortative sign), or as an exhortative sign that transmutes the originary object into nothing more than the particular instance of something else, that is, a reflection of larger historical forces, or universals. Both these moments are performed in Benvenisti's effort at a functionalist presentation of an "earthly Jerusalem"—of a Jerusalem beyond the malevolent excess of "meanings" (or *semiosis*) he seems to work against—but which, in becoming the sign of a Jerusalem beyond or before political connotation, performs its own impossibility and participates in what it would undo.

25 Tomis Kapitan, ed., *Philosophical Perspectives on the Israeli-Palestinian Conflict* (Armonk, N.Y.: M. E. Sharpe, 1997), vii.

26 Ibid. It is important to note, here, that Kapitan's logic has an important pedigree. For example, in her acclaimed study on violence, Hannah Arendt states, "All political institutions are manifestations and materializations of power; they petrify and decay as soon as the living power of the people ceases to uphold them. This is what Madison meant when he said 'all governments rest on opinion.'" Hannah Arendt, *On Violence* (New York: Harcourt, Brace and Ward, 1970), 41.

27 In philosophy, the term "adequation" refers to the very "ends" of reason (in an idealist frame), in the sense of a reality that is adequate to its concept, leaving no supplement, or remainder. See Martin Jay, *Marxism and Totality: The Adventures of a Concept from Lukács to Habermas* (Berkeley: University of California Press, 1984), 56. Similarly, Jacques Derrida has described the meaning of adequation in Hegel as a "felt union between infinite and finite." Jacques Derrida, *Glas*, trans. John P. Leavey Jr. and Richard Rand (Lincoln: University of Nebraska Press, 1986), 48A. For Adorno, this is a historical incommensurability, as well as the very definition of dialectics, which "says no more, to begin with, that objects do not go into their concepts without leaving a remainder, that they come to contradict the traditional norm of adequacy." Adorno, *Negative Dialectics*, 5. The "traditional norm" traverses linguistics as well, which explains adequation as "the process whereby a purely iconic or symbolic image is projected onto an objective reality." *Lore and Language*, 23 January 1979, as cited in the Oxford English Dictionary online, <http://dictionary.oed.com/>.

28 Theodor Adorno, *Minima Moralia: Reflections from Damaged Life*, trans. E. F. N. Jephcott (rpt., London: Verso, 1996), 79.

29 Adorno, *Negative Dialectics*, 145.

30 Shierry Weber Nicholson and Jeremy J. Shapiro, in the introduction to Theodor Adorno, *Hegel: Three Studies*, trans. Shierry Weber Nicholson (Cambridge, Mass.: MIT Press, 1994), xxix.

31 Following E. T. A. Hoffman, Freud presents the *Unheimlich*, or uncanny, as something that should have remained hidden but was somehow brought to light. Sigmund Freud, "The 'Uncanny'" (1919), in *The Standard Edition of the Complete Psychological Works of Sigmund Freud*, 24 vols., ed. James Strachey, trans. under gen. ed. James Strachey (London: Hogarth Press and the Institute of Psycho-Logical Analysis, 1981), 17: 217–252. Following Anthony Vidler's *The Architectural Uncanny*, I am referring here to not only an analogical relation between architecture and the uncanny but a structural one, where the very aspect of the "homely"—of an objective, material form of adequation—presents itself as the dialectically induced unhomely: not merely the opposite of what one expected but the immanent process of its negation, the consequence of the insufficiency already built in to the homely. See "Unhomely Houses," in Anthony Vidler, *The Architectural Uncanny: Essays in the Modern Unhomely* (Cambridge, Mass.: MIT Press, 1992).

32 Benjamin, "Theses on the Philosophy of History," in *Illuminations*, 257.

33 Theodor Adorno to Walter Benjamin, 2 August 1935, reprinted in *Aesthetics and Politics*, by Ernst Bloch et al., trans. and ed. Ronald Taylor (London: NLB, 1977), 116.

34 Robert Hullot-Kentor, "Suggested Reading: Jameson on Adorno," review of *Late Marxism: Adorno, or the Persistence of the Dialectic* (London: Verso, 1990) by Fredric Jameson, *Telos* 89 (fall 1991): 175.

35 "This more is not imposed upon it but remains immanent to it, as that which has been pushed out of it. In that sense, the nonidentical would be the thing's own identity against its identifications." Theodor Adorno, *Negative Dialectics*, 161.

36 Sigmund Freud, "Medusa's Head," in *The Standard Edition of the Complete Psychological Works of Sigmund Freud*, 273–275.

37 In this connection see Neil Hertz, "Medusa's Head: Male Hysteria under Political Pressure," in *The End of the Line: Essays on Psychoanalysis and the Sublime* (New York: Columbia University Press, 1985).

38 Looking to the Gorgon in Greek mythology as a representation of the menacing possibility of castration, Freud suggests that even if the sight of Medusa's head "makes the spectator stiff with terror, turns him to stone," such petrifications are simultaneously compensatory and constructive, because they occasion what he describes as a "consolation to the spectator," offering a "stiffening reassurance of possession." Freud notes, "Observe that we have here once again the same origin from the castration complex and the same transformation of affect." Freud, "Medusa's Head," 273.

39 Erving Goffman, *Frame Analysis: An Essay on the Organization of Experience*, foreword by Bennett Berger (Boston: Northeastern University Press, 1986), 249.

40 Eric Hobsbawm, *The Age of Empire, 1875–1914* (New York: Vintage Press, 1989). The testimony of figures involved in the promotion of Palestine researches made it difficult to establish a distinction between the conceptual territory of "redemption" and the redemption of territory. In 1869, for example, the archbishop of York (chairman of the society) addressed members of the Palestine Exploration Fund, in the following way: "We look on Jerusalem now—we English people—as a city that in some measure belongs to us. Do we not every year pour forth in thousands the documents that attest its history—do we not put forth in thousands and tens of thousands that sacred Book where in is written its rise and its fortunes and its fall? May we not naturally say, when we are so largely occupied in spreading its history, that we have in some measure made it our own? . . . [I]t is with the history of that country, and with what was done upon its soil, that our hopes of salvation have been knit up. [Cheers.]" "Report of Annual General Meeting, held at Willis's Rooms, St. James's, 24th June, 1869," *Quarterly Statement of the Palestine Exploration Fund* [hereafter PEFQ] (1869–70), 90.

41 Beginning, perhaps, with Hurewitz's *The Struggle for Palestine* (1950), histories of the Mandate era established a standard method of periodization that has divided the thirty-one-year span of the era into three (sometimes four) internal phases, which have subsequently been combined and recombined within a limited number of possible arrangements. And these arrangements are themselves based upon the significance ascribed to what have been represented within the historiographic canon as decisive moments of violent historical change. The first of these periods spans between the conquest of Jerusalem on 9 December 1917 and the Nabi Musa riots in Jerusalem of April 1920 and the Jaffa riots of 1921, roughly a year following the establishment of a civil administration in Palestine. Most frequently, this inaugural period of British suzerainty over Palestine is conjoined with a second period extending from the same riots of 1920 and 1921 until the moment of the Wailing Wall, or Buraq disturbances, which once again took place in Jerusalem in

August 1929, then spread to other locations in Palestine (principally Hebron and Safad). A third phase, extending from the riots of August 1929 to the Thawra, or Palestinian-Arab rebellion and general strike (which began in the spring of 1936 and lasted with various pauses and reactivations until 1938), is often included along with the first two phases as one general unit in the historiographic canon. Finally, this same third state is also presented, at times, as the inaugural moment of a fourth, and final period in the history of the Mandate. This last phase is generally marked as having begun with the suppression of the Arab revolt, and then describes a political quietude during the course of World War II, which in turn culminated once again in a time of increasing violence between 1945 and 1948, when the United Nations ratified a partition of the country in November 1947, and when England decided to quit Palestine in May 1948. For examples of this normative historiographic frame at work, see Ann Mosely Lesch, *Arab Politics in Palestine, 1917–1929: The Frustration of a Nationalist Movement* (Ithaca, N.Y.: Cornell University Press, 1979); Martin Kolinsky, *Law, Order, and Riots in Mandatory Palestine, 1928–1935* (London: St. Martin's Press, 1993); Yehoshuah Porath, *The Palestinian Arab National Movement: From Riots to Rebellion, 1929–1939* (London: Frank Cass, 1977); Michael Cohen, "Direction of Policy in Palestine, 1936–1945," *Middle-Eastern Studies* 11, no. 3 (1975): 237–261; Elias Sanbar, "Le Vécu et l'écrit: Historiens-réfugiés de Palestine. Quelques propositions pour la recherche," *Revue d'Etudes Palestiniennes* 1 (fall 1981): 62–65.

42 Kapitan, ed., *Philosophical Perspectives on the Israeli-Palestinian Conflict.*

43 See Adorno, *Aesthetic Theory*, ed. Gretel Adorno and Rolf Tiedemann, trans., ed., and intro. Robert Hullot-Kentor (Minneapolis: University of Minnesota Press, 1997), 252.

44 The role of the Name in Adorno's and Benjamin's thinking about the possibility of "lending voice to suffering" is concisely covered in Susan Buck-Morss, *The Origin of Negative Dialectics: Theodor W. Adorno, Walter Benjamin and the Frankfurt Institute* (New York: Free Press, 1977), 88–90. But see, in particular, Adorno's "A Portrait of Walter Benjamin," in *Prisms*, trans. Samuel Weber and Shierry Weber (Cambridge, Mass.: MIT Press, 1988).

45 Theodor Adorno, "Resignation," in *Critical Models: Interventions and Catchwords*, European Perspectives: A Series in Social Thought and Cultural Criticism, ed. Lawrence D. Kritzman, trans. Henry W. Pickford (New York: Columbia University Press, 1998), 290.

46 Benjamin, "Theses on the Philosophy of History," 257.

1. A Hieroglyph Designed by God

The two epigraphs to this chapter are from W. H. Mallock, "General Gordon's Message," *Fortnightly Review* n.s. 36 (July 1884): 57–74; and Walter Benjamin, *The Origin of German Tragic Drama*, trans. John Osborne (London: NLB, 1977), 232.

1 Lytton Strachey, *Eminent Victorians: Cardinal Manning, Florence Nightingale, Dr. Arnold,*

General Gordon (New York: Harvest/HBJ Books, 1980). For recent Gordon biographies see Roy MacGregor-Hastie, *Never to Be Taken Alive: A Biography of General Gordon* (New York: St. Martin's Press, 1985); and John Charles Pollock, *Gordon: The Man behind the Legend* (London: Constable, 1993). For two differing accounts of Gordon's participation in the suppression of the Taiping revolt, see Andrew Wilson, *The Ever-Victorious Army: A History of the Chinese Campaign under Lt.-Col. C. G. Gordon, C.B. R.E., and of the Suppression of the Tai-ping Rebellion*, Reprint Series: Chinese Materials Center 63, ed. with notes by John Holland (San Francisco: Chinese Materials Center, 1977); and, an excellent recent history of the rebellion itself, Jonathan D. Spence, *God's Chinese Son: The Taiping Heavenly Kingdom of Hong Xiuquan* (New York: W. W. Norton, 1996). Finally, the most recent history of England's intervention in the Sudan is Robin Neillands, *The Dervish Wars: Gordon and Kitchener in the Sudan, 1880–1898* (London: Murray, 1996).

2   Having apparently been left to his own devices with no hope of timely reinforcements by Gladstone's government, the general's death (no less than the fall of Khartoum itself) inaugurated a significant political controversy and a sensation that was eagerly perpetuated by a burgeoning culture industry. Through the efforts of the *London Quarterly Review*, *The Graphic*, the *Fortnightly Review* and other publications, Gordon's ghost joined the phantasmagoria of the commodity form; even copies of a religious text that had been owned by Gordon and then casually given to an acquaintance were reprinted—a *facsimile* of "Gordon's own copy marked in many places with pencil on the margin"—by these executors of Gordon's literary legacy. Such was the case, for example, in Rev. H. Carruthers Wilson's, "The Theology of General Gordon," forming the introduction to a reprint of Gordon's copy of *Christ Mystical, or The Blessed Name of Christ and His Members* by Joseph Hall, bishop of Norwich, A.D. 1654 (1893; London: Hodder and Stoughton, 1908), 12. Another milestone in the hagiography of Gordon is Elizabeth Rundle Charles's *Three Martyrs of the Nineteenth Century: Studies from the Lives of Livingstone, Gordon, and Patterson* (London: SPCK, 1885). It is important to note, however, that Gordon, as both a commodity and a martyr was already "in place" prior to his death, during the period of the siege of Khartoum itself. For example W. H. Mallock's assessment of Gordon's theology (written during the period when Gordon was cut off without the prospect of help) deliberately establishes an image of the general as a near-divine clairvoyant: "It is a fact not generally known, but it is true, nevertheless, that General Gordon, when he left England for the Soudan, did so with the conviction firmly fixed in his mind, that he will never return alive." Mallock, "General Gordon's Message," 57. Following Gordon's death, quasi-religious parallels between Christ's passion on the cross (the betrayal by his intimates, his foreknowledge of Golgotha) and the general's own fate were ratified by Queen Victoria, who, in her published letters to Mary Gordon—Charles Gordon's sister—noted: "*How* shall I write to you or how shall I attempt to express *what I feel!* To think of your dear, noble, heroic Brother, who served his Country and his Queen so truly, so heroically, with a self-sacrifice so edifying to the World, not having been rescued. That the promises of support were not ful-

filled—which I so frequently and constantly expressed on those who asked him to go—*is to me grief inexpressible.*" Letter from Queen Victoria to Miss Gordon, Osborne, 17 February 1885, as reproduced in Charles George Gordon, *Letters of General C. G. Gordon to His Sister, M. A. Gordon*, ed. M. A. Gordon (London: Macmillan, 1888), xv.

3 Strachey, *Eminent Victorians*, 262.

4 In his introduction to the reprint of Joseph Hall's *Christ Mystical, or The Blessed Union of Christ and His Members*, M. Carruthers Wilson notes that "Gordon took a few great truths of Scripture and made them part of his very being. These truths were: The Indwelling of God. . . . This was his favourite topic, and I think it possessed him."

5 Frank Livingstone Huntley, *Bishop Joseph Hall, 1574–1656: A Biographical and Critical Study* (Cambridge: D. S. Brewer, 1979). See also Huntley's "Bishop Joseph Hall and Protestant Meditation in Seventeenth-Century England: A Study with Texts of the Art of Divine Meditation" (1606) and "Occasional meditations" (1633), in *Medieval and Renaissance Texts and Studies*, vol. 1. (Binghamton, N.Y.: Center for Medieval and Early Renaissance Studies, 1981).

6 A supporter of Gordon sought to bypass this aspect of Gordon's persona by turning the strangeness of Gordon's theology back upon an interpreter of that strangeness, arguing that to read Gordon's views literally was to misunderstand him: "'He was not content,' a critic who knew nothing of the man once said, 'if he could not give the exact height, and breadth of the deity.'" Colonel Sir William F. Butler, *Charles George Gordon* (London: Macmillan, 1889), 187.

7 Edward Said, *Orientalism* (New York: Vintage Books, 1979), 238.

8 Ibid., 12.

9 Ibid., 169–170. Regarding this imaginary Orient Said notes: "They planned and projected for, imagined, ruminated about places that were principally in their minds. . . . an Orient of memories, suggestive ruins, forgotten secrets, hidden correspondences, and an almost virtuosic style of being."

10 Ibid., 234.

11 Benjamin, *The Origin of German Tragic Drama*, 183.

12 Charles Gordon, *Reflections in Palestine* (London: Macmillan, 1884), vii–viii.

13 Benjamin, *The Origin of German Tragic Drama*, 166.

14 Francois-René Chateaubriand, *Travels in Jerusalem and the Holy Land through Egypt*, vol. 2, trans. Frederic Shoberl (London: Henry Colburn, 1835), 159. Also see Alphonse de Lamartine, *Voyage en Orient* (1835; rpt., Paris: Hachette, 1887).

15 Benjamin, *Origin of German Tragic Drama*, 232. Compare to Richard Wolin's understanding of the *Trauerspiel*: "The solution to the riddle [of Golgotha] is to be found in the fact that not in spite of but *because of* the utter squalor and despair of its material content, it is ultimately transformed into a theological drama of salvation." Richard Wolin, *Walter Benjamin: An Aesthetic of Redemption* (New York: Columbia University Press, 1982), 70.

16 Benjamin, *The Origin of German Tragic Drama*, 166. For a lucid exposition of Goethe's development of the opposition between allegory and symbol in his "On the Ob-

jects of the Plastic Arts," see Tzvetan Todorov, *Theories of the Symbol*, trans. Catherine Porter (Ithaca, N.Y.: Cornell University Press, 1982), 198–200.

17 Ibid.

18 Georg Friedrich Creuzer, *Symbolik und Mythologie der alten Volker, besonders der Griechen*, 4 vols., in *Vortragen und Entwurfen von Friedrich Creuzer* (Leipzig : K. W. Leske, 1810–1812); See also Todorov, *Theories of the Symbol*, 216–217.

19 "In the process of decay, and in it alone, the events of history shrivel up and become absorbed in the setting. . . . [I]t is fallen nature that bears the imprint of the progression of history." Benjamin, *The Origin of German Tragic Drama*, 179–180. Reading his friend's understanding of dialectical temporality, Theodor Adorno explicated the distinction between Benjamin's presentation of "Nature" and "History" in the following way: "According to Benjamin, nature, as creation, carries the mark of transience. Nature itself is transitory. Thus it includes the element of history. Whenever an historical element appears it refers back to the natural element that passes away with it. Likewise the reverse: whenever 'second nature' appears, when the world of convention approaches, it can be deciphered in that its meaning is shown to be precisely its transience. . . . As transience, all original-history is absolutely present. It is present in the form of 'signification.' 'Signification' means that the elements of nature and history are not fused with each other, rather they break apart and interweave at the same time in such a fashion that the natural appears as a sign for history and history, where it seems to be most historical, appears as a sign for nature." Theodor Adorno, "The Idea of Natural History" (1932; 1973), trans. Robert Hullot-Kentor, *Telos* 60 (summer 1984): 120–121.

20 Benjamin, *The Origin of German Tragic Drama*, 183.

21 Ibid., 218.

22 Edward Said, *Orientalism*, 178. Chateaubriand expresses sentiments quite similar to those of Lamartine when he visits the Church of the Holy Sepulchre. He notes: "All I am certain of is that at the sight of this triumphant tomb I was aware only of my own weakness, and when my guide cried out with St. Paul, 'Death, where is thy victory? Death, where is thy sting?' I listened attentively, as if death were about to respond that it was conquered and chained in that monument." Chateaubriand, *Travels in Jerusalem and the Holy Land*, vol. 2, 159.

23 "Just as earthly mournfulness is of a piece with allegorical interpretation, so is devilish mirth with its frustration in the triumph of matter. This explains the devilish jocularity of the intriguer his intellectuality, his knowledge of significance." Benjamin, *The Origin of German Tragic Drama*, 227.

24 Curzon had witnessed a stampede within the Church of the Holy Sepulchre during the Easter ceremony of the "Holy Fire" (1833). His record of those events scandalized the English public, insofar as it presented Levantine observances as pagan acts. See Robert Curzon, *Visit to Monasteries in the Levant* (London: Humphrey Milford, 1849). See in particular "The Sacred Fire and the Curse of Jerusalem," in chap. 16, 182–197. I believe, however, that in its early modern form, this equation of Eastern practices and idolatry in the Holy Sepulchre was already anticipated in

Henry Maundrell's record of his travels to Palestine in 1697, in which he describes the conclusion of a passion play that took place in the martyrium in this way: "The ceremony of the passion being over, and the guardian's sermon ended, two friars, personating the one Joseph of Arimathea, the other Nicodemus, approached the cross, and, with a most solemn and concerned air, both of aspect and behaviour, drew out the great nails, and took down the feigned body from the cross. . . . These obsequies being finished, they carried off their fancied corpse and laid it out in the sepulchre, shutting up the door till Easter morning." Henry Maundrell, *A Journal from Aleppo to Jerusalem, at Easter, A.D. 1697*, reprinted in *Early Travels in Palestine, comprising the Narratives of Arculf, Willibald, Benard, Saewulf, Sigurd, Benjamin of Tudela, Sir John Maundeville, De La Brocquiere, and Maundrell*, ed. Thomas Wright (New York: Ketav Publishing, 1968), 445.

25 Edward Daniel Clarke, *Travels in Various Countries of Europe, Asia and Africa* (London: T. Cadell, 1812), 542.

26 Adorno, "The Idea of Natural History," 119.

27 Clarke notes, "If Mount Calvary has sunk beneath the overwhelming influence of superstition, studiously endeavouring to modify and to disfigure it, through so many ages; if the situation of Mount Sion yet remains to be ascertained; the Mount of Olives, undisguised by fanatical labours, exhibits the appearance it presented in all the periods of history. . . . The beautiful Gate of the Temple is no more; but Siloa's fountain haply flows, and Kedron murmurs in the Valley of Jehosaphat." Clarke, *Travels in Various Countries of Europe, Asia and Africa*, 547.

28 See Claude Reignier Conder et al., *The Survey of Western Palestine: 1882–1888* ([Slough, England]: Archive Editions in association with Palestine Exploration Fund, 1998). See also Palestine Exploration Fund, *The Survey of Western Palestine*, general index to the memoirs, vols. 1–3; the special papers; the Jerusalem volume; the flora and fauna of Palestine; the geological survey; and the Arabic and English name lists; comp. Henry C. Stewardson (London: Committee of the Palestine Exploration Fund, 1888). One of the many historical ironies of this toponymic strategy is that it was not sanctioned by the Gospels themselves. Only three of the Gospels explicitly refer to Golgotha as a place name (Matthew 27:33, Mark 15:22, John 19:17). The toponymic imperative appears to have originated in the Douay-Rheims New Testament Vulgate "Calvariae locus" (place of the skull) as a translation of the Greek "Kraniou topos." With reference to the position of Golgotha, the *Dictionary of the Bible* notes: "While the events of two thousand years of occupation have altered the topography of the site [of the Church of the Holy Sepulchre] beyond all recognition, it is important to remember that there is no literary or archaeological evidence to support the popular belief that the place of execution was a hill or even a small knoll." "Golgotha," in John L. McKenzie, S.J. *Dictionary of the Bible* (New York: Macmillan, 1965).

29 James Fergusson, *An Essay on the Ancient Topography of Jerusalem* (London: John Weale, 1847); and *The Holy Sepulchre and the Temple at Jerusalem: Being the Substance of*

Two Lectures Delivered at the Royal Institution, Albemarle Street, on the 21st February, 1862, and 3d March, 1865 (London: Murray, 1865), 26.

30 William Smith, Dictionary of the Bible: Comprising Its Antiquities, Biography, Geography, and Natural History, rev. H. B. Hackett; with Ezra Abbot (1858; Boston: Houghton Mifflin, 1881).

31 Elizabeth Rundle Charles, Wanderings over Bible Lands and Seas (New York: Robert Carter and Bros.; 1873), 65–66. Charles takes this point further, noting: "Almost one can fancy one catches the wave of a garment through those olives, or the glimpse of a dim retreating form disappearing over that hill-top, of the little band that went about with him. And then we cast aside fancy altogether, as an unworthy denizen of this land of glorious and terrible truths, and remember, 'He was here.'" Charles was also an avid admirer of General Gordon and participated in his hagiography with the publication of her Three Martyrs of the Nineteenth Century (1885).

32 "The place called Calvary was according to our general idea, the public place of execution. Some have supposed its name—Golgotha, or 'place of the skull'—to be derived from this fact; though others, including many of the early fathers, suppose it to refer to the shape of the ground—a rounded hill, in form like a skull. We look naturally for some spot just outside the city, and beside one of the same roads. . . . These considerations would lead us to fix Calvary—the place of execution, north of Jerusalem, near the main road to Shechem [Nablus], and near the northern cemetery. Now, close to this road, on the east, is a rounded knoll. . . . Thus, to a 'green hill far away, beside the city wall,' we turn from the artificial rocks and marble of the monkish chapel of Calvary. . . . I wish I could bring before the reader's mind as vividly as it now rises in my memory, the appearance of this most interesting spot. The stony road comes out from the beautiful Damascus Gate, and runs beside the yellow cliff, in which are great excavated caverns, perhaps once part of the great Cotton Grotto. Above the cliff, which is some thirty feet high, is the rounded knoll without any building on it, bare of trees, and in spring covered in part with scanty grass, while a great portion is occupied by a Moslem Cemetery." Claude Reignier Conder, Tent Work in Palestine: A Record of Discovery and Adventure, vols. 1 and 2 (New York: D. Appleton, 1878), 374–377.

33 William Simpson, "Transference of Holy Sites," PEFQ (1879): 30.

34 Charles George Gordon, "Notes on Eden and Golgotha," PEFQ (1885): 78–81 (emphasis added). Gordon's exposition on the anamorphic figure continues as follows: "You find also the verse (Ps. XLVIII) 'Zion, on the sides or the North'; the word 'pleura,' same as they pierced His Pleura, and there came blood and water, God took a Pleuron from the side of Adam, and made woman. Now the Church of Christ is made up of, or came from, His Pleura, the Stones of the Temple came from the Quarries, from the chest of the figure, and so on; so that fixed the figure of the body to the skull." In this series of correspondences, the locus of the figure's phallus corresponds with the site of the Temple. As I suggest elsewhere, this is the significance of Gordon's invitation to be "venturesome" in the mapping of the

145

figure. See my essay "The Dimensions of History: On Architecture, between 'Constructive Phenomenology' and Apotropaism," *AA Files* 35 (spring 1998): 46–55.

35 "Based on the assumption that the Ottoman Empire could no longer hold itself together, friend and foe alike engaged in subtle calculations of power politics and considerations of how the spoils would be shared when the time came. The so-called Eastern Question thus was the outsiders' assessment of the troubles facing the Ottoman Empire and how they might benefit from the results." Stanford J. Shaw and Ezel Kural Shaw, *History of the Ottoman Empire and Modern Turkey*, vol. 2: *Reform, Revolution, and Republic: The Rise of Modern Turkey, 1808–1975* (Cambridge: Cambridge University Press, 1977), 133.

36 As Carl Brown has noted, the complexity of Great Power interests, coupled with those of forces within the Ottoman Empire itself, presented a situation during which "no power wanted the risks or the odium of single-handedly pushing the turbanned humpty dumpty off the wall, but neither did any power want to be caught napping in the shade of the wall when the inevitable fall came." L. Carl Brown, *International Politics and the Middle East: Old Rules, Dangerous Game* (Princeton, N.J.: Princeton University Press, 1984), 34–35. From the perspective of the Ottoman Empire, its rulers spent the last hundred years of its existence "trying to confront the growing power of a Europe driven on by the influence of the two great revolutions that it had experienced at the end of the 18th century: the political revolution in France from 1789 onwards; and the industrial revolution in Britain. One result was the nibbling away of the frontiers of the empire in Africa and West Asia, marked by the establishment of European colonies and spheres of influence." Roger Owen, *State, Power and Politics in the Making of the Modern Middle East* (London: Routledge, 1992), 8.

37 Said, "Orientalism Now," in *Orientalism*, 201–255.

38 Edward Said, "Jane Austen and Empire," in *Culture and Imperialism* (New York: Vintage Books, 1994), 80–97.

39 For a cogent presentation of the distinction between culture and society in European intellectual currents, see Adorno, "Cultural Criticism and Society," in *Prisms*, trans. Samuel Weber and Shierry Weber (Cambridge, Mass.: MIT Press, 1988), 27.

40 Neil Asher Silberman, *Digging for God and Country: Exploration, Archaeology, and the Secret Struggle for the Holy Land, 1799–1917* (New York: Anchor Books, 1982), 18.

41 Yehoshua Ben-Arieh, *The Rediscovery of the Holy Land in the 19th Century* (Jerusalem: Magnes Press, 1979).

42 Barbara W. Tuchman, *Bible and Sword: England and Palestine from the Bronze Age to Balfour* (New York: Ballantine Books, 1956), 239–240.

43 "The final years of the mapping of western Palestine under Conder and Kitchener coincided with the renewal of the Russian threat to British interests in the Near East. A memorandum of 1876 written by the British General Wolseley, who later headed the invasion forces in Egypt, indicates that one of Britain's concerns was that the Russians might occupy Syria under the pretext of protecting the Christians of the Holy Land." Naomi Shepherd, *The Zealous Intruders: The Western Rediscovery of*

Palestine (San Francisco: Harper and Row, 1987), 222. Describing England's diplomatic position after 1856, Joseph Heller notes: "The distinctive feature of Britain's Ottoman policy during this period was one of gradual change: the attitude of friendliness, which was evident in the Crimean War and the Eastern Crisis of 1877–8, and which was associated with such eminent British statesmen as Palmerston, Stratford Canning and Disraeli, turned to coolness and occasional hostility." Joseph Heller, *British Policy towards the Ottoman Empire, 1908–1914* (London: Frank Cass, 1983).

44 I elaborate this position in "Orientalism and the Ornament of Mediation," *Design Book Review* [Orientalism Issue] 29/30 (summer/fall, 1993): 32–34.

45 "Little by little the desert grows larger; the ruins of settlements extend further and further, and at the entries of these settlements ever growing cemeteries. Each year another hut collapses and another family dies off so that soon there remains only a cemetery to mark the place where there once was a village." Chateaubriand, *Travels*, 154.

46 JMA/361/A58 [Reproduction of Charles Robert Ashbee Papers in Felicity Ashbee's collection], *Report by Mr. C. R. Ashbee on the Arts and Crafts of Jerusalem and District*. Memorandum to the Chief Administrator, August 1918, 44–45. (C. R. Ashbee is referring to the series of tactical/religious compounds erected in the city during the nineteenth century, each of which was built in its sponsors' national styles.)

47 Theodor Adorno to Walter Benjamin, 2 August 1935, in *Aesthetics and Politics*, ed. Ronald Taylor (London: NLB, 1977), 116.

2. An Unmistakable Sign

The epigraphs to this chapter are from Ernest Tatham Richmond, *The Dome of the Rock in Jerusalem: A Description of Its Structure and Decoration* (Oxford: Clarendon Press, 1924), 4; Ahad Ha'am, "Sacred and Profane," *Selected Essays of Ahad Ha'am* (New York: Atheneum, 1962), 41, quoted in Mitchell Cohen, *Zion and State: Nation, Class and the Shaping of Modern Israel* (Oxford: Basil Blackwell, 1987), 64; and Georg Wilhelm Friedrich Hegel, "The Spirit of Christianity and Its Fate," in *On Christianity: Early Theological Writings*, trans. T. M. Knox, intro. Richard Kroner (New York: Harper, 1948), 196.

1 See Ernest Tatham Richmond, *The Sites of the Crucifixion and the Resurrection* (London: Catholic Truth Society, 1934). The son of the noted painter W. B. Richmond, Ernest Tatham Richmond was born in London in 1874. After studying at Clifton Technical and apprenticing under the architect Gerald C. Horsley (a former pupil of Richard Norman Shaw), he studied at the Royal Academy School of Architecture. Richmond traveled to Egypt in 1895 to assist Richard Somers Clarke (surveyor of St. Paul's Cathedral) in the preparation of drawings for a book on the wall drawings of El Kab. In 1896, he was appointed assistant architect under Herz Bey in the Comité pour la conservation des monuments de l'art Arabe in Cairo, and embarked on a career as a civil servant in Egypt, eventually joining the Ministry of Public

Works of the Egyptian Government in 1900. (Richmond's highest rank there was director general of the Towns and State Buildings Department.) He left Egypt in 1911 and attempted to establish a private architectural practice in England, without great success. During the First World War, Richmond designed hand grenades for the War Office and then joined the War Graves Administration (later the Imperial War Graves Commission). Late in 1917 he was invited by Palestine's military government to report on the structural condition of the monuments on the Haram al-Sharif in Jerusalem, and in consequence of the relationship he established with Arab notables in Palestine, joined the civil administration of the country in the summer of 1920 as assistant secretary for political affairs. His role in the administration between 1920 and 1924, and later between 1927 and 1936 (when he returned to Palestine as director of the Department of Antiquities) is analyzed in this and the following chapter. (The bulk of Richmond's political papers relating to Palestine were reported to have been destroyed in a fire in 1926—see Philip Jones, ed., *Britain and Palestine, 1914–1918, Archival Sources for the History of the British Mandate* (Oxford: Oxford University Press for the British Academy, 1979). However, a significant collection of E.T. Richmond's papers was located by this author, who is now serving as their editor. At the time of the completion of this manuscript, Richmond's own memoirs, entitled "Mammon in the Holy Land" are being prepared for publication. This text is itself organized as a compilation of contemporary letters and diaries, principally from his period of service in Palestine.

2   Ernest Tatham Richmond, "Mammon in the Holy Land: A Description of How We 'Built Up Zion with Blood and Jerusalem with Iniquity,'" 1954, n.p., E. T. Richmond Papers. (All citations to this manuscript refer to the manuscript's own system of pagination.) After Gordon's death, his "Golgotha" was slowly transformed into an Anglican site of devotion, in no small measure because of its associations with him. In 1894 an association was established to purchase the site, which came to be known as the "Garden Tomb." After it was bought, J. Wardle recorded its transformation into a site of pilgrimage, noting: "This rock tomb, it is said, was discovered by my dear old friend and companion, General Gordon. He was for some time exploring and searching for proofs of the real hill of crucifixion and burial, and he seems [sic] satisfied that it was here our dear Lord suffered and died, and was sepulchred and rose again. . . . Rev. Hugh Price Hughes said: 'I was so convinced that this was the veritable place where my dear Lord was laid, that I laid my poor unworthy body in the same place,' and I followed his example." J. Wardle, *A Tour of Palestine and Egypt and Back* (Nottingham, England: H. B. Saxton, 1907). By 1917, the site was unproblematically subsumed within the first British master plan of Jerusalem as a place worthy of inclusion within a prophylactic zone, or greenbelt, that would surround the walls of the city. See William Hannah McLean, *Regional and Town Planning in Principle and Practice* (London: Crosby Lockwood and Son, 1930), 66; and R. K. Home, "British Colonial Town Planning in the Middle East: The Work of W. H. McLean," *Planning History* 12, no. 1 (n.d.): 4–9. On current representations of the Garden Tomb as a Protestant site of devotion, see Rev. Bill White, *A Special*

Place: The Story of the Garden Tomb, Jerusalem (Grantham, England: Stanborough Press, 1989).

3 C. W. Wilson, *Golgotha and the Holy Sepulchre* (London: Committee of the Palestine Exploration Fund, 1906). (This text is a reworking of a series of articles that Wilson published in the Quarterly Statement of the Palestine Exploration Fund between 1902–4.) The compilation was posthumously completed by the Palestine Exploration Fund (PEF). L. H. Vincent, O.P., "Garden Tomb: L'histoire d'un mythe," *Revue Biblique* 34, no. 3 (1 July 1925): 401–431.

4 Vincent, "Garden Tomb: L'histoire d'un mythe," 413: "En 1883, le général américain Gordon, féru d'un mysticisme scripturaire teinté de rabbinisme, arrivait à Jérusalem et du premier coup d'oeil sur la configuration de la cité, il en 'pénétrait tous les arcanes.'" As Vincent makes clear, his own project was in no small measure provoked by a series of articles and letters published in the *Times* in 1924 and 1925, in which the authenticity of the Garden Tomb was reasserted; in the minds of the members of the French School of Archaeology in Jerusalem (the École biblique) these publications continued a tradition of insinuations that they themselves had removed evidence supporting the authenticity of the site. See "Garden Tomb—New Jerusalem Discovery—Shrine Stone and Its Meaning," *Times* (London), 24 July 1924, 15. Richmond presents an entire history of these assertions of Catholic gerrymandering of archaeological evidence in his own *The Sites of the Crucifixion*, 14–15.

5 Wilson suggested that any scientific attempt to authenticate the traditionally accepted sites of the crucifixion and burial of Jesus (i.e., the Church of the Holy Sepulchre) in Jerusalem faced the following issues: (1) It needed to prove "the possibility of a continuous tradition" between the time of the crucifixion and that of Constantine that would have enabled Christians to identify the proper site; (2) it needed to explain "the attitude of early Christians towards holy places," thereby solving the paradox that *as Jews* early followers of Jesus would not have succumbed to a cult of monuments that would have permitted a "continuous tradition" or reverence for monuments to emerge; (3) it needed to locate "the course of the second wall" surrounding the city, since, as a Jew, Jesus could not have been buried within the city's confines. According to this line of thinking, if the Church of the Holy Sepulchre lay within the walls, it could not possibly be authentic. See Wilson, *Golgotha and the Holy Sepulchre*, 48. Incidentally, this last suggestion was already shown to be invalid by Clermont-Ganneau, who presented convincing evidence that the Church of the Holy Sepulchre was located on the site of, and in fact, destroyed a portion of an ancient necropolis. Charles Clermont-Ganneau, "The Holy Sepulchre," PEFQ (1877): 76–84.

6 As Richmond would later elaborate: "There was in England and American circles a great deal of ignorance on the subject of the authenticities of the site of the Crucifixion and the Resurrection. Most English and American people did not believe that the Church was built over those sites. . . . It was for the purpose of dispersing this fog of ignorance and prejudice that I wrote a booklet entitled 'The Sites of the Crucifixion and the Resurrection.'" Richmond, "Mammon in the Holy Land," 289.

7 Wilson, *Golgotha and the Holy Sepulchre*, 48.

8 Richmond, *Sites of the Crucifixion and the Resurrection*, 6. As I noted in part 1 of this study, this is precisely the presupposition that was rendered both explicit and politically productive by James Fergusson in his arguments about the "Transference of Holy Sites" (see chapter 1). Viewed in context, however, Richmond is also thinking of contemporary suggestions that "Romanists" had suppressed historical evidence that would endanger the "cult" of the established Holy Sepulchre.

9 After Herbert Samuel, a Jew, was appointed high commissioner for Palestine during the summer of 1920, and after he in turn selected Wyndham Deedes (a man with strong sympathies with the project of Zionism) to fill the post of chief secretary, Richmond seems to have been considered a necessary political counterweight to lend to the administration the appearance of impartiality. (For Richmond's turbulent career in the Samuel administration, see PRO/CO 733/28.) Until the Richmond papers reviewed by this author are made available to scholars, the most complete presentations of his participation in Samuel's administration will remain Elie Kedourie, "Sir Herbert Samuel and the Government of Palestine," *The Chatham House Version and Other Middle-Eastern Studies* (Hanover, N.H.: University Presses of New England, for Brandeis University Press, 1984), 52–81 (another version of this essay appeared under the same title in *Middle-Eastern Studies* 5, no. 1 [1969]: 44–68); Bernard Wasserstein, *The British in Palestine: The Mandatory Government and the Arab-Jewish Conflict, 1917–1929* (London: Basil Blackwell, 1978); John Richmond, "Prophet of Doom: E. T. Richmond, F.R.I.B.A., Palestine 1920–1924," *Arabic and Islamic Garland: Historical, Educational, and Literary Papers Presented to Abdul-Latif Tibawi* (London: Islamic Cultural Center, 1970), 190–196.

10 ISA/RG2/CS245 (pol. 228721). For two contrasting interpretations of these events see Phillip Mattar, *The Mufti of Jerusalem: Al-Hajj Amin al-Husayni and the Palestinian National Movement* (New York: Columbia University Press, 1988), 19–32; and Zvi Elpeleg, *The Grand Mufti: Haj Amin al-Hussaini, Founder of the Palestinian National Movement*, ed. Shmuel Himelstein, trans. David Harvey (London: Frank Cass, 1993), 7–14. In the next chapter I deal at length with the abortive elections which propelled al-Hajj Amin al-Husayni to the position of grand mufti in 1921.

11 These arguments are analyzed in part 3 of this study.

12 Nominally a contest between the proprietary rights of Muslims and the customary rights of Jews over the wall, the crisis began in earnest in September 1928 and culminated in the mass violence that shocked the country in August 1929. See Great Britain, *Report of the Palestine Commission on the Palestine Disturbances of August, 1929* (London: HMSO, 1930) (this document is also referred to as Cmd. 3530 or the Shaw Report).

13 In his memoirs, Richmond describes his first encounters with Jewish nationalism in 1918 in the following way: "At that time I knew practically nothing about Zionism, whether political or religious; but it was not long before I became alive to the inherent dangers and probable consequences of political Zionism, as well as to the character of the power that backed that movement. That power was, and is, Mam-

mon; rather an inappropriate deity to install in the Holy Land." Richmond, "Mammon in the Holy Land," 1. Richmond seems to have interpreted internal struggles within the Zionist movement—namely, between the general Zionism of Weizmann and the Zionist Organization (ZO), and the various "labor Zionisms" of David Ben-Gurion, Itzhak Ben-Zvi, and others—as duplicity. To him, a monolithic Zionism self-consciously adopted a strategy in which the former presented itself as a predominantly English, and liberal, mask for the latter. For Richmond's equations of Zionism with Bolshevism see his memorandum entitled "Note on the Present Tendencies and Dangers of the Jewish Labour Movement in Palestine," March 1922, ISA/RG2/CS149/Pol. 11. Richmond's understanding of Zionism as a spearhead for a materialist conspiracy only intensified over time. The most striking elaboration of this argument appears in his "Dictatorship in the Holy Land," *Nineteenth Century* 123 (February 1938): 186–192.

14 "Lord Plumer, who was at that time on leave in England, invited me to lunch with him at his Hotel. We had a pleasant luncheon during which he told me that in view of my political past he had felt disinclined to agree to my appointment, but that now he would accept me provided I would give him my word to refrain from all political activities and confine my work to furthering archaeological interests. I replied that I had no desire to have, in Palestine, any further contact with politics and with a policy which I heartily disliked, and I willingly gave him my word to confine my activities there to archaeological affairs. He accepted this." Richmond, "Mammon in the Holy Land," 272.

15 By way of illustration, during the meeting of the commission of inquiry convened by England to assess the causes of the violence in August 1929 (known as the Shaw Commission), the Zionist Executive's attorney argued that the "incitement comes from the top for political reasons. The Mufti makes no bones about being as much against the Balfour Declaration as the rest of the people at the head on his side. None. He is just as much interested in that as he is in consolidating his own position, and in exploiting it just as much. . . . The Burak motif is . . . merely colourable and not genuine at all. That is the case I am making." Great Britain, *Palestine Commission on the Disturbances of August 1929: Minutes of Evidence*, 3 vols., Colonial No. 48 (London, 1930), "Forty-Fifth Sitting," Closing Statement of Sir Boyd Merriman, Tuesday, 24 December 1929, 886. In the report of the Shaw Commission this is recorded as the first of three principal accusations leveled by the Zionist Executive against the grand mufti. The second was that "the innovations in practice which between October, 1928, and July, 1929, were introduced in the neighborhood of the Wailing Wall and also the construction of the Zawiyah [a Sufi hospice] and the building operations as a whole were in reality attempts to provoke the Jews." The third: "by the use of emissaries the Mufti had incited the people in parts of Palestine outside the capital and was having conveyed to them a message that they should come up to Jerusalem." Cmd. 3530, 75.

16 As a case in point, the *Near East* recorded Richmond's return to Jerusalem in the following way: "The Jews remember Mr. Richmond during the O.E.T.A. [Occupied

Enemy Territory Administration] days and the Samuel régime as 'political officer' and as one who, to their minds, overdid his sympathy with Palestinian Arab ideals to such a degree as to be hostile to Zionism; and with his return they see a recrudescence of organised Arab hostility to the British policy of the Jewish National Home—hostility which the Jews are honestly convinced was engineered by certain British residents, officials and non-officials. The sanest of the local Hebrew papers, *Ha'Aretz*, even voiced its conviction that the anti-Jewish malice in the new Director of Antiquities was such that he could be expected so to manipulate the development of Palestinian archaeological research as to minimize the importance of Jewish historical remains and even to argue from the Jewish claims to their national home! But the local Labour Hebrew daily, *Davar*, in a spirit of heroic faith challenged even Mr. Richmond to wipe out from Palestine the traces of Israel's past glories!" "The Director of Antiquities," *Near East*, 10 September 1927.

17 Itamar Ben-Avi, "J'Accuse! A Sequel to 'The Wailing Wall Atrocities,'" *Palestine Weekly*, 23 August 1929, 139. Ben-Avi's "atrocities" actually refer to what proved, in retrospect, to be preliminary skirmishes. The mass violence that would continue for another week and leave over one hundred people dead, actually began on the date of his article's publication.

18 Richmond converted to Catholicism in February 1926. I address the relation between this conversion and his understanding of history in the next chapter.

19 Thomas Carlyle, *Sartor Resartus* (New York: Charles Scribner and Sons, 1921), 63.

20 Belloc argued that the modern condition was not created by the industrial revolution: "No such material cause determined the degradation from which we suffer. It was the deliberate action of men, evil will in a few and apathy of will among the many." Hilaire Belloc, *The Servile State*, as quoted in Raymond Williams, *Culture and Society* (New York: Columbia University Press, 1983), 186. Richmond most closely approaches this same understanding in a letter to his brother, rebuking his sibling for his naïve belief in the "liberal democracy": "If Liberal Democracy is what we have had since the 17th century, it follows that it is *that* that has betrayed our agriculture, drained our countryside in order to flood the ghastly backwaters of our towns with a vast proletariate, wage-slaves deprived of all economic liberty, now sweated, now unemployed, a menace to our national life, pawns used for the enrichment of a few. It has given plenty of freedom to evil doers to enslave mankind to their own greed. Under it, fraternity becomes the oppression of the weak and the reign of the strong. It has spilt the blood of our best and bravest in bolstering up the Industrial Revolution and the financial supremacy of the City of London, the gilded manure heap of modern Progress, and it is now busily engaged under the direction of Mammon, its beloved chief, in establishing by force, the reign of anti-Christ in the Holy Land. No, I cannot enrol myself as a Liberal Democrat. Man is no adequate substitute for God, however 'freely' he may talk and discuss." Correspondence between Ernest Tatham Richmond and Herbert W. Richmond (hereafter ETR to HWR), 28 December 1937, Section D, E. T. Richmond Papers.

21 Allitt suggests that Chesterton came to share Belloc's view that "a Jewish Oli-

garchy, only partially assimilated to British life, was corrupting the Government and Parliament." Patrick Allitt, *Catholic Converts: British and American Intellectuals Turn to Rome* (Ithaca, N.Y.: Cornell University Press, 1997), 173.

22 The author of *The Kingship of Christ* (1931), *The Mystical Body of Christ in the Modern World* (1935), and *The Rulers of Russia* (1938), Fahey is described in his obituary in *Candour* as a thinker responsible for focusing attention on "the subversive activities of the Judaeo-Masonic forces." "A Tribute to the Rev. Father Denis Fahey, C.S. sp." *Candour*, 26 February 1954. In a similar vein, Richmond would come to believe that "the term 'Zionism' did not reflect the age-long desire of religious Jews to return to their Holy Land. It was a term given to the movement for the purpose of bamboozling the innocent into believing that the movement had a religious connotation. Nor in fact was that movement a *national* Jewish movement. It was a movement of quite a different character. It was a step the real purpose of which was to contribute to the same ends as those aimed at by the Jews in Russia. Those ends were revolutionary and anti-religious ends. They implied the ultimate destruction both of Christianity and of Islam, and the furthering of world domination by the Jews who constitute so important an element in international Money Power of the World." Richmond, "Mammon in the Holy Land," 495–496. In his own appreciation of Fahey, Richmond suggests that while "time serving historians" had looked the other way, Fahey had "done much in helping to establish the truth that it [the Balfour Declaration] was in reality the child of New York financiers—Schott, Warburg, and Otto Kahn in their forefront—and that the Russians were merely the midwives of a movement to overthrow the Christian world." Richmond, "Mammon in the Holy Land," 9–10.

For Palestine's importance to this conspiracy, Richmond also turned for confirmation to Delbos's *L'Experience rouge.* "In view of the fact that the Russian Bolshevist revolution was 'organized and worked by Jews'" (in Delbos's words), Richmond suggested, "it is significant that the Holy Land was among the first of the countries, outside of Russia, to become infected with Atheistic Communism; and it cannot be doubted that the revolutionary Jews who organized the destruction of the Christian Faith in Russia, welcomed the opportunity afforded by the Balfour Declaration for getting an effective foothold in the very land where Christian Doctrine was first preached and whence it spread all over the world." Ernest Tatham Richmond, "The Rule of Gerione: A Number of Writings about British Policy in Palestine, 1924–1946," 1946, iii, E. T. Richmond Papers. This text, which Richmond also referred to as "Gerione in the Holy Land," is a compendium of his writings that includes anonymously and pseudonymously published essays.

23 Richmond, "Mammon in the Holy Land," 497.

24 [Ernest Tatham Richmond], "Palestine To-Day, the Old Order, and the New," *Guardian*, 9 April 1926, n.p. See "Gerione," 44–47, E. T. Richmond Papers. From the position expressed here, Richmond would eventually be led to write sympathetically about the fascist regimes of Franco and Mussolini. These, he would later argue, offered the world the only viable political opposition to what he calls "the

Geneva Sanhedrin" (the League of Nations) responsible for the spreading of a "godless politico-economic doctrine." See Ernest Tatham Richmond, "Dictatorship in the Holy Land," *Nineteenth Century* 123 (February 1938): 186–192. This essay would eventually be translated by George Antonious for publication in the Egyptian newspaper *al-Muqattam*, where it appeared on 31 March 1938 under the title "Diktaturiyya fi'l Ard al-Muqqadassa."

25 "The Jew makes a fetish of contract, the bond as such. Once made he will never break it, but he will stick into it some clause which will catch or deceive you. We remember Shylock and the character of Jacob." ETR to HWR, 24 March 1923, Section A, E. T. Richmond Papers.

26 Jacques Derrida, *Glas*, trans. John P. Leavey Jr. and Richard Rand (Lincoln: University of Nebraska Press, 1986), 48.

27 Ibid. Hegel notes that to the Israelites "an image of God was just stone or wood to them; 'it sees not, it hears not,' etc—with this litany they fancy themselves wonderfully wise; they despise the image because it does not manage them, and they have no inkling of its deification in the enjoyment of beauty or in a lover's intuition." Georg Wilhelm Friedrich Hegel, "The Spirit of Christianity and Its Fate," in *On Christianity: Early Theological Writings*, trans. T. M. Knox, intro. Richard Kroner (New York: Harper, 1948), 192. For a history of such claims regarding Jewish aniconism in aesthetics, see Kalman P. Bland, *The Artless Jew: Medieval and Modern Affirmations and Denials of the Visual* (Princeton: Princeton University Press, 2000).

28 Derrida, *Glas*, 44–49.

29 ETR to HWR, 27 October 1927, Section C, E. T. Richmond Papers.

30 Ibid. Elsewhere Richmond notes: "The Jew and a materialistic humanitarianism are now two of the dominant forces in Europe. The only effective counteracting influence is that of the Catholic Church in which are preserved and by which are handed on the traditions and discipline of European civilization, still firmly clung to particularly by the peoples who live round the Mediterranean sea, whence that civilization first sprang—peoples who see no good reasons for exchanging their rich inheritance for Asiatic standards and for the advantage of a people who are Asiatic." [Richmond], "Palestine To-Day, the Old Order and the New."

31 By 1931, many of Richmond's contemporaries in Palestine had already made the leap to such a reflexive claim, insisting for example that in their adversaries' *representations* of holy sites' political uses, history presented itself without mediation. The career of those claims forms part 3 of this study.

32 Jacques Derrida, "My Chances/Mes Chances: A Rendezvous with Some Epicurean Stereophonies," in *Taking Chances: Derrida, Psychoanalysis, and Literature*, ed. Joseph Smith and William Kerrigan (Baltimore, Md.: Johns Hopkins University Press, 1984), 16. There is a temporal dimension to this attempted stereotomy. Richmond's assault on modernity is actually one of the most salient features of that modernity, which resists any successful isolation of the transitory from the unchangeable. Like Baudelaire, he wishes to assign a place to the "ephemeral, the contingent, the half of art whose other half is eternal and immutable." Charles

Baudelaire, as quoted in Marshall Berman, *All That Is Solid Melts into Air: The Experience of Modernity* (New York: Viking Penguin, 1988), 133.

33 Richmond writes, "Thus it happened that a great fog, compounded of inventions, prejudice, ignorance, and inaccuracy was produced. Among the ingredients of this fog we must, it seems, include a *quantium sufficit* of that same slanderous hostility to the Church, as was shown by the opponents of the traditional Calvary and Holy Sepulchre, when they ascribe the basest motives to Constantine the Great and to the then Bishop of Jerusalem. In the great fog created by these methods, large numbers of unsuspecting people, and even of people of whose critical sense more might reasonably have been expected, were misled into believing that the *Garden Tomb* was really the tomb in which Jesus has been laid and whence he rose from the dead. A seventeenth century writer alludes to those befogged western heretics (*nebulones Occidenales haereticos*) who argued that the traditional tomb could not be the true one . . . but the subject of fogs and the befogged is too big a one to pursue further." Richmond, *The Sites of the Crucifixion and the Resurrection*, 16.

34 Ibid., 38.

35 I take up Richmond's efforts to do so in the next chapter.

36 Adorno points out that what distinguishes Sigmund Freud's mass psychology from that of LeBon is the absence in the former of a "contempt for the masses" which exists as the *thema probandum* of the latter. See Theodor Adorno, "Freudian Theory and the Pattern of Fascist Propaganda," in *The Essential Frankfurt School Reader*, ed. Andrew Arato and Eike Gebhardt (New York: Continuum, 1988), 121. For Freud's own critique of LeBon's own *Psychologie des foules* (1895), see Sigmund Freud, "Group Psychology and the Analysis of the Ego," in *The Standard Edition of the Complete Psychological Works of Sigmund Freud*, 24 vols., ed. James Strachey, trans. under gen. ed. James Strachey (London: Hogarth Press and the Institute of Psycho-Analysis, 1981), 18: 65–143.

37 Richmond, *The Sites of the Crucifixion and the Resurrection*, 27–28.

38 Ibid., 22. This is not to imply that Richmond does not make room for a certain kind of toponymy in his own research. In contrast to the toponymics of Gordon, Richmond does not *directly* connect names with unchanged features of landscape. Instead, accounting for historical changes in language, he extrapolates original place-names from contemporary Arabic geographical terms. For example, he suggests that in the Arabic for "promontory"—*ras*, or literally, "head"—one could divine the most probable explanation for the name Golgotha, that is, the place of the skulls (23).

39 Ibid., 32.

40 Ibid., 34.

41 Ibid., 34. Emphasis added.

42 For Richmond's repeated insistence on an iconological relation between essences and appearances see his "Mammon in the Holy Land." There, the term "humbug" normally appears in his descriptions of a false relation between appearances and truth. "Politics," in Richmond's lexicon, along with the terms "drapery" and

"camouflage" allude to the normalization of this false relation, something he also refers to as a "masking." For example, in an appreciation of Sir Thomas Haycraft, the chief justice of Palestine between 1921 and 1927, Richmond reports that "he was a bright spot in the darkness of the administration. . . . He had the rare merit of being an honest man and of making a struggle against the all-pervading & poisonous atmosphere of politics with all that that connotes of bedevilment from which this Administration still suffers. . . . It is infuriating to see a little country like this with all that it has meant and still stands for in the world, sacrificed to a supposed need for bolstering up a great sham and humbug, which is only kept alive by lying Press Propaganda pushed by the international Jews and their friends in England and Europe and in that vast home of cant, dishonesty and greed, the United States of America." ETR to HWR, 3 March 1928, Section C, E. T. Richmond Papers. See also Richmond, "Mammon in the Holy Land," 308.

43 Walter Benjamin, "Trauerspiel and Tragedy," in *Selected Writings, 1913–1926*, vol. 1, ed. Marcus Bullock and Michael W. Jennings (Cambridge, Mass.: Harvard University Press, 1999), 55–57.

3. You Are Blind to the Meaning of the Dome of the Rock

The epigraph to this chapter is from Charles Robert Ashbee, *A Palestine Notebook* (New York: Doubleday, Page, 1923), 237–239.

1 During World War I, many political observers believed that the debilitation of England in the mechanized, Taylorized, horror of this struggle, might imply a corresponding regeneration of the Orient. Some presented this fantasy as the potential beginning of a domino effect that would eventually menace the United Kingdom itself. For example, in what is arguably the "mother" of modern political thrillers, John Buchan's *Greenmantle* presents a scenario in which the Axis powers' attempt to make use of Muslims' reverence for "sacred trinkets"—monuments, figures, and so on—in order to direct their violence against England in a monumental jihad. "Supposing they have got some tremendous sacred sanction—some holy thing, some book or gospel or some new prophet from the desert," one of Buchan's protagonists ruminates, "*supposing there is some Ark of the covenant which will madden the remotest Moslem peasant with dreams of Paradise?*" The response: "Then there will be hell let loose in those parts pretty soon." John Buchan, *Greenmantle* (Ware, England: Wordsworth Classics, 1994), 5–6. (This is not an anxiety that can be dismissed solely as a feature of the author's fiction. Buchan, an intelligence officer during the war, based this scenario on actual intrigues that he would only record later, in his histories of World War I. See John Buchan, *Nelson's History of the War*, vol. 15 (London: Thomas Nelson and Sons, n.d.), and vol. 5, in which Buchan describes the kaiser's efforts to present himself as the legitimate heir of Muhammad for the purpose of instigating a jihad, and for examples of the way Germany looked upon Egypt as a "nursery of sedition.") Buchan's fantasy of the Muslim peril was balanced by visions of a redemptive sort. These argued that the very exhaustion of the

Occident in everything characteristic of the war, that is, mechanization, industrialization, and so on, presupposed the possibility of a new world order. The world would be instructed back into a kind of humanism by regions as yet untainted by the evils of the capitalist West. For example, following a well-worn topos of postwar thought, Richmond's colleague C. R. Ashbee suggested that implicit in the exhaustion of the West lay a redemptive regeneration of the East—redemptive, because in his view this would result in the reassertion of a peaceful synthesis of cultures of the kind once achieved by Islam's subsumption of Byzantium. Melding this faith in a looming age of syncretism with the sociologist Patrick Geddes's quasi-mystical belief in the peaceful reorganization of mankind under a newly formed League of Nations, Ashbee assigned to the Dome of the Rock a role in the reformation of postwar civilization as a whole: "Can't you see our dome [of the Rock] stands for unity and peace as does no other building? Can't you see that this cutting of the knot of trivial theometry, of Graeco-Latin and Hebrew dissension by the word of Mohammed symbolizes unity?. . . . Olympus, Yahweh, Virgin Mary. . . . Keep them because Allah will not mind, but know that in this after-war world for any League of Nations that there can be one God and our Dome is his symbol." C. R. Ashbee, *A Palestine Notebook*, 240. Also see Patrick Geddes to F. Mears, 18 September 1922, NLS/PG/MS 10573; Patrick Geddes, *Cities in Evolution* (New York: Howard Fertig, 1915); and Alessandra Ponte, "Building the Spiral Stair of Evolution: The Index Museum of Sir Patrick Geddes," *Assemblage* 10 (1990): 47–63.

2   Ernest Tatham Richmond, "A Dialogue [Imaginary] about Foreign Dominion," 1912, E. T. Richmond Papers. The manuscript also bears the title "Foreign Dominion: A Dialogue between Abdullah el-Kendahy and Richard Dinsdale." Its dramatis personae were two in number: a thinly veiled version of Richmond himself (Richard Dinsdale), and an Arab (Abdullah Kendahy). Of Dinsdale, Richmond wrote: "His work is in the east. The glittering prizes of official life will not fall to him; not because he would not like them, but, rather, because he is unwilling to pay the price for them" (2). Richmond describes Kendahy as a man "filled with curiosity . . . seeing more in life than the immediate interests of trade. . . . He takes an active interest in political questions. Among Europeans he is considered, by some, to be a "dangerous man" (1). Richmond seems to have framed the outline for this dialogue, or an essay quite like it, several years earlier. In a letter to his bride three years before, he describes an essay whose "gist" is "to show that there is a tendency in this country, not only for Egyptians to become sham Europeans, but for Englishmen to become sham Egyptians. I want to show that the road is sometimes broken through their contact with the West; English people can also find themselves on a broken road as a consequence of their contact with the East! That side of the question is sometimes forgotten. What becomes of England's influence for good if her messengers become half Egyptians?" Correspondence between Ernest Tatham Richmond and Margaret Mary Richmond (hereafter ETR to MMR), 12 June 1909, E. T. Richmond Papers. The completed essay, dated 1912 in the manuscript version, roughly coincides with Richmond's decision to leave Egypt and return to England.

3 Richmond, "A Dialogue [Imaginary] about Foreign Dominion," 14–15.

4 Dinsdale states: "It seems, Abdullah, that you are not so ardent a Nationalist as some believe you to be, and as you, I think, believe yourself to be; also, it seems from what you say that it is not to the rule of foreigners that you object, but to the rule of ignorant foreigners who know nothing and have greedy desires and no real sympathy." Richmond, "A Dialogue [Imaginary] about Foreign Dominion," 51.

5 Richmond, "A Dialogue [Imaginary] about Foreign Dominion," 58. Before being called to a halt by the "dinner cornet . . . playing somewhat lugubriously, 'The Roast Beef of Old England'" the dialogue culminates in an understanding. Receiving assurances from Abdullah that the imperial power would not need to worry about letting go of the tiger's tail, Richmond's "countrymen" would be guaranteed that they would "reassume complete control of their own country without Asiatic assistance or control." Ibid., 65.

6 On 8 March 1918, General Headquarters, Egypt, sent the War Office a secret dispatch claiming that the "Mosque of Al-Aksa and the Mosque of Omar in Jerusalem" were "both in urgent need of repair which if deferred may give rise to a dangerous condition." The brainchild of Ronald Storrs, this dispatch specifically requested the services of Richmond, because of his "experience in superintending the preservation and repair of mosques in Cairo." The "dangerous condition" referred to was political, not structural. Alert to the same concerns, Sir Mark Sykes minuted — i.e., annotated — the file with the recommendation that Richmond should be sent, but stated: "This is dangerous ground. Muslim dignitaries should apply directly to GOCIC [General Officer Commanding] who would inform HMG [His Majesty's Government] who should sanction repairs but assume no responsibility. . . . Any European employed should be employed by authorities of Mosque, and we should not have responsibility." According to a subsequent dispatch sent on 31 March 1918, Richmond was sent for after the grand mufti of Jerusalem, Kamil al-Husayni, formally approached the commander in chief in the way stipulated by Sykes, and offered assurances that "no financial or other responsibility will rest with British authorities and extent of repairs to be undertaken will be determined by report of expert architect." PRO/FO 371/3401/46325.

7 "General Money [Major-General Sir Arthur Wigram Money, chief administrator, Occupied Enemy Territory Administration (OETA), Jerusalem, 1918–19] sent me, for the purpose of finding out whether among the Arab population there existed enough technically competent Arabs to form the nucleus of a Public Works Department. I reported favourably; but in the event the department was for the most part recruited from Jews." Ernest Tatham Richmond, "Mammon in the Holy Land: A Description of How We 'Built Up Zion with Blood and Jerusalem with Iniquity,'" 1954, E. T. Richmond Papers, 12. (All citations to this manuscript refer to the manuscript's own system of pagination.)

8 Ernest Tatham Richmond, "Summary Report upon the Condition of the Dome of the Rock and the Aksa Mosque" (emphasis added), PRO/FO 371/3401/46325.

9 Ernest Tatham Richmond to Ronald Storrs, 3 December 1918, "Further Report on the Dome of the Rock," PRO/FO 371/4203.

10 Ernest Tatham Richmond, *The Dome of the Rock in Jerusalem: A Description of Its Structure and Decoration* (Oxford: Clarendon Press, 1924), 2 (emphasis added).

11 In early September 1918 Richmond completed his initial report on the Dome of the Rock. In it he argued that the supply of replacement tiles for the Dome of the Rock would pose a serious problem. "In peace conditions," he suggested, "the quickest way would probably be to get the tiles made in Europe" and shipped to Palestine. "Conditions of labour transport" during wartime, however, suggested that "it would be preferable to establish a tile factory in Palestine." Consequently, Richmond suggested that "in order to settle the question a skilled tile maker should be engaged to examine the local clays and report upon their suitability. If the report should be favourable; a small experimental plant could be erected." See Richmond, "Summary Report upon the Condition of the Dome of the Rock and the Aksa Mosque." Richmond's "Summary Report" was then forwarded to Whitehall on 10 September 1918, after which D. G. Hogarth was invited to comment upon it. Hogarth's observations were forwarded to OETA in Palestine on 26 October 1918 as follows: "Major Hogarth expresses the opinion that while purely structural consolidation (including the resetting of loose existent tiles) ought of course to be undertaken at once, any attempt to renew the tiling of the Dome of the Rock at the present moment is to be strongly deprecated. He expresses the opinion that the quality of Suleiman's tiles is most unlikely to be attained by any manufactury set up ad hoc in Jerusalem." PRO/FO 371/3401/46325.

12 Richmond to Storrs, "Further Report on the Dome of the Rock": "Commander Hogarth states that adequate facsimiles can only be expected to be produced in first-rate European factories." On 20 December 1918 Hogarth attached a memorandum to Richmond's initial report, stating "Major Richmond seems to have misinterpreted my original Note to imply that I am averse to re-tiling under any circumstances. So far from that, I think it is absolutely necessary to re-tile in the interests of the aesthetic effect of the building; but I do not want it done till the best possible tiles, in imitation of the originals, have been procured," PRO/FO 371/4203.

13 Richmond to Storrs, "Further Report on the Dome of the Rock."

14 Ibid.

15 Ibid. "The Guardians of the Mosque inform me that these tiles came from Germany and that many samples of old tiles were taken to Germany as patterns. . . . In stating the opinion that the quality of Suleiman's tile is most unlikely to be attained by any manufactory set up in Jerusalem, it would seem that Commander Hogarth assumes that the Mosque is, at any rate for the most part, covered with tiles from Suleiman's time. This is not the case. Most of the tiles are of a more recent date." For the nineteenth- and early twentieth-century restorations of the Haram al-Sharif, see Beatrice St. Laurent and Andras Riedlmayr, "Restorations of

159

Jerusalem and the Dome of the Rock and Their Political Significance, 1537–1928,"
Muqarnas 10 (1993): 76–84.

16 In his final report on the Dome of the Rock Richmond maintained: "It is not only
a question of preserving the tiles that exist, it is also a question of preserving and
continuing a system of decoration. . . . Tiles have decayed in the past and will decay in the future, some rapidly, some less so; some by natural causes, others by
reason of neglect or lack of skill. In the past they have always been replaced in
some form or another, and we see to-day the complex results of the efforts made
to preserve the decoration by perhaps as many as fifteen generations of men. In
the lives of these generations, as in those of their predecessors twelve hundred
years ago, and in those of their successors to-day no less, the Dome of the Rock
was, and is, an integral part, but certainly not primarily, as a work of art, but as a
sacred place to be maintained as splendidly as circumstances may allow; *to be
changed if circumstances call for change and to perish if and when it should lose meaning.*"
Richmond, *The Dome of the Rock in Jerusalem*, 71.

17 Richmond's £E80,000 estimate exceeded the annual revenues to the Palestinian Islamic establishment during the majority of the Mandate era. For example, according to Kupferschmidt, the total income of the Supreme Muslim Shariʿa Council
during its first year of existence, 1922, was £E65,056. See Uri Kupferschmidt, *The
Supreme Muslim Council, Islam under the British Mandate for Palestine* (Leiden: E. J. Brill,
1987), 173. Consequently, the grand mufti of Palestine, Kamil al-Husayni, published an appeal in the Arabic press in December 1918. This was paralleled by an
appeal undertaken by C. R. Ashbee (in his capacity as civic adviser to the OETA and
head of the Pro-Jerusalem Society), which appeared in the *Times* on 4–5 December. The text of the grand mufti's message, which includes specific thanks to Richmond, is reproduced in Richmond, "Mammon in the Holy Land," 18. An English
translation appears in Charles Robert Ashbee, ed., *Jerusalem, 1918–1920: Being the
Records of the Pro-Jerusalem Society* (London: John Murray, 1921).

18 "I am encouraged to believe that in approaching you this idea may, on political
grounds, receive favourable consideration. To say that the Dome of the Rock interests the whole of Islam is, too mild a statement. . . . [I]t is to Moslems a place
of much more than mere interest. It is the material symbol of a mighty Religion. . . . [I]t would . . . be lamentable if the results of the sympathetic attitude
taken by us towards Moslem interests in this affair should be buried in a modest
but uncalled for and impolitic obscurity." Ernest Tatham Richmond to Rushbrook
Williams, 19 April 1920, PRO/FO 371/5258.

19 After World War I, England found itself sovereign over the majority of the world's
Muslim population. The politicians in Whitehall were quick to take up Richmond's point concerning the political advantages of a gesture of good will. The
Palestine Government donated £E100 and the India Office five times that. The official correspondence on the subject even shows that the foreign secretary adopted
Richmond's own arguments when he solicited other sources within the British
government for financial support in the publication of the book. For example, on

9 July 1920, G. N. Curzon contacted the Treasury, stating: "As their Lordships are doubtless aware, the Dome of the Rock is a shrine looked upon by Mohammedans with the greatest veneration and for this reason His Lordship is of the opinion that the publication of Mr. Richmond's report would be of Marked political value." The Treasury declined the invitation to contribute. PRO/FO 371/5258.

20 Herbert Samuel to George Nathaniel Curzon, 26 August 1920, PRO/FO 371/5258.

21 Minutes of G. H. Fitzmaurice, 13 September 1920, PRO/FO 371/5258. The rumors to which Fitzmaurice refers had circulated since at least 1918, when British officials in the OETA had attempted to broker a deal to sell the Buraq/Wailing Wall to Jews. While the deal fell through, it is worth noting that some of these officials envisioned a situation in which the proceeds of the sale would be used to finance the restorations to the Haram. ("Attention has especially been drawn to the fact that the amount which the Zionist Commission are prepared to pay for this property would not only enable the persons now living upon it to be suitably accommodated elsewhere, but would furnish a handsome balance which might be devoted to the repair of the buildings of the Dome of the Rock in accordance with the suggestions made by Major Richmond in his report." Gilbert Clayton to General Headquarters, 31 August 1918, PRO/FO 371/3395.) A plan to resettle the residents of the Waqf Abu Madyan, or Maghribi Wakf, is reiterated in the contemporaneous reports of Patrick Geddes, the sociologist/town planner engaged by the Zionist Commission to prepare plans for the Hebrew University. (See his *Jerusalem Actual and Possible: Preliminary Report to the Chief Administrator of Palestine and the Military Governor of Jerusalem on Town Planning and City Improvements*, CZA/A209/132.) Geddes recommended rehousing those who would be displaced either south of the Buraq, or directly outside of the city, to the north of Herod's Gate. A sketch of Geddes's proposal for this new quarter, designed and drawn by his associate Frank Mears, survives among the C. R. Ashbee Papers in the Jerusalem Municipal Archives, JMA/361/A58/IV-10. Despite Geddes's optimism, however, Clayton already anticipated the fate of the project when he noted that "the scheme would meet with great opposition on the part of the Moslems who regard it as a stepping stone to further encroachments on the part of the Jews and even fear that it may lead to attempts upon the Haram enclosure itself." For further data on the Wall deal, see Ronald Storrs to Mark Sykes, 9 August 1918, PRO/FO 800/221.

22 Under Ottoman rule, the Shaykh al-Islam [the Turkish designation was Şeyhül-islâm] was nominally the highest legal authority in Islam. When the Ottoman Empire dissolved, so did the post. (On 3 March 1924 the Turks officially annulled the Ottoman caliphate, and with it their authority in Muslim religious affairs.) In this instance, then, the use of the term in relation to the Shaykh of the Azhar in Cairo assumes prerogatives for Egyptian Muslim authorities that were not explicitly sanctioned anywhere else. See Elie Kedourie, "Egypt and the Caliphate, 1915–52," in *The Chatham House Version and Other Middle-Eastern Essays* (Hanover, N.H.: Brandeis University Press, 1984), 177–207.

23 Ernest Scott to G. N. Curzon, 15 October 1920, PRO/FO 371/5258.

24 Lord Chelmsford (viceroy of India) to Foreign Office (FO), 2 November 1920, PRO/
FO 371/5258. Baghdad's response to this suggestion was that it was "inconsistent"
with the British government's "sound policy" of remaining aloof from the caliphate question. Parenthetically, the question of the restoration of the caliphate would
occasion strong links between Muhammad 'Ali and Shawkat 'Ali (the leaders of
the Indian Khilafat Committee) and Palestinian Islam during the 1920s; these contacts culminated in the Pan-Islamic Congress for the defense of holy places hosted
by the grand mufti of Jerusalem (Muhammad Hajj Amin al-Husayni) in Jerusalem
in 1931. See M. Naeem Qureshi, *Pan-Islam in British Indian Politics : A Study of the Khilafat Movement, 1918–1924* (Leiden: Brill, 1999). See also Martin Seth Kramer, "The
Congress in Modern Islam: On the Origins of an Innovation," Ph.D. diss., Princeton University, 1982.

25 Herbert Samuel to G. N. Curzon, 25 November 1920, PRO/FO 371/5258. A memorandum from Ronald Storrs, governor of Jerusalem, to "Director General of
Wakfs, Wakfs Administration, Jerusalem," indicates that by early March 1921 no
progress toward provisional repairs had been made, however. This was of some
concern to Storrs given the unusually harsh winter that had hit Jerusalem that year.
ISA/RG2/CS191/(Pol. 2259).

26 In his unpublished "Liber Maiorum," which was completed approximately thirty
years after these events transpired, Richmond records that he suggested this fund-
raising initiative to the grand mufti and that it was backed by the administration.
(This should not to be confused with the first appeal in the press of December
1918.) There is some doubt about Richmond's claim to have thought of this initiative, however, because in "Liber Maiorum" he records that he recommended this
plan to the successor of Kamil al-Husayni: "Though during these years in Palestine [1920–24], political harassments took up most of my time, I was able on several occasions to help the Department of Antiquities and also to forward the repair
and conservation of Moslem shrines. The first task was to acquire funds and the
second to establish a technical office. I proposed to the Mufti, then Amin Effendi
al Husaini, that he should personally visit all the Moslem countries and States and
appeal for subscriptions. This proposal was backed by the Authorities with the result that more than £E90,000 were collected." Ernest Tatham Richmond, "Liber
Maiorum," 1949[?], 80, E. T. Richmond Papers.

27 Kedourie, "Sir Herbert Samuel and the Government of Palestine," 64. Richmond
corroborates this understanding of his role. In his memoirs he records that his job
was to serve as a "link between the administration and the Arab population." Richmond, "Mammon in the Holy Land," 37. Richmond was officially offered the post
in September 1920 and arrived in Palestine in November of the same year. PRO/FO
371/5267/8343.

28 The Palin Commission report on the causes of the violence which took place in Jerusalem during the Nabi-Musa festival in Jerusalem on 4–5 April 1920 concluded
that these were spontaneous events, but that "provocateurs" and "political agitators" sought to take advantage of the tensions that were in any event mounting

162

concerning the union of Syria and Palestine. Palin Commission Report, FO 371/ 5121, as cited in Yehoshua Porath, *The Emergence of the Palestinian-Arab National Movement, 1918–1929* (London: Frank Cass, 1974), 98. Having been accused of functioning as "political agitators" of this kind, al-Hajj Amin al-Husayni and 'Arif al-'Arif (later, the author of the classic *al-Nakba*) were sentenced to ten-year prison terms in absentia. (Knowing of an imminent arrest, al-Husayni fled across the Jordan.) Both were later pardoned by Sir Herbert Samuel in July 1920. See also Philip Mattar, *The Mufti of Jerusalem: Al-Hajj Amin al-Husayni and the Palestinian National Movement* (New York: Columbia University Press, 1988), 17.

29 Kedourie, "Sir Herbert Samuel and the Government of Palestine," 65–66. See also Richmond's memorandum, "Grand Mufti," ISA/RG2/CS245.

30 Porath records that the high commissioner "eventually decided that it would be best that such an appointment, being legally suspect, should not receive official confirmation in writing." Porath, *The Emergence of the Palestinian-Arab National Movement*, 193. Porath believes that this fact was "established conclusively" by the authors of the Peel Commission's report (Cmd. 54790), Porath, 193, n. 42. (The Peel Commission was one of two successive commissions established in 1937 and 1938 for the purpose of ascertaining the viability of Palestine's partition.)

31 ISA/RG2/CS245 (emphasis added). For a detailed analysis of the proclamation, and of Sir Alfred Mond's statement concerning the rebuilding of the Temple, see part 3 of this study.

32 See Frederick Kisch to Wyndham Deedes, January 1923, as cited in Kedourie, "Sir Herbert Samuel and the Government of Palestine," 68.

33 "Richmond was so sympathetic to the Palestinian nationalists and to Amin's candidacy that historians such as Elie Kedourie credit him with influencing Samuel in favor of Amin. . . . But there is no documentary or oral evidence to show that he influenced Samuel any more than did the two Zionists in Samuel's administration, Wyndham Deeds [sic], the civil secretary, and Norman Bentwich, the legal secretary and a relative of Samuel. Both of these officials were personally closer to Samuel than Richmond and both were against Amin's candidacy." Mattar, *The Mufti of Jerusalem*, 25–26.

34 In referring to "the sense of the people," or *sensus communis*, I am, of course, returning to publicity, as the bridging principle between "politics" and "morality" ("empirical consciousness" and the "intelligible unity of Consciousness as such"), which is presented in Jürgen Habermas's reading of Immanuel Kant's *Perpetual Peace*. See Jürgen Habermas, *The Structural Transformation of the Public Sphere: An Inquiry into a Category of Bourgeois Society*, trans. Thomas Burger with Frederick Lawrence (Cambridge, Mass.: MIT Press, 1992), 102–117. For Kant, the notion of "common sense" also presents itself as an important factor in the judgment of taste. See Immanuel Kant, *The Critique of Judgement*, trans. Werner S. Pluhar (Indianapolis: Hackett Publishing, 1987), §20. Finally, for a rich, historical examination into this topic see Kathleen Wilson, *The Sense of the People: Politics, Culture, and Imperialism in England, 1715–1785* (1995; Cambridge: Cambridge University Press, 1998).

35 Georg Wilhelm Friedrich Hegel, *Phenomenology of Spirit*, trans. A. V. Miller, analysis and foreword by J. N. Findlay (Oxford: Oxford University Press, 1977), §734, 444–445.

36 According to Richmond, not only is this principal agent of Zionist interests' "legal status to pronounce on such a matter" suspect, but worse, "no opinion emanating from the Legal Secretary or his entourage or from any one dependent in any degree on the favour of his Department will at the present time be regarded as other than suspicious by a very large majority." Richmond to Herbert Samuel, 7 June 1921, ISA/RG2/CS245.

37 Ibid.

38 Here, to follow the Hegelian analogue: Islam's self-actuation only takes place in the context of a naïve empirical "understanding" still transfixed before "the curtain [of appearance] hanging before the inner world." Hegel, *Phenomenology of Spirit*, §165, 103.

39 "Because of its concrete content, sense-certainty immediately appears as the richest kind of knowledge, indeed a knowledge of infinite wealth for which no bounds can be found. . . . But when we look carefully at this *pure being* which constitutes the essence of this certainty, and which this certainty pronounces to be its truth, we see that much more is involved. An actual sense-certainty is not merely this pure immediacy, but an *instance* of it. . . . [I]n sense-certainty pure being at once splits up into what we have called the two 'Thises', one 'this' as 'I', and the other 'this' as object. When *we* reflect on this difference, we find that neither one nor the other is only *immediately* present in sense-certainty, but each is at the same time *mediated*." Hegel, *Phenomenology of Spirit*, §91–92, 58–59.

40 Recognizing the intrusion of the "political" into religion in his own argument, Richmond will eventually resolve the paradox by arguing for the subsumption of the merely political into the suprapolitical. In a private communication concerning the formation of a Supreme Muslim Shariʿa Council [SMC] he would help to establish under al-Husayni's leadership, Richmond suggested: "My main task now is to help the Moslems towards unity and a good organization of their own community. This plan is making good progress, and we shall soon, I hope, have a compact organization dealing with Moslem Religious Affairs. As all Moslem affairs are more or less religious, this body will have great political power. To keep friends with the French and to make Moslems and Christians feel safe from the Jewish intrusion and interference in anything that even remotely touches their religion, are, in my view, very urgent tasks if we are to keep the peace in this country. There are, however, many who, though they [do] not openly deny the wisdom and truth of this contention, only give it lip-service, pretend to want Moslems and Christians to organize their own affairs, pretend to help them do so; but, in 'helping' them, try to leave as many little holes as possible through which Jews may creep and sow discord and disunion. I am conducting an open war against all such traitors." Correspondence between Ernest Tatham Richmond and Herbert W.

Richmond (hereafter referred to as ETR to HWR), 4 September 1921, Section A, E. T. Richmond Papers.

41 A. Quigley to Wyndham Deedes, CID Secret Report, 4 November 1920, ISA/RG2/CS163.

42 Ibid.

43 Ibid. The CID reports implicate Husayni family members among this corps of "agitators." It describes a meeting on 28 October 1920 at ʿAbd al-Latif al-Husayni's house "at which were present a score of leading agitators of Jerusalem. The pan-Islamic movement was discussed at length."

44 Ernest Tatham Richmond, marginalia to CID Report of 4 November 1920, ISA/RG2/CS163.

45 Ibid. In frustration over Quigley of the CID's intelligence assessments Richmond finally penciled a confidential note at the bottom of the 4 November memorandum, stating: "These reports (and I have had several similar) are unsatisfactory in the sense that while on the one hand they denote a serious situation on the other (a) there are no *proofs* or even very convincing arguments and (b) they do not accord with my reading of the situation (for what that is worth). But I cannot go on viewing[?] these reports in this form because *if true* some action appears indicated and if *not true* the ADPS [assistant director of public security] is unfit for his job." Richmond's superior, Wyndham Deedes, responded: "Please see Mr. Quigley quietly yourself . . . and also talk to Colonel Bramley [the director of public security]." Within two years, however, Richmond would remark in his private diaries that Deedes discouraged "frank interviews" with Quigley in the matter of Zionist arms smuggling. See Ernest Tatham Richmond, diary entry of 7 March 1922, "An Administrative Cesspool," E. T. Richmond Papers.

46 Richmond, "Mammon in the Holy Land," 103. In his diary entry of 4 March 1922, Richmond explains the conflict between the legal secretary and the SMC over the Shariʿa courts in the following way: "In spite of the new Law giving over Sharia affairs to the Supreme Moslem Council, Bentwich wanted to retain Administrative supervision of Judges and of Courts, leaving only appointments and dismissals to the Council. Hajj Amin [the grand mufti and president of the SMC] said he could not agree, even if he wanted to. The Moslems in general would object as such a procedure would be against both the intention, as it was understood by Moslems, and the spirit of the new Law, the central idea of which was, as the Moslems understood it, to hand over completely to them the management of their Religious Affairs, both Wakfs and Sharia Courts. It is because the Government is believed to have intended this and to have done it that Moslems in general began to disbelieve a little less in the good will of the Government towards their community. He [the grand mufti] regards Bentwich's proposal as indicating no appreciation of the political atmosphere in Moslem circles, and also as indicating that Bentwich in no way shares the benevolent attitude taken up by the High Commissioner towards Moslems. In a word Bentwich's proposal only serves to confirm

Moslems in their previously formed opinion of him, that is to say that he is working continuously for their destruction as a political and economic force in the country." Richmond, diary entry of 4 March 1922, "An Administrative Cesspool," 24–26ff, E. T. Richmond Papers. See also Kupferschmidt, *The Supreme Muslim Council*, 84–88.

47 Richmond, diary entry of 12 March 1922, "An Administrative Cesspool," E. T. Richmond Papers. Uri Kupferschmidt's authoritative history of the SMC makes no mention of this dispute between Richmond and Bentwich, only to their consensus that the administration should defer any amendments in the council's constitution until the "convening of an electoral college in January 1926, when a new council was to be formed." Kupferschmidt, *The Supreme Muslim Council*, 39.

48 Ernest Tatham Richmond, "Respective Responsibilities of Supreme Muslim Sharia Council and Department of Justice," 11 March 1922, copy in "An Administrative Cesspool."

49 Hegel, *Phenomenology of Spirit*, §755–56, 457. "In so far as self-consciousness one-sidedly grasps only its *own* externalization, then, even though its object is for it just as much Being as Self, and it knows all existence to be spiritual in nature, nevertheless true Spirit has still not yet come to be explicitly *for* self-consciousness, inasmuch as being in general, or Substance, has not equally, on its side, *implicitly* externalized itself and become self-consciousness. . . . Spirit is in this way only *imagined* into existence."

50 Richmond, diary entry of 22 March 1922, "An Administrative Cesspool."

51 Ibid.

52 To Richmond, Deedes was the very exemplar of the "outwardly virtuous" but "inwardly corrupt" colonial official he had described in his own "A Dialogue [Imaginary] about Foreign Dominion" of 1912. He consequently describes Deedes to his wife in the following way: "He is a good fellow, but a stick of sticks. For choice I should compare him to a stick for Sunday use. . . . This virtuous complacency imbued with a Hebrew bias is the materials upon which Deedes works [sic]. You will wonder why I don't counteract the influence. I do to some extent, perhaps to an increasing extent." ETR to MMR, 13 November 1921, reproduced in "Mammon in the Holy Land," 62.

53 Richmond to Deedes, 13 April 1922, as reproduced in "Mammon in the Holy Land," 116–117, emphasis added. Richmond's relations with Deedes had already become quite strained some months earlier. In November of the previous year, after sending Deedes a note about the potential for mass violence in the country unless the administration's positions on Zionism changed, Richmond records that he received a reply from the chief secretary suggesting that he "had very much changed towards him personally." Relating these events to his wife, Richmond continues: "Deedes has got a great deal of information out of me as to Arab thought in this country. He probably fears that, I in my growing distrust and dislike, shall become reticent. Thus he would lose the advantage . . . of knowing what

he regards as the enemy's game." ETR to MMR, 21 November 1921, reproduced in "Mammon in the Holy Land," 64.

54 Richmond, diary entry of 4 March 1922, "An Administrative Cesspool." E. T. Richmond Papers. It is worth noting that during his tenure as assistant secretary for political affairs, Richmond served on the technical committee that the SMC established for the purposes of deciding how best to effect repairs on the Haram. Moreover, he never relinquished the title of consulting architect to the Haram al-Sharif that had been accorded him by the grand mufti, Kamil al-Husayni. In one of his last memoranda to the administration concerning the repair of the Aqsa Mosque, he added the following postscript: "I might add, for your information that, with the approval of the then military gov. of Jerusalem the former Mufti of Jerusalem, Kamil Effendi al Husseini appointed me consulting Architect. That appointment has not been revoked and though, since then, I have assumed, under the Civil Government, other functions, the President of the present Moslem authorities have continued to consult me—I do not know if the present Government recognize and approve this state of affairs." Richmond to Gilbert Clayton, 3 January 1924, ISA/RG2/CSI84.

55 "The state is the actuality of the ethical Idea. It is ethical mind qua the substantial will manifest and revealed to itself, knowing and thinking itself, accomplishing what it knows and in so far as it knows it. The state exists immediately in custom, mediately in individual self-consciousness, knowledge, and activity, while self-consciousness in virtue of its sentiment towards the state, finds in the state, as its essence and the end-product of its activity, its substantive freedom." Georg Wilhelm Friedrich Hegel, *Philosophy of Right*, trans. S. W. Dyde (Amherst, N.Y.: Prometheus Books, 1996), §257, 189.

56 Kupferschmidt, *The Supreme Muslim Council*, 130.

57 "The mission to India . . . promised the Government that it would not take part in political activity of any kind, al-Hajj Amin al-Husayni personally underwriting this pledge. Although not entirely happy about the inclusion of Jamal al-Husayni [the grand mufti's cousin and close political associate] the high commissioner nevertheless lent his full support to the project and did all he could to persuade the British authorities in India to allow the Delegation into that country. Despite the fact that the latter remained opposed to the visit, the High Commissioner permitted the Delegation to leave Palestine, thereby presenting the British Government with a *fait accompli*." Porath, *The Emergence of the Palestinian-Arab National Movement, 1918–1929*, 205–206.

58 The council's annual report of 1922–23 describes these efforts in the following way: "*Preservation of the Al-Aqsa Mosque*: This site occupies an important place in Islam which makes it a jewel of the jewels in the heart of every Muslim and the entire world. Respected by Arabs and non-Arab alike, surviving all ages translating Islamic good will as well as symbolizing the superiority of the Arabs vis-à-vis the rest. . . . Kamal al-Din Bek [Mimas Kemalettin], architectural director at the Min-

istry of Awqaf in Istanbul and well respected architect in the West and in the East, was appointed as the head of this committee. The committee also engaged in fund raising from all over the Muslim world." *Bayan al-Majlis al-Shar'i al-Islami al-A'la fi Falastin li-Sanat 1340–1341 H (1922–1923)*, 5–7.

59 In his diary Richmond describes the work as follows: "The Aqsa Mosque is the first to tackle, because the dome and its supports are in a dangerous state. Above the piers that carry the dome are dangerous tie-beams of timber forming a timer plate upon which, at its four corners, stand the arches that carry the pendentives. The timber is in a doubtful condition, much of it rotten and crushed under the weight on it." Richmond, diary entry of 22 March 1922, "An Administrative Cesspool." Excerpts from Kemalettin's own report are translated and reproduced in Yildirim Yavuz, "The Restoration Project of the Masjid Al-Aqsa by Mimar Kemalettin (1922–26)," *Muqarnas* 13 (1996): 149–164. However, as this study relies only on primary sources held by the Jerusalem waqf authorities and Kemalettin's own materials, it is incomplete in its description and analysis of the project. The author neglects to mention, for example, that Richmond himself had first been approached to serve as the chief architect of the restorations. He declined, suggesting that they engage a Muslim architect. The structural status of the Aqsa would remain a cause of much concern throughout the Mandate era, particularly following an earthquake in October 1937 that left several of its piers cracked, ISA/RG2/24, orig. b/26/37. These latter repairs were undertaken by an Egyptian architect under the direction of Robert W. Hamilton, who succeeded Richmond as director of the Antiquities Department. See Robert W. Hamilton, *The Structural History of the Aqsa Mosque: A Record of Archaeological Gleanings from the Repairs of 1938–1942* (Oxford: Oxford University Press for the Government of Palestine, 1949).

60 "In peace time he had done some work for Mark Sykes, who again came across him during the war as a refugee. It was at Sykes' suggestion that he came to Jerusalem and started a pottery in the hope of ultimately producing glazed tiles of good enough quality to justify their use in repairing the tile decoration of the Dome of the Rock." Richmond, "Liber Maiorum," 77. Ohanessian's early efforts were supported by the Pro-Jerusalem Society, then headed by C. R. Ashbee, who recorded these experiments in tile making in his *Jerusalem 1918–1920*. (See also C. R. Ashbee, *Report by Mr. C. R. Ashbee on the Arts and Crafts of Jerusalem and District*, August 1918, JMA/361/A58.) For example, when the Pro-Jerusalem Society sought to rationalize the naming and numbering system of Jerusalem's streets, Ashbee tried to engage Ohanessian as the manufacturer of new name plates for them. However, Ohanessian was outbid by the Bezalel Academy (the Zionist school of arts and crafts, headed by Boris Schatz). After Ashbee quit Palestine, the city's town planning commission tried to split the tile project between Ohanessian and Bezalel. (See Protocols of the Jerusalem Town Planning Commission, Meeting No. 25, 16 February 1923, JMA/829/EI 1/42/6.) Writing about them in 1919 (and before the rise of the SMC), Richmond himself would record the rise of Armenian potteries of Jerusalem in the following way: "It is hardly conceivable that every effort should

not be made to revive the tile industry. . . . For it is not here [in Jerusalem] alone that there is a demand for tiles. In Constantinople, in Brousa, at Medina, at Konia, and in many other places tiles are needed and have been in demand at least for the last fifteen years or more." Arguing that the demand had begun to be met once again by the Armenians of Kutahia prior to the war, but that the genocide raised some questions about whether the surviving population would wish to remain in Turkey, Richmond then noted: "An Armenian tile-maker from Kutahia is now in Jerusalem. He intends to attempt the establishment of the industry in the city. . . . As a first step it is necessary to import a few Armenian workers from Kutahia. An effort is now being made to do this." Richmond, *The Dome of the Rock*, 73–74. On the history of the Kutahia tradition, see Rifat Cini, *Kutahya in Turkish Tile Making*, trans. Solmaz Turunc and Aydin Turunc (Istanbul: Uycan Yayinlari, 1991).

61 ʿAbdallah Mukhlis and Yaʾqub Abu al-Huda to Herbert Samuel, 5 November 1923, 18 (trans.), ISA/CS/189.

62 Ibid., 1.

63 Ibid.

64 Ibid., 17.

65 Ibid., 18.

66 See, for example, "Monthly Political Report," November 1922, PRO/CO 733/41.

67 For example, immediately following his conflict with Bentwich over the shariʿa courts, Richmond informs his wife: "I am getting on pretty well with my efforts to organize the Moslems in a compact body uncontaminated by the influence of bought people and quite clear of Jewish nominees. . . . I am delighted at breaking down the work of such people." ETR to MMR, 4 September 1921, reproduced in "Mammon in the Holy Land," 58.

68 ETR to MMR, 2 December 1923, reproduced in "Mammon in the Holy Land," 203.

69 Minutes [i.e., annotated comments] of Ernest Tatham Richmond, 29 January 1924, in response to Norman Bentwich to Richmond, in AG to AS (pol.) 10 January 1924, ISA/RG2/CS189.

70 Having tried to turn the attorney general's suggestion that the government didn't have *adequate* oversight over the SMC into an argument that the administration didn't have jurisdiction over the council at all, Richmond found himself surrounded by suggestions that it was time to reform the SMC's relation to government. Responding to Richmond's interpretation of his own views, Bentwich would respond: "My minute does not, I think, in any way support the view that the Gov. has no right of controlling or supervising the execution of the Regulation under which the Supreme Muslim Sharia Council is constituted." Norman Bentwich to Richmond, in AG to AS (pol.), 3 March 1924, ISA/RG2/CS189.

71 On 28 February 1924, Storrs wrote to Gilbert Clayton, the chief secretary of the Palestine government, in order to express the view that Mukhlis and Abu al-Huda's claims of administrative negligence "appear to be a logical and not unreasonable criticism." He then added: "As mentioned by me in my political report, no. 4475/G of 31 October, 1923, the Council is unique (among other respects) among admin-

istrative for judicial councils, in that it is subjected to no control whatever, in consequence of which there is an increasing body of criticism and complaint levelled against its activities and inactivities. These complaints, like many others in Palestine, may be not altogether genuine and are doubtless exaggerated in part for political and personal motives, but I think they are worthy of examination and possibly of action in the direction above indicated, especially as the discredit and odium resulting from the charges made ultimately fall upon the Government, which, it need hardly be added, has received practically no acknowledgement or appreciation for its generous and sympathetic handling of the general Sharia Question." Ronald Storrs to Gilbert Clayton, 28 February 1924, ISA/RG2/CS189.

72 See, for example, ETR to MMR, 4 December 1923: "I learn that District Governors in general and Ronald Storrs in particular have made representatives at Government House to the effect that their influence and authority are undermined by me and that I have too much power etc: that I receive 'natives,' talk to them and let them air their views and grievances too much. Ronald Storrs is at present engaged in a campaign against the Mufti, Hajj Amin, and the Moslem Supreme Council. What he expects to gain by all this folly I cannot imagine." Reproduced in Richmond, "Mammon in the Holy Land," 198.

73 Ronald Storrs to Gilbert Clayton, Secret Report, 8 December 1923, ISA/RG2/CS184.

74 "I do not know what may be the sources of information from which the Daily Intelligence Summaries are compiled. It is, however, safe to assume that the information comes from informers. The reputation enjoyed by those who follow that pursuit is well known. It would clearly be injudicious to assume that everything they say necessarily represents the exact truth. It is even possible that, on occasion, it may be the exact opposite of the truth. . . . To accept . . . the communication under reference as undoubtedly true, without further enquiry is, in my opinion, much to be deprecated." Richmond to Gilbert Clayton, 13 December 1923, ISA/RG2/CS184.

75 Richmond to Gilbert Clayton, 13 December 1923, ISA/RG2/CS184. After reviewing Richmond's minutes, on 18 December 1923 Storrs noted on its margins that Richmond's argument was "eminently applicable to all unpalatable information."

76 Ernest Tatham Richmond, "Report on the Work Done by the Political Office During the Calendar Year 1922," reprinted in "Mammon in the Holy Land," 174–184, E. T. Richmond Papers. Early in 1923, the chief secretary, Wyndham Deedes, asked Richmond to submit a report on the activities of his office for the previous year. This was a document that the Palestine government intended to forward to the Colonial Office. In response to this request, Richmond produced a document so startling to his superiors that it was, to my knowledge, never directly referred to again in any official correspondence.

77 Among the "tendencies" he felt himself obligated to oppose, Richmond includes the "suggestion" that "Arab Nationalism is not as legitimate a political creed as Jewish Nationalism and that adherents of Arab Nationalism should be treated by the Police and by the Administration generally as potential criminals while adher-

ents to Jewish Nationalism are regarded as comparatively law-abiding citizens." Richmond, "Report on the Work Done" in "Mammon in the Holy Land."

78 Richmond, "Report on the Work Done," 181.

79 Ibid., 180. Elsewhere he notes: "I want to dispel the fog that is obscuring what is going on to England's discredit in this country. Jews are not Englishmen however English they may seem when in an English atmosphere. I am astonished at my discovery of the fact of the Jew. No wonder Arabs here regard the Palestine Government as Jewish camouflaged as British." ETR to HWR, 24 March 1923, Section A, E. T. Richmond Papers.

80 Richmond, "Report on the Work Done," 178. Richmond also believes himself to have had some success in this matter. Noting "the change that has taken place during the year in the point of view held by the Arab Nationalists in this country," he submits that "the tendency has been for Arab Palestinian Nationalism to become less parasitic in character, that is to say, local Arab Nationalists appreciate more and more that it is by their own efforts that the hoped for and desired Arab renaissance in Palestine must be brought about . . . and that they must depend rather upon hard work than upon political agitation and intrigue." Ibid., p. 183.

81 Richmond, *The Dome of the Rock in Jerusalem*, 5.

82 Contrary to Elie Kedourie's and Bernard Wasserstein's chronologies, Richmond did not announce his intention to quit the administration abruptly in response to a dinner invitation from the high commissioner in March 1924. He did so some two months earlier. The high commissioner had kept Richmond in limbo concerning his status in the administration after the Colonial Office (CO) unilaterally changed his title earlier in 1922, and after Richmond protested this as a demotion. In addition to this, Richmond's efforts to communicate with the CO directly on the state of affairs in Palestine (bypassing his superiors) had been discovered, and they occasioned a prolonged correspondence between Samuel and Sir John Shuckbrugh concerning his future in the administration. (See PRO/CO 733/60.) The officials were assessing whether there was any need for this publicly pro-Arab official to stay on, given the fact that the pro-Zionist chief secretary, Wyndham Deedes, had already departed the administration the previous summer. According to Richmond, in late December 1923, Samuel held an interview with Richmond in which he asked Richmond if he had not been "rather shocked" by the things he himself had said in his memorandum (the memorandum concerning the activities of his office in 1922, although in his letters Richmond confusingly refers to it as the "July" memorandum). Richmond replied that he "adhered to every word of it." (ETR to MMR, 20 December 1923, reproduced in "Mammon in the Holy Land," 202–203.) On 16 January 1924, Richmond informed Samuel—via Clayton— of his intention to leave Palestine in April. While Samuel previously confided to Shuckbrugh of the CO that he "thought it difficult for Richmond to remain," given his "attitude on the chief subject of political controversy" in Palestine, upon learning of Richmond's intentions to leave he seems to have informed Richmond that he had changed his views and that Richmond's presence in Palestine was "essen-

171

tial." (ETR to MMR, 17 January 1924, reproduced in "Mammon in the Holy Land," 205–209.) Richmond's official letter of resignation, dated 13 March 1924 (to be found in ISA/HS/11 and discussed in Kedourie, "Sir Herbert Samuel and the Government of Palestine," *Middle-Eastern Studies* 5, no. 1 [1969]: 44–68), was preceded by leaks of his imminent departure in the press. See, for example, "Resignations," *Near East*, 21 February 1924, and "Mr. Richmond," in *Sawt al-Sha'b*, February 1924.

83 Richmond to Herbert Samuel, 13 March 1924, ISA/HS/11. Despite entreaties from Samuel and Storrs requesting him to stay on through the spring, Richmond refused, believing the administration wished to use him as a symbol of its empathy to Arabs during the politically tense Easter and Nabi Musa festivals.

84 See (1) Ernest Tatham Richmond, "British Policy in Palestine and the Mandate," parts 1–3, *Near East* (1925), 26 March, 329–330; 2 April, 350–352; 9 April, 381–382; (2) Ernest Tatham Richmond, "'England' in Palestine," *Nineteenth Century* (July 1925); 46–51; (3) [Ernest Tatham Richmond], "Palestine To-Day, The Old Order, and the New," *Guardian*, 9 April 1926, n.p. "'England' in Palestine" was first delivered as a speech at the Near and Middle East Association. *Near East* did not publish the whole of Richmond's essay, the original of which may be found in Ernest Tatham Richmond, "The Rule of Gerione: A Number of Writings about British Policy in Palestine, 1924–1946" (1946), E. T. Richmond Papers.

85 "International Jewry and British crankiness—here, then, are the forces (obvious, not merely to Arabs, but to all who live round the Mediterranean Sea) which, combining together, were able to impose upon the League of Nations outward responsibility for that iniquitous document known as the Mandate for Palestine, and to represent the course that has been taken as something sacred, something that cannot be changed, something that embodies the combined political wisdom of the civilised world." Richmond, "'England' in Palestine," 49.

86 ETR to MMR, 13 December 1923, reproduced in Richmond, "Mammon in the Holy Land," 201.

87 Ernest Tatham Richmond, *Moslem Architecture, 632–1516: Some Causes and Consequences* (London: Royal Asiatic Society, 1926), 9, 15.

88 Ibid., 36. "Muqaddasi, in his description of the mosque refers to these famous monuments. He says: 'this mosque (of Jerusalem) is even more beautiful than that of Damascus; for, during the building of it, they had for a rival and as a comparison the great church belonging to the Christians at Jerusalem; and they built the mosque to be even more magnificent than that other." Ibid., 20. Something resembling this "political" interpretation of the monument's significance has been sustained by the architectural historian Oleg Grabar and his students. See for example, Oleg Grabar, "The Meaning of the Dome of the Rock," in *The Medieval Mediterranean: Cross Cultural Contacts*, ed. Marilyn Chiat and Kathryn L. Reyerson, Medieval Studies at Minnesota 3 (St. Cloud, Minn.: Northstar Press, 1988); Nasser Rabat, "The Meaning of the Ummayad Dome of the Rock," *Muqarnas* 6 (1990): 12–21.

89 Richmond, *Moslem Architecture*, 20.

90 Ibid., 47.
91 Ibid., 7.
92 Herbert Plumer to Leo Amery, 8 November 1926, PRO/CO 733/129. For Plumer's opinion of P. L. O. Guy, see CO to Plumer, 16 June 1927, PRO/CO 733/133.
93 "I should be blind if I were not aware that exception might be taken to him [ETR] as the [*illegible*] of his attitude towards political questions in Palestine, but in that matter I would say that archaeology or antiquities are ill suited . . . at politics and no man would conflate[?] the two." Admiral H. W. Richmond to Leo Amery, 8 February 1927, PRO/CO 733/133. E. T. Richmond would later record that he had no wish to uproot his family and move to Palestine, nor was he happy at the prospect of renewing his associations "with the Government of that misgoverned land." Given these sentiments, the reasons he lists among those prompting his return are significant: "The post would enable me to continue a job that much interested me: the reconditioning of the Moslem Holy Places. It would also, I hoped, enable me to do something for the Christian Holy Places, particularly for the churches of the Holy Sepulchre and of the Nativity." Richmond, "Mammon in the Holy Land," 271.
94 Gilbert Clayton to Leo Amery, 7 March 1927, PRO/CO 733/133.
95 Minutes of Sir John Shuckbrugh, 9 June 1927, PRO/CO 733/133.
96 Richmond, "Mammon in the Holy Land," 272. However, in this context Richmond's definition of "politics" was fascinating. Among the reasons he lists for occasioning his return, he mentions that he wished to revise the Antiquities Law of Palestine, which, in his words, had been "devised by Bentwich" so that its terms "were politically poisoned in that they reflected his Socialistic ideology." Ibid., 273. To thwart the intrusion of politics into the realm of antiquities was not, in Richmond's thinking, a political act. While Richmond's actual labors as director of antiquities are beyond the scope of this study, it is worthwhile to note that he did pursue a certain policy of noncooperation in matters that he perceived to hinder Christian and Muslim interests, and to advance Zionism's "Socialistic ideology." Soon after his arrival, Richmond learned that the attorney general, in concert with the town planning adviser, Clifford Holliday, was endeavoring to create a green belt around the Old City of Jerusalem. Since 1918, the Jerusalem municipality—on instructions from the government—had repeatedly failed in its various attempts to achieve this prophylactic zone (in which construction would be restricted if not banned outright), because it could not legally freeze development on private land adjoining the walls without providing compensation to owners (most of whom were Arab). Bentwich and Holliday advanced a novel idea: to declare an "archaeological zone" in which development would be proscribed, but without any obligation on the government's part towards landowners. Richmond refused to cooperate with this scheme, arguing that it was really a question for "authorities who deal with matters of public amenity rather than an archaeological question." Richmond to Norman Bentwich, 17 November 1927, ISA/RG2/M24/B/10/3. For the career of the "archaeological zone" see Protocols of the Jerusalem

173

Local Town Planning Commission, Meetings 80–88 (July-October 1927), JMA/
829/EI/I/42/6.

97 ETR to HWR, 27 October 1927, Section C, E. T. Richmond Papers.

98 Ibid.

99 ETR to HWR, 12 August 1928, Section C, E. T. Richmond Papers, emphasis added.
For the program of the celebrations to which Richmond refers, see al-Jami'a
al-'Arabiyya, 27 August 1928.

100 "This Becoming presents a slow-moving succession of Spirits, a gallery of images, each of which, endowed with all the riches of Spirit, moves thus slowly just
because the Self has to penetrate and digest this entire wealth of its substance. As
its fulfilment consists in perfectly knowing what it is, in knowing its substance,
this knowing is its withdrawal into itself in which it abandons its outer existence
and gives its existential shape over to recollection. Thus absorbed in itself, it is
sunk in the night of its self-consciousness; but in that night its vanished outer
existence is preserved, and this transformed existence—the former one, but now
reborn of the Spirit's knowledge—is the new existence, a new world and a new
shape of Spirit. In the immediacy of this new existence the Spirit has to start
afresh to bring itself to maturity as if, for it, all that preceded were lost and it had
learned nothing from the experience of the earlier Spirits. But recollection, the in-
wardizing, of that experience, has preserved it and is the inner being, and in fact
the higher form of the substance." Hegel, Phenomenology of Spirit, §808, 492.

101 The principal primary sources on the wall crisis are Great Britain, House of Com-
mons Sessional Papers, The Western or Wailing Wall in Jerusalem, Memorandum
by the Secretary of State for the Colonies (Cmd. 3229), 1928; Great Britain, Report
of the Palestine Commission on the Palestine Disturbances of August 1929 (Cmd. 3530),
(London: HMSO, 1930); Great Britain, Palestine Commission on the Disturbances of
August 1929: Minutes of Evidence, 3 vols. (Colonial 48), (London: HMSO, 1930); International Commission for the Wailing Wall, The Rights and Claims of Moslems and
Jews in Connection with the Wailing Wall at Jerusalem, Institute for Palestine Studies,
Basic Documents Series, no. 4. (1931; rpt., Beirut: Institute for Palestine Studies,
1968).

102 As Mosely Lesch notes: "The wall and pavement belonged to the Islamic waqf,
but the Jewish community had traditionally used it for prayers. They did not, however, have permission to place a screen there, and the British authorities feared
that permitting it to remain would establish a precedent and inflame the Muslim
community." Ann Mosely Lesch, Arab Politics in Palestine: The Frustration of a
Nationalist Movement (Ithaca, N.Y.: Cornell University Press, 1979), 208. See
also Great Britain, The Western or Wailing Wall in Jerusalem.

103 On the origin of the "Status Quo" see Article 13 of the Council of the League of
Nations Mandate to Great Britain over Palestine, which states: "All responsibility
in connection with the Holy Places and religious buildings or sites in Palestine,
including that of preserving existing rights and securing free access to the Holy

Places, religious buildings and sites and the free exercise of worship, while ensuring the requirements of public order and decorum, is assumed by the Mandatory, who shall be responsible solely to the League of Nations in all matters concerned herewith." League of Nations, Council, *Mandate for Palestine* (Geneva: League of Nations, 1926).

104 Bernard Wasserstein, *The British in Palestine: The Mandatory Government and the Arab-Jewish Conflict, 1917–1939* (London: Royal Historical Society, 1978), 222.

105 Mosely Lesch, *Arab Politics in Palestine*, 208.

106 J. M. N. Jeffries, *Palestine: The Reality* (London: Longmans, Green, 1939), 603. I do not present Jeffries as a particularly impartial historian of this conflict. But I do introduce his sentiments as representative of the unquestioned norm. Remaining content to debate the *causes* of that escalation, both the witnesses to these events and later historians have left intact a presupposition of causality according to which the instigation of history is reduced to the matter of locating an "appropriate catalyst" to arouse the masses. This is the presupposition whose career I examine in part 3 of this work.

107 *Bayan ila Ikhwanina al-Muslimin 'Amattan* (Jerusalem, 1347 A.H./1928–29), 6–10. The English translation of this proclamation is to be found in Great Britain, Colonial 48, Exhibit No. 86, 1082–1083. The "first method" referred to here is one I presented earlier in this chapter, when the Zionist Commission attempted to purchase the Waqf Abu Madyan with British assistance.

108 "If the desire of Jews to pray at that place peacefully . . . be misrepresented as the establishment of a strategic platform for an attack against the Moslem Mosques within the Haram area, this can only be the fruit of false imagination or willful calumny." Va'ad Hale'umi, as quoted in Great Britain, Colonial 48, 1102.

109 Great Britain, Colonial 48, Exhibit No. 108, 1101. Muslim countercharges to Jewish countercharges confirm that the performative horizon of each side's claims is the untruth of the other side's assertions: "We hold the whole world witness of what the Jews commit of the transgressions and ambitions in the Moslem Holy Places in which, by *false propaganda* and trouble making they endeavour to establish for themselves rights which have no origin. We charge the Jews alone with all the serious consequences and responsibility which ensue from their continuation in these transgressions and ambitions despite what the Moslems have done and still do for the preservation of security and tranquility." From *Bayan ila Ikhwanina*, trans. in Great Britain, Colonial 48, 1036.

110 ETR to HWR, 7 September 1929, Section C, E. T. Richmond Papers.

111 Robert Hullot-Kentor, "Suggested Reading: Jameson on Adorno," review of *Late Marxism: Adorno, or the Persistence of the Dialectic* by Fredric Jameson, Telos 89 (fall 1991): 175.

112 Theodor Adorno, "Aspects of Hegel's Philosophy," in *Hegel: Three Studies*, trans. Shierry Weber Nicholsen, intro. Shierry Weber Nicholsen and Jeremy J. Shapiro (Cambridge, Mass.: MIT Press, 1994), 26.

4. Cataclysm and Pogrom: An Exergue on the Naming of Violence

The epigraphs to this chapter are from Richard Meinertzhagen, "Report of April 9, 1920," in Richard Meinertzhagen, *Middle East Diary, 1917–1956* (London: Cresset Press, 1959), 79–84; reprinted in *The Rise of Israel: A Documentary Record from the Nineteenth Century to 1948*, vol. 12: *Riots in Jerusalem–San Remo Conference April 1920*, ed. Isaiah Friedman (New York: Garland Publishing, 1987), 18 (emphasis added); and from FO371 5118/85. "Memoranda circulated by the Zionist Executive among some members of Parliament concerning the riots in Jerusalem and Jabotinsky's arrest," reprinted in Friedman, *The Rise of Israel*, 12:155 (emphasis added).

1 "Violence, not for the first or last time in the history of the Palestine conflict, was in 1929 the catalyst which produced a new political situation." Bernard Wasserstein, *The British in Palestine: The Mandatory Government and the Arab-Jewish Conflict, 1917–1929* (London: Royal Historical Society, 1978), 235. Martin Kolinsky similarly argues that a "major turning-point was the riots in August 1929 . . . [which] . . . shattered nearly a decade of relative tranquility, and led to announced changes of policy by the British Government." Martin Kolinsky, *Law Order and Riots in Mandatory Palestine, 1928–1935* (London: St. Martin's Press, 1993), xiv–xv.

2 CZA/Z4/16084. "The Anti-Jewish Riots in Jerusalem," Memorandum by the Zionist Commission on 11 April 1920, reprinted in Friedman, *The Birth of Israel*, 12:24–25. Edmund Allenby (1861–1936) was the commander in chief of the Egyptian Expeditionary Force that conquered Palestine in the military campaigns of 1918–19. After the war, he remained in Egypt, as high commissioner, until 1925.

3 FO371/5118/85. "Report of the Official Court of Inquiry on the April Riots, 1 July 1920" [Palin Commission Report], reprinted in Friedman, *The Birth of Israel*, 12:113 (emphasis added).

4 Testimony of Major Alan Saunders in Great Britain, *Palestine Commission on the Disturbances of August 1929: Minutes of Evidence*, 3 vols., Colonial No. 48 (London: HMSO, 1930), "Third Sitting, Afternoon Sitting: Testimony of Major Alan Saunders," Tuesday, 29 October 1929, Question Nos. 946–947, p. 43.

5 The importance of the "pogrom" in the Zionist imaginary was crystallized by Chaim Nahman Bialik in his "On the Slaughter," a poem written in 1903 in response to the Kishiniev pogrom. See Chaim Nahman Bialik, "Al Hash'chitah," in *Kol Shirei Bialik* (Tel-Aviv: Devir, 1970), 152. Historians have also argued that the pogroms triggered and intensified the Zionist response to the so-called Jewish Question in Europe. See Howard Sachar, *A History of Israel: From the Rise of Zionism to Our Time* (New York: Knopf, 1976).

6 See Ranajit Guha, "The Prose of Counter-Insurgency," in Ranajit Guha and Gayatri Chakravorty Spivak, eds., *Selected Subaltern Studies* (New York: Oxford University Press, 1988), 45–86.

7 Guha, "The Prose of Counter-Insurgency," 46.

8 Friedrich Nietzsche, "On Truth and Lies in a Nonmoral Sense," in *Philosophy and Truth: Selections from Nietzsche's Notebooks of the Early 1870's*, ed. and trans. Daniel Breanzenle (Atlantic Highlands, N.J.: Humanities Press, 1979), 84.

176

9   See the "Memoranda circulated by the Zionist executive among some members of Parliament." See also FO371/5114/61, "Arab-Moslem-Christian Society to the Military Governor, April 1920, accusing the Jews of disturbing the peace in Jerusalem," reprinted in Friedman, *The Birth of Israel*, 12:55.

10 See Guha, "The Prose of Counter-Insurgency," 77.

11 The fact that a normative historiography privileges mass violence as the principal vehicle of historical transformation (as opposed to changes in mode of production, for example) may be shown in a cursory fashion, simply by noting the standard periodization of most of the historical texts on the subject. The majority move from one such violent crisis to the next, usually employing as their conclusion or as their beginning the instances of either the 1929 Buraq, or Wailing Wall, riots or the Palestinian *thawra*, or revolt, which took place between 1936 and 1939. See for example, Bernard Wasserstein's *The British in Palestine*; Yehoshuah Porath's two volumes on Palestinian-Arab political leadership, divided respectively between 1918–1929 and 1929–1939: *The Emergence of the Palestinian-Arab National Movement: 1918–1929* (London: Frank Cass, 1974) and *The Palestinian Arab National Movement: From Riots to Rebellion, 1929–1939* (London: Frank Cass, 1977); and Ann Mosely Lesch's *Arab Politics in Palestine, 1917–1939: The Frustration of a Nationalist Movement* (Ithaca, N.Y.: Cornell Univesity Press, 1979).

12 Yehoshua Porath, *The Emergence of the Palestinian-Arab National Movement, 1918–1929*, 269.

13 Philip Mattar, *The Mufti of Jerusalem: Al-Hajj Amin al-Husayni and the Palestinian National Movement* (New York: Columbia University Press, 1988), 35.

14 Ibid., 36. Mattar is referring here to an article published on 28 September 1928.

15 Ibid., 47. The normative response to this exoneration (it is not new) is that the incitement was primed over weeks and months before the actual violence by the SMC—and that it could consequently not be stopped by its leaders. Their "exoneration" is their indictment. Against this charge, defenders of the grand mufti argue that the responsibility for incitement (the trigger to violence) ultimately rests with Zionists, whose insensitivities to the relation between Palestinian Muslims with their holy sites caused the violence. Here, a dramaturgy of recrimination presents itself to view. I address this same dramaturgy at length in part 3 of this study.

16 Fredric Jameson, "Marx's Purloined Letter," *New Left Review* 209 (January/February 1995): 94.

17 John Marlowe, *The Seat of Pilate: An Account of the Palestine Mandate* (London: Cresset Press, 1959), 1.

18 Theodor W. Adorno, *Negative Dialectics*, trans. E. B. Ashton (New York: Continuum, 1987), 120.

19 "The Russian word 'pogrom' (pronounced with stress on the final syllable) is generally translated 'desolation, devastation'. The word is related to the Russian words *grom*, thunder, the thunder-clash, and to *gromit*, to thunder, to batter down as with a thunderbolt, to destroy without pity." *Oxford English Dictionary*, online edition, s.v. "pogrom."

20 "Contradiction is nonidentity under the aspect of identity . . . the principle of con-

tradiction makes the thought of unity the measure of heterogeneity . . . What is differentiated will appear divergent, dissonant, negative just as long as consciousness is driven by its own formation towards unity; just as long as it measures what is not identical with itself against its own claim for totality," Adorno, *Negative Dialectics*, 5–6.

21 "Address by the Va'ad Hale'umi [National Council]," Great Britain, *Report of the Commission on the Palestine Disturbances of August 1929*, Cmd. 3530 (London: HMSO, 1930) [Shaw Report], 30. The Va'ad Hale'umi was an executive council of elected representatives that "concerned itself primarily with the local issues of the Yishuv." For an excellent outline of its place in the Zionist infrastructure in Palestine, see Mitchell Cohen, *Zion and State: Nation, Class, and the Shaping of Modern Israel* (Oxford: Basil Blackwell, 1987), 76–77.

22 For example, neither Porath nor Mattar can entertain the possibilities discussed by Gramsci long before them, or by a historiographic tradition since: that in effect, all those who are, or are putatively causing or not causing the uprising from behind the scenes are part of a political condition within which even their semblance of agency is questioned by the same uprising, since its violence may not represent a simple response to incitement, or an organic outpouring, but an attempt to take consequences beyond what those who stand in positions of leadership had hoped for: in essence, to take advantage of such moments in order to make a play for hegemony. For Gramsci, a "common sense" that presents itself in the apparent superstition of the masses (such as the kind of rumor that coordinates their collective action) becomes the model for philosophy: "it is the conception of a subaltern social group, deprived of historical initiative, in continuous but disorganic expansion, unable to go beyond a certain qualitative level, which still remains below the level of the possession of the State and of the real exercise of hegemony over the whole of society which alone permits a certain organic equilibrium in the development of the intellectual group. The philosophy of praxis has itself become 'prejudice' and 'superstition.' As it stands, it is the popular aspect of modern historicism, but it contains in itself the principle through which this historicism can be superseded." Antonio Gramsci et al., *Selections from the Prison Notebooks of Antonio Gramsci*, ed. and trans. Quintin Hoare and Geoffrey Nowell Smith (New York: International Publishers, 1971), 396.

23 Gayatri Chakravorty Spivak, "Introduction," in Guha and Spivak, *Selected Subaltern Studies*, 6. "There is always a counterpointing suggestion in the work of the [subaltern studies] group that subaltern consciousness is subject to the cathexis of the elite, that is never fully recoverable, that it is always askew from its received signifiers, indeed that it is effaced even as it is disclosed, that it is irreducibly discursive. It is, for example, chiefly a matter of 'negative consciousness'?" Gayatri Chakravorty Spivak, "Subaltern Studies: Deconstructing Historiography," in *In Other Worlds: Essays in Cultural Politics* (New York: Methuen, 1988), 203. See also Gayatri Chakravorty Spivak, "Can the Subaltern Speak?" in *Marxism and the Interpreta-*

tion of Culture, ed. Cary Nelson and Lawrence Grossberg (Urbana: University of Illinois Press, 1988), 271–313.

24 Adorno, Negative Dialectics, 32.

25 "The [subaltern studies] group, as we have seen, tracks failures in attempts to displace discursive fields. A deconstructive approach would bring into focus the fact that they are themselves engaged in an attempt at displacing discursive fields, that they themselves 'fail' (in the general sense) for reasons as 'historical' as those they adduce for the heterogeneous agents they study; and would attempt to forge a practice that would take this into account. Otherwise, refusing to acknowledge the implications of their own line of work because that would be politically incorrect, they would, willy-nilly, 'insidiously objectify' the subaltern (2.262), control him through knowledge even as they restore visions of causality and self-determination to him (2.30), become complicit, in their desire for totality (and therefore totalization) (3.317), with a 'law [that] assign[s] a[n] undifferentiated [proper] name' (EAP 159) to the 'subaltern as such.'" Spivak, "Introduction," in Guha and Spivak, Selected Subaltern Studies, 9. Numbered citations in parentheses refer to volume numbers and pages of Selected Subaltern Studies.

26 Ibid., 4. Spivak, then, recuperates the subaltern historiography by arguing that the very problem of agency emerges in conjunction with a "subaltern subject effect" that could only be brought to scrutiny via a performative, strategic use of essentialism of the kind practiced by the collective.

27 Adorno, Negative Dialectics, 160.

28 Ibid., 149–150.

5. Sir Alfred Mond's After-Dinner Eloquence

The first epigraph in this chapter is from ['Abd al-Qadir al-Muzaffar], Nida' 'Amm ila al-'Ammat al-Islamiyya min Ikhwanihum Muslima Bayt al-Maqdis wa Sa'ir Filastin [Public Call to the Muslim People from your Brethren the Muslims of Jerusalem and the Rest of Palestine] (Jerusalem, 1922), ISA/AE65/1721; the version in this epigraph comes from the translation of a version published in al-Nahda on 13 July 1922 and reproduced in James Morgan to FO, 4 August 1922, PRO/CO 733/31, "Manifesto of the Palestinean Moslem Mission." The second epigraph is from Lord Melchett [Henry Ludwig Mond], Thy Neighbor (New York: H. C. Kinsey, 1937), 174.

1 In part the consequence of a coalition between Muhammad al-Hajj Amin al-Husayni and the leaders of the Khilafat movement in India, the conference has variously been interpreted as the grand mufti's play for broader Muslim support of the Palestinian cause (Mosely Lesch), or as a feature of Palestinian Islam on the "defensive" (Kupferschmidt). The meeting was boycotted by Turkey—out of concerns that the meeting would attempt to raise the matter of the caliphate—and by the Egyptian Islamic orthodoxy for fears that the meeting would challenge the hegemony of the Azhar Mosque, because one of the stipulated aims of the meeting

was to establish a parallel Islamic university in Jerusalem. Concerns about the meeting were expressed by the government of Italy and by elements within the British colonial administration, which feared the political potential of a pan-Islamic movement. However, contemporary interpreters, such as the orientalist H. A. R. Gibb and the author George Antonious, were much impressed with the meeting and saw it as a potentially important political event. Finally, the meeting has also been interpreted as a decisive moment of failure for the mufti and his Majlissiyyun (the group associated with the Supreme Muslim Council) because, while the congress represented the pinnacle of the mufti's own political prestige, it was nevertheless a failed effort to construct a global pan-Islamic coalition under the banner of Palestine and its holy sites. See Ann Mosely Lesch, *Arab Politics in Palestine, 1917–1939: The Frustration of a Nationalist Movement* (Ithaca, N.Y.: Cornell University Press, 1979), 140; Uri M. Kupferschmidt, *The Supreme Muslim Council: Islam under the British Mandate for Palestine* (Leiden: E. J. Brill, 1987), 187–253; Alfred Nielsen, "The International Islamic Conference at Jerusalem," *Moslem World* (London), Nile Mission Press by Christian Literature Society for India, 22, no. 4 (October 1932): 340–354. The most comprehensive analysis of this congress, and of the congress in Modern Islam appears in Martin Seth Kramer, "The Congress in Modern Islam: On the Origins of an Innovation," Ph.D. diss., Princeton University, 1982, 167–310; and Martin Seth Kramer, *Islam Assembled: The Advent of the Muslim Congresses* (New York: Columbia University Press, 1986). Finally, for a striking contemporary evaluation see H. A. R. Gibb, "The Islamic Congress at Jerusalem in December 1931," in *Survey of International Affairs 1934*, ed. Arnold J. Toynbee (London: Humphrey Milford and Oxford University Press, 1935), 99–105.

2 Chaim Arlozorov, *'al-Sahyuniyya wa'l-Amakin al-Islamiyya al-Muqaddasa fi Falastin* [Zionism and the Islamic Holy Places in Palestine] (Jerusalem: Jewish Agency for Palestine, November 1931). For the Political Department of the Jewish Agency's efforts to challenge the imperatives of the congress, see Chaim Arlozorov, *Yoman Yerushalayim* (Tel Aviv: Mifleget Po'alei Israel, 1949), 135–136. For the grand mufti's claims that the Zionists were attempting to take over Islamic holy sites in Jerusalem, and that for this reason a pan-Islamic defense was needed, see "The Islamic Congress, Views of Sayed el Husseini," *Egyptian Gazette* (Cairo, 14 November 1931), 5–6.

3 CZA/S25/2976. The Political Department of the Jewish Agency records that "with the opening of the Islamic Congress in Jerusalem, the pamphlet was sent to all of the participants whose names and addresses (place of accommodation) the Arab bureau of the Jewish Agency could locate."

4 This is apparently a revision of a pamphlet that already existed in 1929, published by the Jam'iyyat Hirasat al-Masjid al-Aqsa wa'l-Amakin al-Islamiyya al-Muqaddasa and entitled *Bayan ila al-'Alam al-Islami* [Proclamation to the Muslim World] (Jerusalem, 1929), but it also adds a series of direct rebuttals of Arlozorov's charges. In the 1929 pamphlet, the Society for the Protection of the Aqsa Mosque and the Islamic Holy Places calls itself the "Jam'iyyat Histasat al-Masjid al-sqsa wa'l-Amakin al-Islamiyya al-Muqaddasa." In 1931, with the timing of the publication of the pamphlet to coincide with an international congress for the protection of Muslim holy

places in Jerusalem, the organization added "bi'l Quds" [in Jerusalem] to its name. For the sake of simplicity, I refer to the 1931–32 version as the *Proclamation of the Society for the Protection of the Aqsa Mosque.*

5 Kupferschmidt foregrounds what he calls the "defensive" character of Palestinian Islam, relying on the prevalence of the word difa' (defense) in the names of committees, publications, and speeches, as evidence for that conclusion. See Kupferschmidt, *The Supreme Muslim Council*, 221, n. 2.

6 Colonel Frederick Hermann Kisch to E. Morris, assistant chief secretary, Palestine Government, 30 December 1927, CZA/S25/704/1. I examine these communications later in this chapter.

7 Arlozorov, *'al-Sahyuniyya.*

8 See Erving Goffman, *Frame Analysis: An Essay on the Organization of Experience*, foreword by Bennett Berger (Boston: Northeastern University Press, 1986), 11.

9 Arlozorov, *'al-Sahyuniyya.*

10 In its formal outlines, the Palestinian response to Arlozorov's assertion was already in place during the commission of inquiry on the causes of the August 1929 disturbances, when the Zionist charge that Arab leaders incited masses through rumors was itself turned back upon Zionist accusers as suspect. Summarizing the grand mufti's position during the inquiry, a lawyer states: "All you can tell us about it is: that it was alleged by the Zionists that these disturbances had been started by certain Arab leaders, but that suggestion or allegation is not true. That is all you can tell us?" The mufti then replies, "I wish to add that this is a habit to make such a suggestion." See Great Britain, *Palestine Commission on the Disturbances of August 1929: Minutes of Evidence*, 3 vols., Colonial No. 48 (London: HMSO, 1930), "Twenty-Eighth Sitting: Testimony of Muhammad Hajj Amin al Husseini," Monday, 2 December 1929, Question No. 12,527, p. 493 (hereafter Colonial 48).

11 From the perspective offered by a dramaturgical analysis of politics, Arlozorov appears close to "flooding out," or in other words, close to abandoning the formalized political system in which he is a player, because he "discovers that . . . [he] is lodged into cognition and action on false assumptions," 357. To the degree that he refuses to accept this formal code of self-presentation—by attempting to address participants in the Congress directly—he occasions a crisis at the level of the dramaturgy that the other side responds to by "shifting key," that is, via "a mounting cycle of response to him," 359. Their refusal to "break frame" incorporates the attempted frame break as the frame's own patch. In doing so, they simultaneously cast doubt upon the genuineness of Arlozorov's gesture, so that even his effort to discredit "the appearance of reserve" of the other side is disclosed to be a performance that can itself be discredited, 375. All quotations from Goffman, *Frame Analysis.s*

12 J. L. Austin, *How to Do Things with Words*, ed. J. O. Urmson and Marina Sbisa (1962; Cambridge, Mass.: Harvard University Press, 1975), 21–22.

13 Goffman, *Frame Analysis*, 395.

14 *Bayan Jam'iyyat Hirasat al-Masjid al-Aqsa wa'l-Amakin al-Islamiyya al-Muqaddasa bi'l Quds* (Jerusalem, 1931–32), 7.

181

15　Arlozorov, ʿal-Sahyuniyya, 7. Arlozorov also believed that the mufti's strategies had frustrated legitimate political development of Palestine's Arabs. See Arlozorov, "Nisayon Lesikum" (1929), in Kitvei Chaim Arlosorov, vol. 1, Choma Shel Zchuchit [Glass Curtain] (Tel-Aviv: A. J. Steybel, 1934?), 102–104. Arlozorov repeats his claim—uttered as early as 1921—that in the Arab movement in Palestine there exists the "nucleus" of a legitimate political movement. He goes on to note that this development was weakened, in part, by the politics of notables and other forces (namely religious) that worked in the opposite direction, and which were in turn weakened by resisting the latent forces of modernization. He notes for example, that between 1922 and 1930 "the power of the Husaynis and their 'prestige' was decreased," 104.

16　Erving Goffman, Strategic Interaction (Philadelphia: University of Pennsylvania Press, 1969), 101.

17　Goffman, Strategic Interaction, 85.

18　So it is apparent that there is a certain art to these bayan—to both Zionist and Arab proclamations about monuments and holy places, just as it is also evident that in the very aesthetic of these performances "social development is reproduced without being imitated." "Nothing" here—to paraphrase Adorno's understanding of the social situation of art—is "immediately social, not even when this is its aim." See Theodor W. Adorno, Aesthetic Theory, ed. Gretel Adorno and Rolf Tiedemann; trans., ed., and intro. Robert Hullot-Kentor (Minneapolis: University of Minnesota Press, 1997), 226.

19　Ernest Tatham Richmond, The Dome of the Rock in Jerusalem (Oxford: Clarendon Press, 1924), 4–5.

20　For my first discussion of "stereotomy," see chapter 3.

21　As I have already noted in an earlier chapter, Richmond achieved this coup despite the irregularities associated with such an action under the status quo policies that the British administration in Palestine had adopted with respect to the country's religious affairs, and in contravention of the anticipated terms of Great Britain's mandate over Palestine. Articles 13 and 14 of the League of Nations Mandate specifically referred to the autonomy of Muslim religious affairs and holy places, and ensured that "nothing in this mandate shall be construed as conferring upon the Mandatory authority to interfere with the fabric or the management of purely Moslem shrines, the immunities of which are guaranteed." For the uses of this paragraph in the context of the mufti's allegations that the Jews were influencing Great Britain and intended to demolish the Haram monuments and rebuild the temple in their place, see Palestine Royal Commission, Minutes of Evidence (Peel Commission), Colonial No. 134 (London: HMSO, 1937), "Evidence of Haj Amin Eff. El-Husseini," Question Nos. 4618–4632, p. 296.

22　See Bernard Wasserstein, The British in Palestine: The Mandatory Government and the Arab-Jewish Conflict, 1917–1929 (Oxford: Basil Blackwell, 1991), 98–101.

23　ISA/RG2/CS245 (Pol. 228721). This proclamation also appears in PRO/CO 733/3 dispatch no. 92 (secret), 9 May 1921 (Political Report for April). Copies of the proclamation itself were apparently posted in the Old City of Jerusalem on the night of 19–20 April 1921. They were translated by the police into English by the CID (Criminal Investigations Division). The full text reads:

"WAKE UP MOSLEMS." The Jews are interfering in the election of the Mufti. Awake and prevent danger before it occurs. The accursed traitors whom you all know, have combined with the Jews to have one of their party appointed Mufti on the following conditions:

[1] To assist the Jews in the exchange of Moslem Wakfs and theirs sale to the specially the Wakf Abu Midien [sic] near the Wailing Place.

[2] To assist the Jews in killing the national spirit in the country.

[3] To agree to all Jewish Zionist claims and accept them on behalf of the Moslems.

[4] To help in handing over [to] the Jews the Haram Esh-Sherif, the Dome of the Kock [sic] and el Aksa that they might pull them down and build in their place the Temple and the place of sacrifice as stated by Alfred Mond and the president of the Zionist Commission Dr. Eder. Moslems you must know what you have been brought to in your own country in the Jews mock your religious feelings and public opinion and use their influence in appointing the man of their choice who would be under their orders.

The pride of Islam is dead, but God wants to punish you for having opposed the Moslem Government of the Caliphate which protected the religion. Will you accept the shame to have a Jewish Zionist Mufti and that your religious affairs should become a plaything in their hands.

For a comprehensive overview of these events see Elie Kedourie, "Sir Herbert Samuel and the Government of Palestine," *Middle-Eastern Studies* 5, no. 1 (1969): 63. Another significant overview of the same events is presented in Kupferschmidt, *The Supreme Muslim Council*, 20.

24 Herbert Samuel to Winston Churchill, 1 July 1921, PRO/CO 733/4. Following is the original of the exchange of Bellairs with Leo Amery in Parliament (Great Britain, Colonial 48, "Forty-Sixth Sitting: Extract from *Hansard* of the 5 of April, 1921," 26 December 1929, 919): "Commander Bellairs asked the Prime Minister whether his attention had been drawn by the proposal put forward at a meeting to the Palestine Foundation Fund to erect a great temple on the site of the Temple of Solomon; whether he is aware that the site is now occupied by the mosque of Omar; and whether, in view of the difficulties which such proposals cause to the mandatory powers he will state that in no circumstance will Mohammedan institutions be interfered with? Mr. Amery: 'My attention has been drawn to a passage in a speech delivered by my right Hon. Friend the Minister of Health, to which the Hon. and gallant Member apparently alludes. I think it is clear that my right Hon. Friend was speaking figuratively and did not intend so literal an interpretation to be given to his words . . .' [and then he refers to Article 13 of the draft mandate regarding holy places]. Earl Winterton follows up by asking Amery to convey to the Minister of

Health 'the undesirability of making the sort of figurative speech which he did, in view of Mohammedan sensibilities?' To which Amery responds: 'I cannot be responsible for the extent of misinterpretation which may be put on figurative speeches.'"

25 Winston Churchill to Herbert Samuel, 13 July 1921, PRO/CO 733/4. Mond's own statement had been delivered only a few weeks before the election of the mufti, on 22 March 1921, at a dinner hosted in his honor by the Palestine Foundation Fund's Central Committee for the United Kingdom. His words were paraphrased in the *Daily Telegraph* on the following day, which reported that Mond expressed the belief that "there was not in the world today any movement so idealistic, so free from personal feeling or personal ambition, nor one which would be so magical in its effect as the building up of a national home for the Jews. He believed that Palestine could once more send out a great message to the world. A great new epoch was starting, and he was willing to concentrate the remainder of his energies on the building up of a great edifice where once stood the Temple of Solomon. [Cheers]." *Daily Telegraph*, 13 July 1921.

26 Winston Churchill to Herbert Samuel, 7 July 1921, PRO/CO 733/4.

27 Muhammad Amin al-Husayni, *Haqaʾiq ʿan Qadhiyyat Filastin* (Cairo: Maktab al-Haya al-ʿArabiyah al-Ulya li-Filastin, 1954), 118–119. Hajj Amin al-Husayni (1897–1970) served as grand mufti of Jerusalem and president of the Supreme Muslim Council from 1921 to 1936. Although appointed to a permanent post by the British, al-Husayni was removed from office in 1936 after the unified Arab High Committee, which he chaired, rebelled against British authority. In October 1937 he fled to Lebanon, where he continued the committee and retained the support of many Palestinian Arabs.

28 Al-Husayni, *Haqaʾiq ʿan Qadhiyyat Filastin*. "Sir Alfred announced that the widow of Mr. Joseph Fels had given $600,000 to the fund for the purchase of land in Palestine." (Perhaps this is the "building" referred to in the Colonial Office's response?) "Future of Palestine," *Daily Telegraph*, 23 March 1921.

29 See Erving Goffman, *The Presentation of Self in Everyday Life* (New York: Doubleday, 1959), 77–105, for "performance fears."

30 See ibid., 216, for "dramaturgical discipline." In fairness, Goffman does not exactly address what I describe since no "informal" communication or "realigning action" is attempted by Mond, initially, though it is—in the sense of nonconfrontational speech—attempted by the Colonial Office. However he approximates what I am trying to show when he states: "When two teams establish an official working consensus as a guarantee for safe social interaction we may usually detect an unofficial line of communication which each team directs at the other. This unofficial communication may be carried on by innuendo, mimicked accents, well-placed jokes, significant pauses, veiled hints, purposeful kidding, expressive overtones, and many other sign practices. Rules regarding this laxity are quite strict. The communicator has the right to deny that he 'meant anything' by his action,

should his recipients accuse him to his face of having conveyed something unacceptable, and the recipients have the right to act as if nothing, or only something innocuous, has been conveyed." In *The Presentation of Self in Everyday Life*, 190.

31 Friedrich Nietzsche, "On Truth and Lies in a Nonmoral Sense," in *Philosophy and Truth: Selection for Nietzsche's Notebooks of the Early 1870's*, ed. and trans. Daniel Breanzenle (Atlantic Highlands, N.J.: Humanities Press, 1979).

32 Ibid., 84.

33 Kupferschmidt, in so doing, in turn implies that the "truth" of the quote is manipulated into an untruth by virtue of the fact that a private utterance was treated as if it were a public proclamation. See Kupferschmidt, *The Supreme Muslim Council*, 239. See Zvi Elpeleg, *Minekudat Re'uto Shel Hamufti* [*In the Eyes of the Mufti: The Essays of Hajj Amin, Translated and Annotated*] (Tel Aviv: Tel Aviv University Press, 1995), especially the chapter entitled "Misgad Al-Asqa Veheichal Shlomo," 157–162.

34 According to Yehosha Porath, al-Muzaffar (apparently formerly al-Muzghr) had been the president of the Damascus chapter of the nationalist organization al-Nadi al-ʿArabi. See Yehosha Porath, *The Emergence of the Palestinian-Arab National Movement, 1918–1929* (London: Frank Cass, 1974), 77–78.

35 Kramer, *Islam Assembled*, 83. For protests see PRO/CO 733/25 and PRO/CO 733/160, 57540. Porath also notes that: "When Skeih ʿAbd al-Qadir al-Muzaffar tried in late 1922 to enlist the support of the Kemalist Turks and the representatives of Persia and Afghanistan in the Arab Struggle in Palestine, he stressed the danger to the al-Aqsa mosque and the need for Pan-Islamic Defense of it." Porath, *The Emergence of the Palestinian-Arab National Movement, 1918–1929*, 263.

36 See ʿAbd al-Qadir al-Muzaffar, *Nidaʾ ʿAmm ila al-ʿAmmat al-Islamiyya min Ikhwanihum Muslima Bayt al-Maqdis wa Saʾir Filastin* [hereafter *Nidaʾ ʿAmm*] (Jerusalem, 1922), ISA/AE65/1721.

37 See the Report of the Hejaz delegation activities to the Arab Executive, 5 Tammuz, 1922, ISA/RG2/AE65/1721. In his unpublished memoirs, Ernest Tatham Richmond describes a private conversation with al-Muzaffar soon after the shaykh returned from the pilgrimage congress in the Hejaz. According to Richmond, al-Muzaffar told him: "The Arabs, even in Palestine, still cling to England, still say in their hearts 'Hell with the English is better than Paradise with the French.' Let England know that their patience cannot last for ever. We have reached a parting of the ways. Let England now decide whether she will allow the Arabs in Palestine to be free to work for their own and England's ends and against Turkish, Russian and French intrigue." Interview of Shaykh ʿAbd al-Qadir al-Muzaffar and Richmond, 28 October 1922, as recorded in Ernest Tatham Richmond, "Mammon in the Holy Land," 1954, E. T. Richmond Papers, 165.

38 Secret Memorandum, 7 November 1922, Storrs to Governorate 5213/G, PEM Storrs Papers Box III/3.

39 Ibid. For the similarities between Storrs's prose and that of standard imperial policing see Ranajit Guha, "The Prose of Counterinsurgency," in *Selected Subaltern*

Studies, ed. Ranajit Guha and Gayatri Chakravorty Spivak (New York: Oxford University Press, 1988), 59.

40 Nida' 'Amm, ISA/AE65/1721.

41 "The Zionist Organization—which is trying to found the Jewish Kingdom in Palestine and steal the Aqsa from Muslims because it was built on the remnants of Solomon's Temple (peace be upon him) and transform the Mosque into their great Temple—is aiming to make Palestine a base for the purpose of enlarging its influence throughout the Arabic Peninsula and the East in its entirety." Ibid.

42 Ibid.; al-Muzaffar's Nida' 'Amm is itself among the first Palestinian political pamphlets of the period to contain images of disputed monuments, though it does not actually reproduce the image it refers to as evidence of Zionist ambitions. The distribution of the image with the crown of Zion in the Hejaz is traceable to 'Abd al-Qadir Rashid, editor of the newspaper al-Jami'a al-'Arabiyya, who apparently bought fifty copies of this image at Jewish shops in Jerusalem and passed them on to the delegation. He also reprinted it in al-Jami'a al-'Arabiyya in December 1928. See Great Britain, "Twenty-Sixth Sitting, Afternoon Sitting: Examination of Abdel Khader Rashid," Friday, 29 November 1929, Colonial 48, Question Nos. 12,006–12,024, p. 477. For detailed analysis of this and other figures of this kind, see chapter 6.

43 Ibid. See also the version in PRO/CO 733/31. British Consulate in Aleppo to FO, 4.8.1922: "The Sionists have gone so far as to publish pictures of the Jerusalem showing sionist flags on its walls, and the crescent on the dome replaced by a sionist crown. They distribute such illustrations to their followers. Their dreams will never be realised as long as there are Moslems who foresee the danger, and as long as the Moslems of the whole world who venerate these holy places consider it a religious and patriotic duty to defend them. The Christians, too, of the East and of the West have [been] alarmed and the political world also. Protests have been made even in the British house of lords. Why do not the Moslems nations make their protests heard[?] The time when the Sionists will see their ambition realised or wrecked is close at hand. On July 15 the League of Nations is to examine the mandate which contains the ill fated promise of Balfour—a promise which is a mortal blow to all the Moslems. We beg all Moslems to think on this fateful date to protest against any violation of our most lawful rights."

44 "Troubles in al-Aqsa Mosque and Muslim World Response: Big Islamic Demonstration at Mecca," al-Qibla (Mecca), 15 July 1922, in ISA/RG2/AE65/1721.

45 PRO/CO 733/31. James Morgan, British consul in Aleppo, to FO, 4 August 1922.

46 PRO/CO 733/31. John Perowne to Arthur James Balfour, 11 July 1922.

47 CID Intelligence Report, 23 August 1922, PEM/Storrs Papers/Box III/3.

48 Colonel Frederick Hermann Kisch (1888–1943) served as director of the Political Department of the Palestine Zionist Executive between 1922 and 1931. As an Anglo-Jewish officer and diplomat, Kisch was selected by Chaim Weizmann for this position for the purpose of improving relations between Zionists and the British administration. He also served as head of the Palestine Executive, Jewish

Agency, 1929–1931. Musa Kazim al-Husayni (1853–1934), a graduate of the Istanbul School of Administration, served as mayor of Jerusalem from March 1918 until he was dismissed by Ronald Storrs in April 1920 for his opposition to British policies toward Zionism. He served as head of the Palestinian Arab Executive from 1920 to 1928, and as head and member of the Palestinian Delegations to London in the 1920s and 1930s. He was a leader and spokesperson for Palestinian national movement until his death in 1934.

49 Frederick Kisch interview of Musa Kazim al-Husayni, 26 April 1923, CZA/S25/518/1 [Tikei Kisch (Kisch diaries)].

>[Kisch]—"You exaggerate. . . . You were just now speaking of them in saying that it is necessary to think about what [or who] brings together and not about what divides. One was wrong [it was a mistake] to inculcate in the spirit of the simplistic masses the idea that the Jews want to seize the Mosque of Omar."
>
>[Musa Kazim al-Husayni]—"It's not us, it's the Jews themselves who had the mosque photographed with the Zionist flag waving over the top of the dome."
>
>[Kisch]—"Say, rather, that it's the work of imbecile enemies of both Jews and Muslims. I myself can assure you that the Jews will always respect the Mosque of Omar and all the Muslim and Christian holy places. Don't Muslims have guard over the tombs of Jewish prophets, of Jewish kings, and even of the great lawgiver, Moses?"
>
>[Musa Kazim al-Husayni]—"Exactly! The Muslims recognize all the prophets and respect them. From all time they have guarded all the Holy Places, those of Christians as well as those of Israelites."

50 In his essay "Regions and Region Behavior," Erving Goffman defines a backstage of social interaction as a "place, reactive to a given performance, where the impression fostered by the performance is knowingly contradicted as a matter of course." In *The Presentation of Self in Everyday Life*, 122. Goffman states: "There tends to be one informal or backstage language of behavior, and another language of behavior for occasions when a performance is being presented. . . . In general, then, backstage conduct is one which allows minor acts which might easily be taken as symbolic of intimacy and disrespect for others present and for the region, while front region conduct is one which disallows such potentially offensive behavior," 128–129.

51 A few months later, at a social gathering at the house of the painter Anna Ticho, Kisch would meet Musa Kazim al-Husayni again, only to record that "he expressed himself as a pure anti-Semite." Kisch, 13 July 1923, CZA/S25/518/1 [Tikei Kisch]. Following the disturbances of August 1929, Kisch recorded what he perceived to be the legacy of the politics of monuments he had himself attempted to work through in the debate with Musa Kazim. Describing the tense week before the actual violence that took place on 23 August 1929, Kisch noted: "The stage was now set for an outbreak of Moslem fanaticism on a grand scale, and although no

serious person could for a moment believe that a single Jew had any idea of menacing the Mosques, the Jews had by systematic provocation been put apparently in the wrong." Frederick H. Kisch, *Palestine Diary*, foreword by Rt. Hon. D. Lloyd George (London: Victor Gollancz, 1938), 250–251. To my knowledge, Musa Kazim al-Husayni left no record of this exchange.

52 The translation of the article in *al-Hurriya* reproduced in *al-Jami'a al-'Arabiyya* states: "Jewish propaganda announces that the Zionists are endeavoring to rebuild Solomon's Temple on the ruins of the Moslem Mosque, second to that of Mecca and Medina. It is even alleged by that propaganda that the various parts of the Temple made of stone, and Iron have been completed in Europe and American and will shortly be gathered in Palestine for the final erection of the building. . . . Those who have raised this Jewish question are quite aware that the fact of announcing the project constitutes a menace to peace in Palestine and fortiori the attempt to carry it out. . . . Should Zionism not be able to bring about the materialisation of all these dreams and imaginary project, it would be satisfied with the donations it could collect among Jews in America and in other countries." CZA/ S25/704/I [Tikei Kisch].

53 Gershon Agronsky to Frederick Kisch, 29 December 1927, CZA/S25/704/I [Tikei Kisch].

54 Kisch to Luke[?], 30 December 1927, CZA/S25/704/I [Tikei Kisch].

6. *Designs on Our Holy Places*

The epigraphs to this chapter are from Great Britain, *Palestine Commission on the Disturbances of August 1929: Minutes of Evidence*, 3 vols., Colonial No. 48 (London: HMSO, 1930), "Twenty-Third Sitting, Afternoon Sitting: Examination of Abdel Khader Rashid by Mr. Silley before the Shaw Commission," Tuesday, 26 November 1929, Question No. 10,699, p. 423 (hereafter Colonial 48); and al-Hajj Amin al-Husayni, grand mufti of Jerusalem, as quoted in the *Egyptian Gazette*, 14 November 1931, 6.

1 Theodor W. Adorno, "Society," in *Aesthetic Theory*, ed. Gretel Adorno and Rolf Tiedemann, trans., ed., and intro. Robert Hullot-Kentor (Minneapolis: University of Minnesota Press, 1997), 236.

2 Ibid.

3 For histories of these indices, see Tzvetan Todorov, *Theories of the Symbol*, trans. Catherine Porter (Ithaca, N.Y.: Cornell University Press, 1982), particularly chap. 6, "Romantic Crisis"; W. J. T. Mitchell, *Picture Theory* (Chicago: University of Chicago Press, 1994); Michael Podro, *Critical Historians of Art* (New Haven, Conn.: Yale University Press, 1982).

4 See Michael Camille, *The Gothic Idol*, for a discussion of idolatry as an ideologeme of the "other." Camille notes: "Ever since its most influential appearance in the Old Testament, idolatry has been invariably regarded as something practiced by someone else—by those 'Philistines' who lack knowledge of 'the truth.'" Michael

Camille, *The Gothic Idol: Ideology and Image-Making in Medieval Art* (Cambridge: Cambridge University Press, 1989), xxv.

5 On the concept of a performative figure, see James Rubin, "Disorder/Order: Revolutionary Art as Performative Representation," in *The French Revolution, 1789–1989: Two Hundred Years of Rethinking*, special issue of *The Eighteenth Century: Theory and Interpretation*, ed. Sandy Petrey (1989): 83–111; and "Jacques-Louis David et la main du peuple: Saisir le site de la représentation," in *David contre David: Actes du Colloque du Musée du Louvre*, vol. 2 (Paris: Documentation Française, 1993), 783–803. For an elaboration of the same concept in the context of architecture, see K. Michael Hays, "Allegory unto Death: An Etiology of Eisenman's Repetition," in *Cities of Artificial Excavation: The Work of Peter Eisenman, 1978–1988*, ed. Jean-François Bédard (Montreal: Canadian Center for Architecture, 1994).

6 Lajnat al-Difaʿ ʿan al-Buraq al Sharif, *Bayan ila Ikhwanina al-Muslimin ʿAmmatan* (Jerusalem, 1347 A.H./1928–29). It appears that the Lajnat al-Difaʿ ʿan al-Buraq al-Sharif, or Defense Committee for the Noble Buraq, formed in 1928 with the emerging conflict over the Buraq/Wailing Wall. After 1928 the SMC established the Jamʿiyyat Hirasat al-Masjid al-Aqsa waʾl-Amakin al-Islamiyya al-Muqaddasa, or Society for the Protection of the Aqsa Mosque and the Islamic Holy Places. On the mufti's clarifications of the differences between them, see Great Britain, Colonial 48, Question Nos. 12,905–12,920, p. 515. For additional sources on the Society for the Protection of the Aqsa Mosque and the Islamic Holy Places, see Philip Mattar, *The Mufti of Jerusalem: Al-Hajj Amin al-Husayni and the Palestinian National Movement* (New York: Columbia University Press, 1988), 42–43.

7 *Bayan ila Ikhwanina al-Muslimin ʿAmmatan.* In the translation of this text, I have relied on the version presented in Colonial 48, because all evidence and translations had to be ratified by the opposing parties. See Great Britain, Colonial 48, Exhibit No. 86, "Translation of a Pamphlet issued in October, 1928, by the Defense Committee of the Noble Burak," 1081–1082.

8 *Bayan ila Ikhwanina al-Muslimin ʿAmmatan.*

9 Ibid.

10 According to the Arab Bureau of the Political Department of the Jewish Agency this pamphlet of 1931 was apparently printed in two versions, one of which was distributed to members of the Islamic Conference and a second shortly thereafter in 1932. See CZA/S25/2967. "T'shuvat Shomrei Misgad al-Aqsa Lehatzharato shel Hadoktor Ch. Arlozorov al 'Hatziyonut Vehamekomot Ha'islami'im Hak'doshim Be'Eretz-Israel" [Response of the Society for the Protection of the Aqsa Mosque to Doctor Chaim Arlozorov's pamphlet, *Zionism and the Islamic Holy Places in Eretz-Israel*].

11 Mahmud al-Abidi, *Mihnat Bayt al-Maqdis* (Cairo: n.p., n.d.).

12 See Great Britain, *Palestine Commission on the Palestine Disturbances of August 1929: Report* (London: HMSO, 1930), Cmd. 3530 [Shaw Report]. The commission was appointed on 13 September 1929 to "inquire into the immediate causes which led to the . . . outbreak in Palestine and to make recommendations as to the steps neces-

189

sary to avoid a recurrance," 3. The commission also produced the three-volume set of the evidence heard in its twenty-nine sittings, encompassing the record of exactly 22,082 questions put to witnesses between 24 October 1929 and 24 December 1929. See Great Britain, Colonial 48. For a secondary source on this, see Pinhas Ofer, "The Commission on the Palestine Disturbances of August 1929: Appointment, Terms of Reference, Procedure and Report," *Middle-Eastern Studies* 21, no. 3 (1985): 349–361.

13 Great Britain, Colonial 48. The representatives of the Zionist Executive before the Shaw Commission were Sir Boyd Merriman, Viscount Erleigh, S. Horowitz, W. A. Davies, S. E. Iaminnski, and L. J. Stein.

14 W. H. Stoker, in Great Britain, Colonial 48, "Forty-Sixth Sitting," Thursday, 26 December 1929, 918. The representatives of the Arab Executive before the Shaw Commission were two English and two Palestinian Arab lawyers: W. H. Stoker, Reginald Silley, ʿAwni ʿAbd al-Hadi, and M. E. Moghannam.

15 Theodor W. Adorno, *Negative Dialectics*, trans. E. B. Ashton (New York: Continuum, 1987), 10.

16 Paul de Man, "Hegel on the Sublime," in *Aesthetic Ideology*, ed. and intro. Andrzej Warminski (Minneapolis: University of Minnesota Press, 1996), 107. The outlines of what would have been his likely response to de Man appear in Adorno's "Skoteinos, or How to Read Hegel," in *Hegel: Three Studies*, trans. Shierry Weber Nicholsen, intro. Shierry Weber Nicholsen and Jeremy J. Shapiro (Cambridge, Mass.: MIT Press, 1994).

17 Great Britain, Colonial 48, "Twenty-Eighth Sitting: Testimony of Haj Amin al-Husseini," Monday, 2 December 1929, Question Nos. 12,572–74, p. 496.

18 Ibid., Question No. 12,591, p. 497.

19 The figure appeared in the newspaper *Dos Yiddishe Folk*, 30 April 1920.

20 Merriman, in Great Britain, Colonial 48, "Forty-Fifth Sitting: Closing statement of Sir Boyd Merriman," Tuesday, 24 December 1929, 879. Here Merriman is referring to the reprint of the image in the 1929 pamphlet *Bayan ila al-ʿAlam al-Islami*. This was the template for the Society for the Protection of the Aqsa Mosque's response to Arlozorov in 1931.

21 See Michael Berkowitz's analysis of this image, which appears first in "Art in Zionist Popular Culture and Jewish National Self-Consciousness," in *Art and Its Uses: The Visual Image and Modern Jewish Society*, Studies in Contemporary Jewry 6, ed. Ezra Mendelsohn (Oxford: Oxford University Press, 1990); and also in his *Zionist Culture and West European Jewry before the First World War* (Chapel Hill: University of North Carolina Press, 1993), 119–143. Believing that Herzl's image helped to "bridge the gap between secular national aspirations and Jewish messianism," Berkowitz states: "One of the most reproduced pictures of Herzl was a photograph taken by E. M. Lilien. It shows Herzl leaning over the balcony of his hotel room in Basel, overlooking the Rhine. It placed Herzl in the present—in Basel, the site of the early Zionist congresses, the temporary hub of the national life of the Jews—but

he was undoubtedly fixed on the future. . . . After his death, this image was imposed on a Jerusalem scene, with Herzl looking towards the Tower of David rising above the walls of the Old City, as a team of Jewish pioneers march to work in the valley between Herzl and the walls. This variation was used for pictures and Jewish National Fund stamps, which along with photographs from Herzl's journey to Palestine in 1898, helped associate Herzl with the Jewish national landscape of *Eretz Israel*," 136–137. Berkowitz does not trace the career of the image after World War I.

22 Great Britain, Colonial 48, "Forty-Sixth Sitting: Closing Statement of Mr. H. Stoker," Thursday, 26 December 1929, 919–920.

23 Ibid., 919.

24 *Bayan Jamʿiyyat Hirasat al-Masjid al-Aqsa waʾl-Amakin al-Islamiyya al-Muqaddasa biʾl Quds*, 1931.

25 CZA/S25/2967, "T'shuvat Shomrei Misgad al-Aqsa Lehatzharato shel Hadoktor Ch. Arlozorov al 'Hatziyonut," 11.

26 Great Britain, Colonial 48, "Twenty-Eighth Sitting: Testimony of Haj Amin al-Husseini," Monday, 2 December 1929, Question No. 12,588, p. 497.

27 Ibid., Question No. 12,611, p. 498 (emphasis added).

28 Ibid., "Twenty-Ninth Sitting, Afternoon Sitting: Testimony of Haj Amin al-Husseini," Tuesday, 3 December 1929, 520.

29 Ibid., Question No. 13,042, p. 520.

30 Ibid., "Thirtieth Sitting, Afternoon Sitting: Testimony of Haj Amin al-Husseini," Wednesday, 4 December 1929, Question Nos. 13,487–91, p. 542.

31 Ibid., Question No. 13,488, p. 542.

32 Eliash was referring to a text published by Marco Antonio Guistiniani in 1546. He also introduced others into evidence from the mid-nineteenth century published by "the old fashioned Jewish rabbis . . . books on ethics." See Great Britain, Colonial 48, "Forty-Third Sitting, Afternoon Sitting: Testimony of Dr. Mordecai Eliash," Question No. 21,052, p. 841.

33 Ibid., Question No. 21,045, p. 840.

34 After Rashid gave this explanation, Sir Boyd Merriman sought clarification of this understanding of the Hebrew writing on the represented monument, asking again if the "Hebrew inscription is [in itself] an offence." One of the Arab Executive's attorneys, Reginald Silley, intervened, saying, "He said taken in conjunction with the rest." Ibid., "Twenty-Fourth Sitting. Cross-Examination of 'Abd al Khader Rashid," Wednesday, 27 November 1929, Question Nos. 10,741–42, p. 425.

35 Ibid., "Forty-Third Sitting, Afternoon Sitting: Testimony of Dr. Mordecai Eliash," Friday, 20 December 1929, Question Nos. 21,057–58, p. 841.

36 Ibid., Question No. 21,058, p. 841.

37 Ibid., Question No. 21,059, p. 841 (emphasis added).

38 Ibid., 841.

39 Ibid. According to the Arab Bureau of the Political Department of the Jewish

Agency for Palestine, this image was drawn by a man named Moshe Ben-Itzhak Mizrahi, an elderly immigrant from Persia who had been living in Jerusalem for over thirty years.

40 Ibid., "Forty-Fifth Sitting: Closing statement of Sir Boyd Merriman," Tuesday, 24 December 1929, 878.

41 Ibid., 879.

42 Ibid., 879.

43 Gayatri Chakravorty Spivak, "Subaltern Studies: Deconstructing Historiography," in *In Other Worlds: Essays in Cultural Politics* (New York: Methuen, 1988), 197. Recognizing that I have reached a somewhat different conclusion from Spivak concerning that "space for a change" (see chapter 4), I am not, in any sense attempting to present myself as a metacritical "Merriman" to her "Silley," so much as I am trying to trace the "profane illumination achieved by the dialectical image, dislocating chains of concordance with one hand, reconstellating in accord with a mimetic snap, with the other." See Michael Taussig, *Mimesis and Alterity: A Particular History of the Senses* (New York: Routledge, 1993), 12.

44 Paul de Man, "Rhetoric of Temporality," in *Blindness and Insight: Essays in the Rhetoric of Contemporary Criticism*, 2d ed. rev.; intro. Wlad Godzich (Minneapolis: University of Minnesota Press, 1983), 189.

45 Ibid., 208.

46 W. H. Stoker in Great Britain, Colonial 48, "Twenty-Eighth Sitting: Testimony of Muhammad Hajj Amin al Husseini," Monday, 2 December 1929, Question No. 12,594, p. 497.

47 Ibid. See also the grand mufti's presentation of this figure in the *Egyptian Gazette*, reproduced in the second epigraph of this chapter.

48 Great Britain, Colonial 48, "Twenty-Ninth Sitting, Afternoon Sitting: Testimony of Haj Amin Al Husseini," Tuesday, 3 December 1929, Question No. 13,063, p. 521. This presentation is repeated in 1931, where, in the bayan of the Society for the Protection of the Aqsa Mosque, the figure appears with a caption reading: "The Jews distribute a picture printed on thick paper. On one side of this picture, is the Noble Buraq and in it, a door leading to the Haram al-Sharif in the form of a Jewish synagogue," in *Bayan Jamʿiyyat Hirasat al-Masjid al-Aqsa waʾl-Amakin al-Islamiyya al-Muqaddasa biʾl Quds*, 1931–32. (The Arab Bureau of the Political Department of the Jewish Agency is discussing a children's flag for the holiday of Simhat Torah.)

49 Great Britain, Colonial 48, "Twenty-Ninth Sitting, Afternoon Sitting: Testimony of Haj Amin Al Husseini," Tuesday, 3 December 1929, Question Nos. 13,064–67, p. 521.

50 Ibid., Question No. 13,065, p. 521. The Arab Bureau of Political Department of the Jewish Agency identifies the artist as a certain Rubinstein and the press as Klinkstein. See CZA/S25/2976, 17.

51 Great Britain, Colonial 48, "Twenty-Ninth Sitting, Afternoon Sitting: Testimony of Haj Amin Al Husseini," Tuesday, 3 December 1929, Question No. 13,070, p. 521.

52 Ibid., Question No. 13,071, p. 521.

53 "Conflict between a conception of the self in its authentically temporal predicament and a defensive strategy that tries to hide from this self-knowledge," Paul de Man, "Hegel on the Sublime," in *Aesthetic Ideology*, 208.

54 Great Britain, Colonial 48, "Twenty-Fourth Sitting: Cross-Examination of 'Abd al Khader Rashid," Wednesday, 27 November 1929, Question Nos. 10,707–10,776, pp. 424–426.

55 "All of these pictures were found for the SMC by [Rashid] (husband to a Jewish woman and someone who knows the Hebrew language [a comment made by a reporter in the Bureau]), during the Shaw Commission who was at one time a secretary of the Arab Executive and Hebrew translator for the board of the *al-Jami'a al-'Arabiyya* publication. At his request the artist Pikovsky prepared the picture for press." See CZA/S25/2967.

56 See Great Britain, Colonial 48, "Twenty-Eighth Sitting: Testimony of Haj Amin Al Husseini," Monday, 2 December 1929, Questions Nos. 12,582–87, pp. 496–497.

57 Ibid., Question no. 12,586, p. 496.

58 Ibid.

59 Ibid.

60 Ibid., Question No. 12,587, p. 497.

61 Let me note that I am aware of the fact that in allegory, the problem of intention is unavoidable. As Peter Burger has noted, "The allegorist pulls one element of the totality of the life context, isolating it, depriving it of its function. Allegory is therefore essentially fragment. . . . [T]he allegorist joins the isolated fragments of reality and thereby creates meaning. This is posited meaning; it does not derive from the original context of the fragments." Peter Burger, *Theory of the Avant-Garde* (Minneapolis: University of Minnesota Press, 1984), 69. But here, I argue, in Merriman's working theory there is a kind of indictment of an allegory of a second order: the indictment of an intention in the sense that someone feigns the labor of the original allegorist, by relying on the index of another's allegorical performance, or worse, by modifying the "original context"—the figure—in advance in such as a way to guarantee a very specific "posited meaning."

62 Roman Jakobson and Morris Halle, *Fundamentals of Language*, 2d rev. ed. (The Hague: Mouton, 1971), 90.

63 Great Britain, Colonial 48, "Forty-Fifth Sitting: Closing Statements of Sir Boyd Merriman," Tuesday, 24 December 1929, 879. (Merriman is referring to the index superimposed upon the image in "the little grey book," the *Bayan ila Ikhwanina al-Muslimin 'Ammatan* (fig. 4), a publication in whose making the lawyer tried to implicate the mufti via the organization, and the printer, who published it.) See closing statement of Sir Boyd Merriman in Great Britain, Colonial 48, "Forty-Fifth Sitting: Closing statement of Sir Boyd Merriman," Tuesday, 24 December 1929, 872–906.

64 Edmund Leach, *Claude Lévi-Strauss* (Harmondsworth, England: Penguin Books, 1974), 48.

65 All present at the inquiry seemed to concur that on 15 August 1929 the picture was

193

published in al-Jami'a al-'Arabiyya with the caption reading: "Jewish ambitions with regard to the Mosque of Omar and the Holy Dome of the Rock. The Dome of the Mosque and above it the Jewish Crown and the Jewish religious symbols as it appears to them in their ambitions and dreams. The reader may see in the picture other Moslem religious places, which the Jews in their ambitions seek to acquire and to own." However, after reviewing two different microfilm versions of al-Jami'a al-'Arabiyya, I was not able find this cropped figure and its caption as described by Merriman in the issue of 15 August 1929. Instead, an image quite like it appeared on 11 October 1928. Having no access to originals of the newspaper, I was incapable of reconciling this discrepancy.

66　Great Britain, Colonial 48, Question No. 12,993, p. 517. To this, the mufti simply retorted that Merriman's revelation meant that the original picture was itself only "a souvenir for their ambitions."

67　Ibid., "Twenty-Ninth Sitting, Afternoon Sitting: Testimony of Haj Amin Al Husseini," Tuesday, 3 December 1929, Question No. 13,056, p. 521.

68　Ibid., "Forty-Fifth Sitting: Closing Statement of Sir Boyd Merriman," Tuesday, 24 December 1929, 879–80.

69　Theodor W. Adorno, "Cultural Criticism and Society," in Prisms, trans. Samuel Weber and Shierry Weber (1967; Cambridge, Mass.: MIT Press, 1988), 31.

70　James George Frazer, The Golden Bough: A Study in Magic and Religion, part 1, 3d ed. (Vienna, 1950), chapter 3, as cited in Jakobson and Halle, Fundamentals of Language, 95.

Conclusion: A Terrible Caricature

The epigraph is from Theodor W. Adorno, Minima Moralia: Reflections from Damaged Life, trans. E. F. N. Jephcott (rpt., London: Verso, 1996), 74.

1　Chaim Arlozorov, as cited in Shlomo Avineri, Arlosoroff (London: Weidenfeld and Nicholson, 1989), 72. Arlozorov suggested that "revisionist propaganda created, especially among certain younger circles, a nationalistic phraseology about rule by force, without having created—or being able to create—the means for such a rule," Ibid. The response of Vladimir Jabotinsky, the leader of the Zionist Revisionist Movement, to this kind of argument was that Labor Zionists (and specifically, David Ben-Gurion): "underestimate the value of a gesture and a slogan; the word, the formula possess enormous power." David Ben-Gurion, Zikhronot, vol. 2 (Tel-Aviv: Am Oved, 1976), 186, as quoted in Mitchell Cohen, Zion and State: Nation, Class, and the Shaping of Modern Israel (Oxford: Basil Blackwell, 1987), 140.

2　Chaim Arlozorov, K'tavim, vol. 1 (Tel-Aviv: Devir, 1934), 105, 120 respectively, as cited in Avineri, Arlosoroff, 70–72. Arlozorov is specifically referring here to the provocations of the Revisionist right in Zionist politics, and in particular, to those of the Society for the Defense of the Kotel in 1928. For al-Qassam's remarkable, if apocryphal rebuke of the mufti, see Ann Mosely Lesch, Arab Politics in Palestine, 1917–

1939: The Frustration of a Nationalist Movement (Ithaca, N.Y.: Cornell University Press, 1979), 108.

3 Theodor W. Adorno, *Negative Dialectics*, trans. E. B. Ashton (New York: Continuum, 1987), 404.

4 An immanent procedure "takes seriously the principle that it is not ideology in itself which is untrue, but rather its pretension to correspond to reality." Theodor W. Adorno, "Cultural Criticism and Society," in *Prisms*, trans. Samuel Weber and Shierry Weber (1967; Cambridge, Mass.: MIT Press, 1988).

5 Adorno, "Cultural Criticism and Society," 31.

6 The standpoint of freedom, according to this model, would lie in one's political renunciation of a fetishism of objects, thereby associating a sophisticated resignation with reason's triumph over appearances, or mere ideology.

7 Adorno, "Cultural Criticism and Society," 31.

195

I. ARCHIVAL AND MANUSCRIPT SOURCES

Israel

Central Archives for the History of the Jewish People (CAHJ), Jerusalem
P3   Judah Leon Magnes Papers

Central Zionist Archives (CZA), Jerusalem
A175, A175a   Personal Files, Richard Kauffmann
A209   Personal Files, Gershon Agron [Agronsky]
L3   Zionist Commission, Jerusalem, 1918–1921
L4   Zionist Commission, Jaffa, 1918–1921
L18   Palestine Land Development Company, Tel-Aviv, Jerusalem, Berlin, 1918–1921
S2   Executive of the World Zionist Organization and the Jewish Agency for Palestine, Education Department, 1913–1932

S14	Executive of the World Zionist Organization and the Jewish Agency for Palestine, Technical Department, 1926–1948
S25	Executive of the World Zionist Organization and the Jewish Agency for Palestine, Political Department, 1921–1948
S53	Eliezer Kaplan, "Shikun" Ltd., 1933–1948
S90	Executive of the World Zionist Organization and the Jewish Agency for Palestine, Economic Research Bureau, 1936–1952
Z4	Central Office of the World Zionist Organization and the Jewish Agency for Palestine, Central Office, London, 1911–1920

Israel Antiquities Authority (IAA), Jerusalem
Folios of photographs and architectural materials originally belonging to Austen
St. Barbe Harrison, government architect

Israel State Archives (ISA), Jerusalem

RG 2	Palestine Government, Office of the Chief Secretary; series CS, CS Pol., and CS Admin.
RG 3	Palestine Government, Office of the Attorney General
RG 12	Palestine Government, Public Works Department; series 2, Police and Prisons; 3, Schools; 21, Antiquities; 11, untitled files on government structures
RG 23	Palestine Government, District Commissioner's Office, Jerusalem
RG 65	"Abandoned" Papers; Supreme Muslim Shariʿa Council (SMC), and Arab Executive (AE) series
RG 103	Private Papers of Edwin Samuel

City of Jerusalem Municipal Archives (JMA), Jerusalem

RG361–62	Felicity Ashbee Papers (Reproductions of Charles Robert Ashbee Papers undertaken by JMA)
RG362	Pro-Jerusalem Society, Minutes, 1919–1921
RG829	Jerusalem Local Building and Town Planning Commission [JBTPC], Minutes, 1921–1937 (including minutes of Central Town Planning Commission)
RG830	Jerusalem Local Building and Town Planning Commission [JBTPC], Minutes, 1937–1948 (including minutes of Jerusalem District Town Planning Commission)
RG1107	City Engineer's Office, 1933–1948
RG1108	
RG1109	
RG3583	
RG848	
RG850	
RG853	

United Kingdom

Kings College Library (KCL), Modern Manuscript Centre, Cambridge
Charles Robert Ashbee Papers

Pembroke College Library (PEM), Cambridge, England
Sir Ronald Storrs Papers

Middle East Centre (MEC), St. Antony's College, Oxford
Frederick Wentworth Foster-Turner Papers
Sir Charles Tegart Papers
Humphrey Bowman Papers

National Library of Scotland (NLS), Edinburgh
10516   Sir Patrick Geddes Papers, Correspondence, 1919–1924
10517   Sir Patrick Geddes Papers, Correspondence, 1925–1928
10518   Sir Patrick Geddes Papers, Correspondence, 1928–1932
10546   Sir Patrick Geddes Papers, Correspondence received, 1918
10573   Sir Patrick Geddes Papers, Correspondence with Frank Mears
10613   Sir Patrick Geddes Papers, *The Proposed Hebrew University of Jerusalem, Preliminary Report*, December 1919
10629   Lectures and Papers of Sir Frank Mears
10658–82 Sketchbooks of Sir Frank Mears, 1900–1953

Public Record Office (PRO), Kew, London
CO733   Colonial Office, Palestine Original Correspondence, 1921–1945
FO371   Foreign Office, Palestine Original Correspondence
FO800   Records of Private Office and Private Papers; Sir Mark Sykes Papers

Strathclyde University (STR), Glasgow
T-Ged   Sir Patrick Geddes Papers

United States

Columbia University, Rare Book and Manuscript Library (CU), New York
MSS73–90 Julian Clarence Levi Papers

Columbia University, Avery Drawings Collection (CU-AV), New York
Taylor and Levi Architects, drawings for the Rosenbloom Building, Hebrew University, Jerusalem, 1930–1931

II. PLANNING REPORTS

Ashbee, Charles Robert. *Jerusalem Park System*. 17 October 1918. JMA/CRA-FA/361/A58/IV-I.

———. *Report by Mr. C. R. Ashbee on the Arts and Crafts of Jerusalem and District.* August 1918. JMA/CRA-FA/361/A58.

————. *Report on the Antiquities of Jerusalem*. 13 March 1920. Lambeth Palace Library (15309/P).

Baramki, Dimitri. *Report of Chief Inspector of Department of Antiquities re Condition of the Old City Walls and Citadel Grounds*. From a field inspection carried out on 2 August 1934. JMA/850/ Unnumbered file entitled "Condition of the City Walls, 34–35."

Geddes, Patrick. *Jerusalem Actual and Possible, A Preliminary Report to the Chief Administrator of Palestine and the Military Governor of Jerusalem on Town Planning and City Improvements*. November 1919. CZA/A209/132.

————. *Proposed Hebrew University of Jerusalem, Preliminary Report by Patrick Geddes, Assisted by Captain Frank Mears*. December 1919. NLS/PG/TS10613.

Geddes, Patrick, and Frank Mears. *Interim Report on the Hebrew University, Jerusalem*. 6 July 1920. STR/PG/121200.

Kemalettin, Mimar. "Harem-i Şerīf." Unpublished report, Jerusalem, 1922.

McLean, William Hannah. *Jerusalem Town Planning Scheme, Explanatory Note*. 20 August 1918. Report to the Commander in Chief at Advanced General Headquarters in Palestine. JMA/CRA-FA/361/A58.

III. GREAT BRITAIN: OFFICIAL PUBLICATIONS OF
THE BRITISH GOVERNMENT CONCERNING PALESTINE

First Report on Agricultural Development and Land Settlement in Palestine [French Report]: Palestine, 1931.

Government of Palestine, Annual Reports of the Public Works Department, 1924–1932. 1924–1927 by H. B. Lees; 1927, by F. Pudsey.

Government of Palestine, Town Planning Adviser, Annual Reports, 1936–1938. By H. Kendall.

Palestine: Disturbances in May 1921. Report of the Commission of Inquiry with Correspondence Relating Hereto. Cmd. 1540, 1921 [Haycraft Report].

Palestine Commission on the Disturbances of August 1929: Minutes of Evidence. 3 vols. Colonial No. 48. London: HMSO, 1930.

Report of the Palestine Commission on the Disturbances of August 1929. Cmd. 3530. London: HMSO, 1930 [Shaw Report].

Palestine: Statement of Policy with Regard to British Policy, Cmd. 3582, 1930 [White Paper on the Shaw Report].

Palestine Royal Commission, Minutes of Evidence. Colonial No. 134 London: HMSO, 1937 [Peel Commission Evidence].

The Western or Wailing Wall in Jerusalem. Memorandum by the Secretary of State for the Colonies. Cmd. 3229. 1928.

IV. PAMPHLETS AND REPORTS

Arabic

Ahad Fudala' al-Muslimin, *Bayan wa-Radd ʿala Bayan al-Majlis al-Islami al-A ʿla muwajjah li-Kull Muslim fi al-ʿAlam al-Islami ʿAmmatan wa-fi Filastin Khassatan*. Jerusalem, 1924.

Arlozorov, Chaim. ʿAl-Sahyuniyya waʾl-Amakin al-Islamiyya al-Muqaddasa fi Falastin. Jerusalem: Jewish Agency for Palestine, 1931.

Idarat al-Awqaf wa-Lajnat ʿImarat al-Haram al-Sharif. Bayan fi al-Dakhl waʾl-kharj li-ʿImarat al Haram al-Sharif. Jerusalem, 1924.

Jamʿiyyat Hirasat al-Masjid al-Aqsa waʾl-Amakin al-Islamiyya al-Muqaddasa. Bayan ila al-ʾAlam al-Islami. Jerusalem, 1929.

Jamʿiyyat Hirasat al-Masjid al-Aqsa waʾl-Amakin al-Islamiyya al-Muqaddasa biʾl-Quds. Bayan Jamʿiyyat Hirasat al-Masjid al-Aqsa waʾl-Amakin al-Islamiyya al-Muqaddasa biʾl-Quds. Jerusalem, 1931–32.

al-Khalidi, Raghib. ʿArif Hifkmat al-Nashashibi, Hasan al-Budayri, Bayan ila al-ʿAlam al-Islami ʿAmmatan ʿan al-Amakin al-Muqaddasa al-Islamiyya fi Filastin. Jerusalem, n.d.

Lajnat al-Difaʿ ʿan al-Buraq al-Sharif. Bayan ila Ikhwanina al-Muslimin ʿAmmatan. Jerusalem, 1928–29.

al-Majlis al-Sharʿi al-Islami al-Aʿla. Bayan al-Majlis al-Sharʿi al-Islami al-Aʿla fi Filastin li-Sanat 1340–1 hijriyya. Jerusalem, 1923.

al-Majlis al-Sharʿi al-Islami al-Aʿla. Bayan al-Majlis al-Sharʿi al-Islami al-Aʿla fi Filastin li-Sanat 1341-2 hijriyya. Jerusalem, 1924.

al-Majlis al-Sharʿi al-Islami al-Aʿla. Bayan al-Majlis al-Islami al-Aʿla li-Sanat 1342–1343 wafqa 1924–1925. Jerusalem, n.d.

al-Majlis al-Sharʿi al-Islami al-Aʿla. Bayan al-Majlis al-Islami al-Aʿla li-Sanat 1344 hijriyya wafqa 1925–1926. Jerusalem, n.d.

al-Majlis al-Sharʿi al-Islami al-Aʿla. Bayan al-Majlis al-Islami al-Aʿla li-Sanat 1345–47 H. wafqa 1928. Jerusalem, n.d.

al-Majlis al-Sharʿi al-Islami al-Aʿla. Bayan al-Majlis al-Islami al-Aʿla li-Sanat 1347–8 hijriyya wafqa 1929. Jerusalem, n.d.

al-Majlis al-Sharʿi al-Islami al-Aʿla. Bayan al-Majlis al-Islami al-Aʿla li-Sanat 1349–50 hijriyya wafqa 1931. Jerusalem, n.d.

al-Majlis al-Sharʿi al-Islami al-Aʿla. Bayan al-Majlis al-Sharʿi al-Islami al-Aʿla fi-Filastin ʿan ʿImarat Qubbat al-Masjid al-Asqa al-Mubarak wa-Ma Tamma min ʿImara fi al-Amakin al-Ukhra min al-Haram al-Sharif waʾl Barnamaj al-Muqarrar li-Itman al-ʿImara. Jerusalem, 1928.

al-Majlis al-Sharʿi al-Islami al-Aʿla. Majmuʿat Taqarir al-Taftish 1940. Jerusalem, n.d.

al-Muzaffar, ʿAbd al-Qadir. Nidaʾ ʿAmm ila al-ʾAmmat al-Islamiyya min Ikhwanihum Muslima Bayt al-Maqdis wa Saʾir Filastin. Jerusalem, 1922.

English

An Appeal to the Friends of Jewish Culture. New York, 1922.

Canaan, Tawfiq. Conflict in the Land of Peace. Jerusalem: 1936.

———. The Palestine Arab Cause. Jerusalem: 1936.

Comments on Dr. Canaan's Pamphlet "The Palestine Arab Cause," by a Native of Palestine. Jerusalem, 1936.

The Jerusalem Young Men's Christian Association. Jerusalem: Palestine, 1933.

Jewish Agency for Palestine. *Memorandum on Jerusalem Under Partition.* Jerusalem, August 1938.

Supreme Moslem Council. *A Brief Guide to al-Haram al-Sharif, Jerusalem.* Jerusalem, 1924; repr. in 1925, 1930.

Hebrew

Misrad le'inyanei datot, Reshut hamekomot hak'dushim, Hakeren lemoreshet hakotel hama'aravi. *Minheret Hakotel Hama'aravi.* Jerusalem, n.d.

V. MISCELLANEOUS UNPUBLISHED MANUSCRIPTS AND PRIVATE PAPERS

Ernest Tatham Richmond Papers [E. T. Richmond Papers]

Correspondence

Series ETR-HWR. Correspondence between Ernest Tatham Richmond and Admiral Herbert W. Richmond.

Section A: Letters 1–31. 11 November 1920 to 3 October 1923.

Section B: Letters 32–33. 6 February 1924 and 13 June 1927 [1926?].

Section C: Letters 34–78. 7 September 1927 to 24 January 1937 [plus unnumbered letter of 18 May 1937].

Section D: Letters 79–99. 28 August 1937 to 4 May 1939.

Section E: Letters 100–175. 6 January 1940 to 11 April 1946.

Series ETR-RS. Correspondence between Ernest Tatham Richmond and Sir Ronald Storrs. 12 October 1951 to 20 October 1953.

Series ETR-MMR. Correspondence between Ernest Tatham Richmond and Margaret Mary Richmond (née Muriel Lubbock).

Unpublished manuscripts

Richmond, Ernest Tatham. "An Administrative Cesspool." 103 pp., diary of 1922, introduction 1946. Also titled "Palestine Notes Made between February 1922 and November 1922."

———. "A Dialogue [Imaginary] about Foreign Dominion." 66 pp., 1912. Also titled "Foreign Dominion: A Dialogue between Abadallah el-Kendahy and Richard Dinsdale."

———. "Gerione in the Holy Land." 1946. Also referred to as "The Rule of Gerione: A Number of Writings about British Policy in Palestine, 1924–1946." Compendium of Richmond's writings that includes anonymously and pseudonymously published essays.

———. "Liber Maiorum, ETR and MMR." N.d., after 1949, 270 pp.

———. "Mammon in the Holy Land." 1954, 545 pp.

Miscellaneous unpublished records

Memento Album Given as Gift to ETR by Technical Office of Architects Restoring the Aqsa Mosque, 1924, photo album, 17 pp.

Miscellaneous Unpublished Manuscripts and Private Papers

Chapman, Rupert. "British Levantine Archaeology, 1918–1939: The Intellectual Framework." London: Palestine Exploration Fund, n.d.

Gibson, Shimon. "British Archaeology in the Holy Land during the Mandate Period." London: Palestine Exploration Fund, n.d.

Goldman, Shalom. "Building the Jerusalem YMCA: American Perceptions and Mandate Palestine Realities." Dartmouth College, 7 June 1992.

Keith-Roach, Edward. "Pasha of Jerusalem." Pembroke College, Cambridge.

VI. INTERVIEWS

Professor Roy Gazzard, Durham, 17 December 1992.

Professor Julius Posener, New York, 10 September 1992.

VII. NEWSPAPERS AND PERIODICALS

al-Ahram (Cairo)

Daily Telegraph

Do'ar Hayom (Tel-Aviv)

Egyptian Gazette

Ha'aretz (Tel-aviv)

al-Jami'a al-'Arabiyya (Jerusalem)

The Times (London)

Observer (London)

Oriente Moderno (Rome)

Dos Yiddishe Folk (New York)

VIII. BOOKS AND ARTICLES

al-Abidi, Mahmud. Mihnat Bayt al-Maqdis. Cairo: n.p., n.d.

———. Qudsunah. Cairo: Ma'had al-Buhuth wa al-Dirasat al-'Arabiyya, 1972.

Abu-Amr, Ziad. Islamic Fundamentalism in the West Bank and Gaza: Muslim Brotherhood and Islamic Jihad. Bloomington: Indiana University Press, 1994.

Abu-Ghazaleh, Adnan. Arab Cultural Nationalism in Palestine During the British Mandate. Beirut: Institute for Palestine Studies, 1973.

Abu-Lughod, Janet. "Moroccan Cities: Apartheid and the Serendipity of Conservation." In African Themes, Northwestern University Studies in honour of G. M. Carter, ed. Ibrahim Abu-Lughod. Evanston, Ill.: 1975.

———. Rabat: Urban Apartheid in Morocco. Princeton, N.J.: Princeton University Press, 1980.

Adorno, Theodor W. "The Actuality of Philosophy." Telos 31 (spring 1977): 120–133.

———. Aesthetic Theory. Ed. Gretel Adorno and Rolf Tiedemann. Trans., ed., and intro. Robert Hullot-Kentor. Minneapolis: University of Minnesota Press, 1997.

————. *Critical Models: Interviews and Catchwords*. Trans. Henry W. Pickford. New York: Columbia University Press, 1998.

————. "Cultural Criticism and Society." In *Prisms*, trans. Samuel Weber and Shierry Weber. 1967; Cambridge, Mass.: MIT Press, 1988.

————. "Extorted Reconciliation: On Georg Lukacs' Realism in Our Time." In *Notes to Literature*, vol. 1, trans. Shierry Weber Nicholsen. New York: Columbia University Press, 1992.

————. "Freudian Theory and the Pattern of Fascist Propaganda." In *The Essential Frankfurt School Reader*, ed. Andrew Arato and Eike Gebhardt. New York: Continuum Books, 1988.

————. "Functionalism Today." *Oppositions* 17 (summer 1979): 31–41.

————. *Hegel: Three Studies*. Trans. Shierry Weber Nicholsen, intro. Shierry Weber Nicholsen and Jeremy J. Shapiro. Cambridge, Mass.: MIT Press, 1994.

————. "The Idea of Natural History" (1932; 1973), trans. Robert Hullot-Kentor. *Telos* 60 (summer 1984): 111–124.

————. *The Jargon of Authenticity*. Trans. Knut Tarnowski and Fredric Will. Evanston, Ill.: Northwestern University Press, 1973.

————. *Kierkegaard: Construction of the Aesthetic*. Trans., ed., and foreword by Robert Hullot-Kentor. Minneapolis: University of Minnesota Press, 1989.

————. *Minima Moralia: Reflections from Damaged Life*. Trans. E. F. N. Jephcott. Rpt., London: Verso, 1996.

————. *Negative Dialectics*. Trans. E. B. Ashton. New York: Continuum, 1987.

————. "A Portrait of Walter Benjamin." In *Prisms*, trans. Samuel Weber and Shierry Weber. Cambridge, Mass.: MIT Press, 1988.

————. "Resignation." In *Critical Models: Interventions and Catchwords*. European Perspectives: A Series in Social Thought and Cultural Criticism, ed. Lawrence D. Kritzman, trans. Henry W. Pickford. New York: Columbia University Press, 1998.

————. "Subject and Object." In *The Essential Frankfurt School Reader*, ed. Andrew Arato and Eike Gebhardt. New York: Continuum Books, 1988.

————. "Theses upon Art and Religion Today." *Kenyon Review* 7 (fall 1945): 677–682.

————. "What Does Coming to Terms with the Past Mean?" (1960). In *Bitburg in Moral and Political Perspective*, ed. G. Hartmann. Indianapolis: Indiana University Press, 1986.

Adorno, Theodor W., et al. *Aesthetics and Politics: Debates between Ernst Bloch, Georg Lukacs, Bertolt Brecht, Walter Benjamin and Theodor Adorno*. Afterword by Fredric Jameson. London: NLB, 1977.

Ahad Ha'am [Asher Ginzberg]. "Sacred and Profane." In *Selected Essays of Ahad Ha'am*. New York: Atheneum, 1962.

Alcalay, Ammiel. *After Jews and Arabs: Remaking Levantine Culture*. Minneapolis: University of Minnesota Press, 1993.

Alexander Baerwald, 1877–1930, Architect and Artist. Exh. Cat. National Museum of Science, Planning and Technology, Haifa: n.d.

Allitt, Patrick. *Catholic Converts: British and American Intellectuals Turn to Rome.* Ithaca, N.Y.: Cornell University Press, 1997.

Alsberg, P. A. "Hama'avak al Iriyat Yerushalayim Bit'kufat Hamandat." In P'rakim Betoldot Yerushalayim Bazman Hachadash, Sefer Zikaron LeYa'acov Herzog, ed. E. Shaltiel. Jerusalem: Yad Ben-Zvi, 1981.

Althusser, Louis. "Ideology and Ideological State Apparatuses." In *Lenin and Philosophy and Other Essays.* London: New Left Books, 1971.

Andrews, Fannie Fern. *The Holy Land under Mandate.* Westport, Conn.: Hyperion Press, 1976.

Antonius, George. *The Arab Awakening: The Story of the Arab National Movement.* New York: G. P. Putnam and Sons, 1946.

Appadurai, Arjun. *Modernity at Large: Cultural Dimensions of Globalization.* Minneapolis: University of Minnesota Press, 1996.

Apter, Emily. "Female Trouble in the Colonial Harem." *Differences* 4, no. 1 (1992): 205–234.

———. *Feminizing the Fetish: Psychoanalysis and Narrative Obsession in turn-of-the-century France.* Ithaca, N.Y.: Cornell University Press, 1991.

Apter, Emily, and William Pietz, eds. *Fetishism as Cultural Discourse.* Ithaca, N.Y.: Cornell University Press, 1993.

Arato, Andrew, and Eike Gebhardt, eds. *The Essential Frankfurt School Reader.* New York: Continuum Books, 1988.

Arendt, Hannah. *On Violence.* New York: Harcourt, Brace and Ward, 1970.

al-'Arif, 'Arif. *A Brief Guide to the Dome of the Rock and al-Haram al-Sharif.* Jerusalem: Supreme Awqaf Council, 1959.

———. *al-Mufassal fi Tarikh al-Quds.* 1961; rpt., Jerusalem: F. Yusuf, 1986.

———. *al-Nakba: Nakbat Bayt al-Maqdis wa al-firdaws al-mafqud, 1947–1952.* Sayda: al-Maktaba al-Misriyya, 1962.

———. *Ta'rikh Qubbat al-Sakhra al-Musharifa wa'l Masjid al-Aqsa al-Mubarak wa'l-Mahatt 'an Ta'rikh al-Quds.* Jerusalem, 1955.

Arlozorov, Chaim. "Nisayon Lesikum" (1929). In *Kitvei Chaim Arlosorov,* vol. 1, *Choma Shel Zchuchit* [Glass Curtain]. Tel-Aviv: A. J. Stybel, 1934.

———. *Yoman Yerushalayim.* Tel-Aviv: Mifleget Po'alei Israel, 1949.

Armstrong, Karen. *Jerusalem: One City, Three Faiths.* New York: Ballantine Books, 1997.

Arnon-Ohanah, Yuval. *Fal'achim Bamered Ha'aravi Be'Eretz-Israel, 1936–1939.* Tel-Aviv: Mahon Shiloach, 1978.

Asali, K. J. "Jerusalem under the Ottomans, 1516–1831 A.D." In *Jerusalem in History,* ed. K. J. Asali. New York: Olive Branch Press, 1990.

Ashbee, Charles Robert, ed. *Jerusalem, 1918–1920, Being the Records of the Pro-Jerusalem Society.* London: John Murray, 1921.

———. ed. *Jerusalem, 1920–1922, Being the Records of the Pro-Jerusalem Society.* London: John Murray, 1924.

———. *The Kings of Min Zaman.* London: Oxford University Press, 1938.

————. *Kingfisher out of Egypt: A Dialogue in an English Garden*. London: Humphrey Milford and Oxford University Press, 1934.

————. *A Palestine Notebook*. New York: Doubleday, Page, 1923.

————. *Where the Great City Stands: A Study in the New Civics*. London: Essex House Press, 1917.

Austin, J. L. *How to Do Things with Words*. Ed. J. O. Urmson and Marina Sbisa. 1962; Cambridge, Mass.: Harvard University Press, 1975.

Avineri, Shlomo. *Arlosoroff*. London: Weidenfeld and Nicholson, 1989.

El-Awaisi, Abd Al-Fattah Muhammad. *The Muslim Brothers and the Palestine Question, 1928–1947*. London: Tauris Academic Studies, 1998.

Baedeker, Karl. *Palestine and Syria, with the Chief Routes through Mesopotamia and Babylonia: Handbook for Travellers*. Leipzig: Karl Baedeker, 1906.

Baltrusaitis, Jurgis. *Aberrations: An Essay on the Legend of Forms*. Cambridge, Mass.: MIT Press, 1989.

Baramki, Dimitri C. *The Art and Architecture of Ancient Palestine, A Survey of the Archaeology of Palestine from the Earliest Times to the Ottoman Conquest*. Palestine Books 23. Beirut: Palestine Liberation Organization Research Center, 1969.

Barkai, Gabriel. "The Garden Tomb: Was Jesus Buried Here?" *Biblical Archaeology Review* 12, no. 2 (1986): 40–56.

Barnett, Michael N. *Dialogues in Arab Politics: Negotiations in Regional Order*. New York: Columbia University Press, 1998.

Barshai, Bezalel. "Hahachana Lep'tichat Ha'universita B'Yerushalayim Ush'noteiha Harishonot." [In Hebrew] *Cathedra* 25 (September 1982): 65–78.

Bartlett, W. H. *Jerusalem Revisited*. London: Arthur Hall, Virtue, 1855.

————. *Walks about the City and Environs of Jerusalem*. London: Longman, 1825.

Baudrillard, Jean. *For a Critique of the Political Economy of the Sign*. Trans. and intro. Charles Levin. Telos Press: St. Louis, Mo.: 1981.

Behor, Gai, and the Sokhnuyot hayedi'ot [News Services]. "Arab League: The Aim of Israel Is to Undermine the Aqsa Mosque and to Build the Temple." *Ha'aretz*, 26 September 1996, A4.

Bellamy, Edward. *Looking Backward, 2000–1887*. Boston: Ticknor, 1888.

Belloc, Hilaire. *The Servile State*. 1912; New York: Gryphon Editions, 1998.

Ben, Aluf. "Netanyahu Places the Responsibility for the Riots with Arafat." *Ha'aretz*, 26 September 1996, A4.

Ben-Arieh, Yehoshua. *Jerusalem in the 19th Century: Emergence of the New City*. New York: St. Martin's Press, 1986.

————. *The Rediscovery of the Holy Land in the 19th Century*. Jerusalem: Magnes Press, 1979.

————. "The Sanjak of Jerusalem in the 1870's." *Cathedra* 36 (1985): 73–122.

Ben-Avi, Itamar. "J'Accuse! A Sequel to 'The Wailing Wall Atrocities.'" *Palestine Weekly*, 23 August 1929, 139.

Ben-Gurion, David. *My Talks with Arab Leaders*. Ed. Misha Louvish, trans. Aryeh Rubenstein and Misha Louvish. New York: Third Press, 1973.

206

Benhabib, Seyla. *Critique, Norm, and Utopia: A Study of the Foundations of Critical Theory.* New York: Columbia University Press, 1986.

Benjamin, Walter. *The Correspondence of Walter Benjamin, 1910–1940.* Ed. and ann. Gershom Scholem and Theodor W. Adorno, trans. Manfred R. Jacobson and Evelyn M. Jacobson. Chicago: University of Chicago Press, 1994.

———. "Critique of the New Objectivity." In *Selected Writings,* vol. 2, 1927–1934, ed. Michael W. Jennings, Howard Eiland, and Gary Smith, trans. Rodney Livingstone et al. Cambridge, Mass.: Harvard University Press, 1999.

———. *The Origin of German Tragic Drama.* Trans. John Osborne. London: NLB, 1977.

———. *Reflections: Essays, Aphorisms, Autobiographical Writings.* Trans. Edmund Jephcott. New York: Schocken Books, 1986.

———. *Selected Writings.* Vol. 1, 1913–1926, and vol. 2, 1927–1934. Ed. Marcus Bullock and Michael W. Jennings. Cambridge, Mass.: Harvard University Press, 1999.

———. "Theses on the Philosophy of History." In *Illuminations,* trans. Harry Zohn. New York: Schocken Books, 1969.

———. "Traverspiel and Tragedy." In *Selected Writings,* vol. 1, 1913–1926, ed. Marcus Bullock and Michael Jennings. Cambridge, Mass.: Harvard University Press, 1999.

Bentwich, Norman. *For Zion's Sake: A Biography of Judah L. Magnes.* Philadelphia: Jewish Publication Society of America, 1954.

———. *The Hebrew University of Jerusalem, 1918–1960.* London: Weidenfeld and Nicholson, 1961.

Bentwich, Norman de Mattos, and Helen Bentwich. *Mandate Memories, 1918–1948.* New York: Shocken Books, 1965.

Benvenisti, Meron. *City of Stone: The Hidden History of Jerusalem.* Trans. Maxine Kaufman Nunn. Berkeley: University of California Press, 1996.

Berkowitz, Michael. "Art in Zionist Popular Culture and Jewish National Self-Consciousness." In *Art and Its Uses: The Visual Image and Modern Jewish Society.* Studies in Contemporary Jewry 6, ed. Ezra Mendelsohn. Oxford: Oxford University Press, 1990.

———. *Zionist Culture and Western European Jewry before the First World War.* Chapel Hill: University of North Carolina Press, 1993.

Berman, Marshall. *All That Is Solid Melts into Air: The Experience of Modernity.* New York: Viking Penguin, 1988.

Bevis, Rochard, ed. *Bibliotheca Cisorientalia: An Annotated Checklist of Early English Travel Books on the Near and Middle East.* Boston: G. K. Hall, 1973.

Bhabha, Homi. "Articulating the Archaic: Notes on Colonial Discourse." In *Literary Theory Today,* ed. Peter Collier and Helga Geyer-Ryan. Cambridge: Polity Press, 1990.

———. "Difference, Discrimination, and the Discourse of Colonialism." In *The Politics of Theory,* ed. Frances Barker et al. Colchester, England: University of Essex, 1983.

———. "DissemiNation. . . ." In *Nation and Narration,* ed. Homi K. Bhabha. London: Routledge, 1990.

————. *The Location of Culture.* London: Routledge, 1994.

————. "Narrating the Nation." In *Nation and Narration,* ed. Homi K. Bhabha. London: Routledge, 1990.

————. "Of Mimicry and Man: The Ambivalence of Colonial Discourse." In *October, the First Decade, 1976–1986,* ed. Annette Michelson et al. Cambridge, Mass.: MIT Press, 1987.

————. "Representation and the Colonial Text: A Critical Exploration of Some Forms of Mimeticism." In *The Theory of Reading,* ed. Frank Gloversworth. Brighton: Hawkins Press, 1984.

Biale, David. *Eros and the Jews: From Biblical Israel to Contemporary America.* New York: BasicBooks, 1992.

Bialik, Chaim Nahman. "Al Hash'chita." In *Kol Shirei Bialik.* Tel-Aviv: Devir Publishing, 1970.

Biger, Gidon. *Moshevet Keter o Bayit Le'umi, Hashpa'at Hashilton Habriti al Eretz-Israel, 1917–1930.* Jerusalem: Yad Ben-Zvi, 1983.

————. "The Spatial Diffusion of Jerusalem's Population in the Early Mandatory Period." *Cathedra* 39 (1986): 125–141.

————. "Urban Planning and the Garden Suburbs of Jerusalem, 1918–1925." *Studies in Zionism* 7, no. 1 (1986): 1–9.

Bland, Kalman P. *The Artless Jew: Medieval and Modern Affirmations and Denials of the Visual.* Princeton, N.J.: Princeton University Press, 2000.

Boardman, Philip. *Patrick Geddes, Maker of the Future.* Chapel Hill: University of North Carolina Press, 1944.

————. *The Worlds of Patrick Geddes: Biologist, Town Planner, Re-Educator, Peace Warrior.* London: Routledge and Kegan Paul, 1978.

Bois, Yves-Alain. "Metamorphoses of Axonometry." In *Daidalos* 1: *De Stijl: Neo-Plasticism in Architecture* (September 1981): 41–58.

Briner, William M., and Moses Rischlin, eds. *Like All the Nations? The Life and Legacy of Judah L. Magnes.* Albany: State University of New York Press, 1987.

Brown, L. Carl, *International Politics and the Middle East: Old Rules, Dangerous Game.* Princeton, N.J.: Princeton University Press, 1984.

Buber, Martin. *I and Thou.* Trans. Walter Kaufmann. New York: Charles Scribner and Sons, 1970.

Buchan, John. *Greenmantle.* Ware, England: Wordsworth Editions, 1994.

————. *Nelson's History of the War.* Vols. 5 and 15. London: Thomas Nelson and Sons, n.d.

Buckingham, James Silk. *The Greatest Reform Yet Remaining to Be Accomplished.* London: Ridgeway, 1846.

————. *National Evils and Practical Remedies.* London: Peter Jackson, Late Fisher and Son, 1849.

————. *Travels among the Arab Tribes.* London: Longman, 1825.

————. *Travels in Palestine through the Countries of Bashan and Gilead, East of the River Jordan: Including a Visit to the Cities of Gerasa and Gamala, in the Decapolis.* Vol. 1. London: Longman, Hurst, Rees, Orme, and Brown, 1822.

Buck-Morss, Susan. *The Dialectics of Seeing: Walter Benjamin and the Arcades Project*. Cambridge, Mass.: MIT Press, 1989.

————. *The Origin of Negative Dialectics: Theodor W. Adorno, Walter Benjamin and the Frankfurt Institute*. New York: Free Press, 1977.

Bulloch, John Malcolm. *Bibliography of the Gordons*. Aberdeen, Scotland: University Press, 1924.

Burckhardt, John Lewis. *Travels in Syria and the Holy Land*. London: John Murray, 1822.

Burger, Peter. *Theory of the Avant-Garde*. Minneapolis: University of Minnesota Press, 1984.

Burke, Edmund. "Moroccan Resistance, Pan-Islam and German War Strategy, 1914–1918." *Francia* (1975): 434–464.

Busch, Briton Cooper. *Britain, India, and the Arabs, 1914–1921*. Berkeley: University of California Press, 1971.

Butler, [Colonel Sir] William F. *Charles George Gordon*. London: Macmillan, 1889.

Camille, Michael. *The Gothic Idol: Ideology and Image-Making in Medieval Art*. Cambridge: Cambridge University Press, 1989.

Canaan, Tawfiq. *The Palestinian Arab House, Its Architecture and Folklore*. Jerusalem: Syrian Orphanage Press, 1933.

Canetti, Elias. *Crowds and Power*. Trans. Carol Stewart. New York: Seabury Press, 1978.

Carlyle, Thomas. *Sartor Resartus*. New York: Charles Scribner and Sons, 1921.

Caspi, Yehoshuah "Prisons in Palestine During the Mandatory Period." *Cathedra* 32 (1984): 141–74.

Chakrabarty, Dipesh. "Invitation to a Dialogue." In *Subaltern Studies: Writings on South Asian History and Society*, ed. Ranajit Guha, vol. 4. Delhi: Oxford University Press, 1985.

Charles, Elizabeth Rundle. *Three Martyrs of the Nineteenth Century: Studies from the Lives of Livingstone, Gordon, and Patterson*. London: SPCK, 1885.

————. *Wanderings over Bible Lands and Seas*. New York: Robert Carter and Bros., 1873.

Charters, David A. *The British Army and Jewish Insurgency in Palestine, 1945–1947*. London: Macmillan, 1989.

Chateaubriand, Francois-René [Viscomte de]. *Travels to Jerusalem and the Holy Land through Egypt*. 2 vols. Trans. by Frederic Shoberl. London: Henry Colburn, 1835.

Chatterjee, Partha, "Caste and Subaltern Consciousness." In *Subaltern Studies: Writings in South Asian History and Society*, ed. Ramajit Guha, vol. 6. Delhi: Oxford University Press, 1988.

————. "More on Modes of Power and the Peasantry." In *Subaltern Studies: Writings on South Asian History and Society*, ed. Ranajit Guha, vol. 2. Delhi: Oxford University Press, 1983.

Cini, Rifat. *Kutahya in Turkish Tile Making*. Trans. Solmaz Turunc and Aydin Turunc. Istanbul: Uycan Yayinlari, 1991.

Clarke, Edward Daniel. *Travels in Various Countries of Europe, Asia and Africa*. London: T. Cadell, 1812.

Clarke, Thurston. *By Blood and Fire: The Attack on the King David Hotel.* New York: G. P. Putnam's Sons, 1981.

Clermont-Ganneau, Charles. *Archaeological Researches in Palestine During the Years 1873–1874.* Vol. 1. Trans. Aubrey Stuart. Rpt., Jerusalem, 1971.

———. "The Holy Sepulchre." *Quarterly Statement of the Palestine Exploration Fund* [PEFQ] (1877): 76–84.

"Clinton on Prospects for Peace Agreement in Mideast: Comment." Washington, 26 July 2000 (Bloomberg). <http://www.Bloomberg.net>.

Clutterbuck, Richard. *Protest and the Urban Guerrilla.* London: Cassell, 1973.

Cohen, Michael J. "Direction of Policy in Palestine, 1936–45." *Middle-Eastern Studies* 11, no. 3 (1975): 237–261.

———. "Sir Arthur Wauchope, the Army, and the Rebellion in Palestine, 1936." *Middle-Eastern Studies* 9, no. 1 (1973): 19–34.

Cohen, Mitchell. *Zion and State: Nation, Class, and the Shaping of Modern Israel.* Oxford: Basil Blackwell, 1987.

Collins, George R., and Christiane Crasemann. *Camillo Sitte: The Birth of Modern City Planning.* New York: Rizzoli, 1986.

Conder, Claude Reignier. *Tent Work in Palestine: A Record of Discovery and Adventure.* Vols. 1 and 2. New York: D. Appleton, 1878.

Conder, Claude Reignier, et al. *The Survey of Western Palestine: 1882–1888.* [Slough, England]: Archive Editions in association with Palestine Exploration Fund, 1998.

Coward, Harold, and Toby Foshay, eds. *Derrida and Negative Theology.* Conclusion by Jacques Derrida. Albany: State University of New York Press, 1992.

Crawford, Alan. *C. R. Ashbee: Architect, Designer, and Romantic Socialist.* New Haven: Yale University Press, 1985.

Creswell, K. A. C. *The Origin of the Plan of the Dome of the Rock.* Jerusalem: British School of Archaeology, 1924.

———. *A Short Account of Early Muslim Architecture.* London: Penguin Books, 1958.

Creuzer, Georg Friedrich. *Symbolik und Mythologie der alten Volker, besonders der Griechen.* 4 vols. In *Vortragen und Entwurfen von Friedrich Creuzer.* Leipzig : K. W. Leske, 1810–1812.

Crinson, Mark. "Victorian Architects and the Near East: Studies in Colonial Architecture, Architectural Theory and Orientalism, 1840–1870." Ph.D. diss., University of Pennsylvania, 1989.

Curzon, Robert. *Visits to Monasteries in the Levant.* London: Humphrey Milford, 1849.

Defries, Amelia. *The Interpreter: Geddes, the Man and His Gospel.* London: Routledge, 1927.

Deleuze, Gilles. *The Fold, Leibniz and the Baroque.* Trans. Tom Conley. Minneapolis: University of Minnesota Press, 1993.

Deleuze, Gilles, and Guattari, Félix. *Anti-Oedipus: Capitalism and Schizophrenia.* Trans. Robert Hurley, Mark Seem, and Helen R. Lane. Minneapolis: University of Minnesota Press, 1983.

———. *A Thousand Plateaus: Capitalism and Schizophrenia.* Trans. Brian Massumi. Minneapolis: University of Minnesota Press, 1987.

De Man, Paul. *Aesthetic Ideology.* Ed. and intro. Andrzej Warminski. Minneapolis: University of Minnesota Press, 1996.

———. *Blindness and Insight: Essays in the Rhetoric of Contemporary Criticism.* 2d ed. rev. Intro. Wlad Godzich. Minneapolis: University of Minnesota Press, 1983.

———. *The Resistence to Theory.* Foreword by Wlad Godzich. Theory and History of Literature 33. Minneapolis: University of Minnesota Press, 1986.

———. *The Rhetoric of Romanticism.* New York: Columbia University Press, 1984.

Derrida, Jacques. *Dissemination.* Trans. with intro. and notes by Barbara Johnson. Chicago: University of Chicago Press, 1981.

———. *Glas.* Trans. John P. Leavey Jr. and Richard Rand. Lincoln: University of Nebraska Press, 1986.

———. "How to Avoid Speaking, Denials." In *Derrida and Negative Theology,* ed. Harold Coward and Toby Foshay. Albany: State University of New York Press, 1992.

———. *Margins of Philosophy.* Trans. with notes by Alan Bass. Chicago: University of Chicago Press, 1982.

———. "My Chances/*Mes Chances*: A Rendezvous with Some Epicurean Stereophonies." In *Taking Chances: Derrida, Psychoanalysis, and Literature,* ed. Joseph Smith and William Kerrigan. Baltimore, Md.: Johns Hopkins University Press, 1984.

———. "Of an Apocalyptic Tone Newly Adopted in Philosophy." In *Derrida and Negative Theology,* ed. Harold Coward and Toby Foshay. Albany: State University of New York Press, 1992.

———. *Of Grammatology.* Trans. Gayatri Chakravorty Spivak. Baltimore: Johns Hopkins University Press, 1976.

———. "Passages from Traumatism to Promise." In *Points: Interviews, 1974–1994,* trans. Peggy Kamuf. Stanford: Stanford University Press, 1995.

———. *Positions.* Trans. Alan Bass. Chicago: University of Chicago Press, 1981.

———. *The Post Card: From Socrates to Freud and Beyond.* Trans. Alan Bass. Chicago: University of Chicago Press, 1987.

———. *The Truth in Painting.* Trans. Geoff Bennington and Ian Mcleod. Chicago: University of Chicago Press, 1987.

"The Director of Antiquities." *Near East,* 10 September 1927.

Dorfles, Gillo. " 'Innen' et 'Aussen' en Architecture et en Psychanalyse." *Le Dehors et le Dedans: Nouvelle Revue de Psychanalyse* 8 (spring, 1974): 229–238.

Doughty, Charles M. *Travels in Arabia Deserta.* Intro. T. E. Lawrence. New York: Boni and Liveright, 1920.

Eliade, Mircea. *Traité d'histoire des religions.* Preface by Georges Dumezil. Paris: Payot, 1949.

Elpeleg, Zvi. *The Grand Mufti: Haj Amin al-Hussaini, Founder of the Palestinian National Movement.* Ed. Shmuel Himelstein, trans. David Harvey. London: Frank Cass, 1993.

———. *Minekudat Re'uto Shel Hamufti.* [In the Eyes of the Mufti: The Essays of Hajj Amin, Translated and Annotated] Tel Aviv: Tel Aviv University Press, 1995.

Esco Foundation for Palestine. *Palestine, A Study of Jewish, Arab, and British Policies.* 2 vols. New Haven: Yale University Press, 1947.

Eusebius. *The History of the Church from Christ to Constantine.* Trans. G. A. Williamson. London: Penguin Books, 1965.

Ezrahi, Yaron. *Rubber Bullets: Power and Conscience in Modern Israel.* New York: Farrar, Straus and Giroux, 1997.

Fahey, Denis. *The Kingship of Christ, According to the Principles of St. Thomas Aquinas.* Dublin: Brown and Nolan, 1931.

———. *The Mystical Body of Christ in the Modern World.* Waterford: Browne and Nolan, 1935.

———. *The Rulers of Russia.* Dublin: Trader Publishing, 1938.

Faludi, Andreas, ed. *A Reader in Planning Theory.* Oxford: Pergamon Press, 1973.

Fanon, Frantz. *Black Skin, White Masks.* Trans. Charles Lam Markmann. New York: Grove Weidenfeld, 1967.

———. *The Wretched of the Earth.* Preface by Jean-Paul Sartre. Trans. Constance Farrington. New York: Grove Weidenfeld, 1963.

Fergusson, James. *An Essay on the Ancient Topography of Jerusalem.* London: John Weale, 1847.

———. *A History of Architecture.* London: Ridgway, 1846.

———. *The Holy Sepulchre and the Temple at Jerusalem: Being the Substance of Two Lectures Delivered in the Royal Institution, Albemarle Street, on the 21st February, 1862, and 3rd March, 1865.* London: John Murray, 1865.

Flappan, Simha. *The Birth of Israel, Myths and Realities.* New York: Pantheon Books, 1987.

Frampton, Kenneth. *Modern Architecture: A Critical History.* New York: Oxford University Press, 1980.

Frazer, James George. *Folk-Lore in the Old Testament, Studies in Comparative Religion Legend and Law.* Vol. 1. London: Macmillan, 1918.

———. *The Golden Bough: A Study in Magic and Religion.* Part 1, 3d ed. London: Macmillan, 1925.

French, Charles Chemenix. *Charley Gordon, An Eminent Victorian Reassessed.* London: Allen Lane, 1978.

Freud, Sigmund. "Fetishism." In *The Standard Edition of the Complete Psychological Works of Sigmund Freud,* vol. 21, ed. James Strachey, trans. under gen. ed. James Strachey. London: Hogarth Press and the Institute of Psycho-Analysis, 1981.

———. "Group Psychology and the Analysis of the Ego." In *The Standard Edition of the Complete Psychological Works of Sigmund Freud,* vol. 18, ed. James Strachey, trans. under gen. ed. James Strachey. London: Hogarth Press and the Institute of Psycho-Analysis, 1981.

———. "Medusa's Head." *The Standard Edition of the Complete Psychological Works of Sigmund Freud,* vol. 18, ed. James Strachey, gen. ed. James Strachey. London: Hogarth Press and the Institute of Psycho-Analysis, 1981.

———. "The 'Uncanny.'" In *The Standard Edition of the Complete Psychological Works of Sigmund Freud,* vol. 17, ed. James Strachey, trans. under gen. ed. James Strachey. London: Hogarth Press and the Institute of Psycho-Analysis, 1981.

Friedman, Isaiah, ed. *The Rise of Israel: A Documentary Record from the Nineteenth Century to*

1948: A Facsimile Series Reproducing over 1,900 Documents in 39 Volumes. New York: Garland Publishing, 1987.

Fromkin, David. *A Peace to End All Peace: The Fall of the Ottoman Empire and the Creation of the Modern Middle East.* New York: Avon Books, 1989.

Gallop, Jane. "Lacan's 'Mirror Stage': Where to Begin." *SubStance* 37/38 (1983): 120–121.

———. *Reading Lacan.* Ithaca, N.Y.: Cornell University Press, 1985.

Garber, Marjorie. "Fetish Envy." *October* 54 (1990): 45–56.

"Garden Tomb—New Jerusalem Discovery—Shrine Stone and Its Meaning." *Times* (London), 24 July 1924, 15.

Gavish, Dov. *Karkah Umapah, Mehesder Karka'ot Le Mapat Eretz-Israel, 1920–1948.* Jerusalem: Yad Ben-Zvi, 1991.

Geddes, Patrick. "The Charting of Life." *Sociological Review* 19 (January 1927): 40–63.

———. *Cities in Evolution.* New York: Howard Fertig, 1915.

———. "Palestine in Renewal." *Contemporary Review* 670 (October 1921): 475–484.

"General Gordon." *London Quarterly Review* (July 1884): 353–371.

Gibb, H. A. R. "The Islamic Congress at Jerusalem in December 1931." In *Survey of International Affairs, 1934,* ed. Arnold J. Toynbee. London: Humphrey Milford and Oxford University Press, 1935.

Gilman, Sander. *Freud, Race, and Gender.* Princeton: Princeton University Press, 1993.

Goffman, Erving. *Frame Analysis: An Essay on the Organization of Experience.* Foreword by Bennett Berger. Boston: Northeastern University Press, 1986.

———. *The Presentation of Self in Everyday Life.* New York: Anchor Books, Doubleday, 1959.

———. *Strategic Interaction.* Philadelphia: University of Pennsylvania Press, 1969.

———. "Where the Action Is." In *Interaction Ritual: Essays on Face-to-Face Behavior.* New York: Pantheon Books, 1967.

Goldschmidt-Lehmann, R. "The Western Wall—Selected Bibliography." *Cathedra* 12 (1979): 207.

"Golgotha." By John L. McKenzie, S.J. *Dictionary of the Bible.* New York: Macmillan Publishing, 1965.

Gordon, Charles George. *Letters of General C. G. Gordon to His Sister, M. A. Gordon.* Ed. M. A. Gordon. London: Macmillan, 1888.

———. "Notes on Eden and Golgotha." *Quarterly Statement of the Palestine Exploration Fund* [PEFQ] (1885): 78–81.

———. *Reflections in Palestine, 1883.* London: Macmillan, 1884.

Goren, Arthur, ed. *Dissenter in Zion: From the Writings of Judah L. Magnes.* Cambridge, Mass.: Harvard University Press, 1982.

Gorni, Yosef. "Utopian Elements in Zionist Thought." *Studies in Zionism* 15, no. 1 (1984): 19–27.

Gosset, Alphonse. *Les Coupoles d'Orient et d'Occident.* Paris: A. Lewy, 1889.

Goux, Jean-Joseph. "The Phallus: Masculine Identity and the 'Exchange of Women.'" *Differences: A Journal of Feminist Cultural Studies* 4, no. 1 (1992): 40–75.

———. *Symbolic Economies: After Marx and Freud.* Trans. Jennifer Curtiss Gage. Ithaca, N.Y.: Cornell University Press, 1990.

Grabar, Oleg. "The Meaning of the Dome of the Rock." In *The Medieval Mediterranean: Cross Cultural Contacts*, ed. Marilyn Chiat and Kathryn L. Reyerson. Medieval Studies at Minnesota 3. St. Cloud, Minn.: Northstar Press, 1988.

————. "The Umayyad Dome of the Rock." *Ars Orientalis* 3 (1959): 33–62.

Gramsci, Antonio, et al. *Selections from the Prison Notebooks of Antonio Gramsci.* Ed. and trans. Quentin Hoare and Geoffrey Nowell Smith. New York: International Publishers, 1971.

Graves, Robert Massey. *Experiment in Anarchy.* London: Victor Gollancz, 1949.

Greenblatt, Stephen. *Marvelous Possessions: The Wonder of the New World.* Chicago: University of Chicago Press, 1991.

Guest, A. R., and Ernest Tatham Richmond. "Misr in the Fifteenth Century." *Journal of the Royal Asiatic Society* (October 1903): 791–817.

Guha, Ranajit, and Gayatri Chakravorty Spivak, eds. *Selected Subaltern Studies.* New York: Oxford University Press, 1988.

H., R. F. "Notes on Our Lord's Tomb." *Quarterly Statement of the Palestine Exploration Fund* [PEFQ] (1870): 379–381.

Habermas, Jürgen. *The Structural Transformation of the Public Sphere: An Inquiry into a Category of Bourgeois Society.* Trans. Thomas Burger with Frederick Lawrence. Cambridge, Mass.: MIT Press, 1992.

Hall, Joseph. *Christ Mystical, or The Blessed Union of Christ and His Members; from General Gordon's copy with an Introduction on the theology of General Gordon by M. Carruthers Wilson.* London: Hodder and Stoughton, 1908.

Halper, Jeff. *Between Redemption and Revival: The Jewish Yishuv of Jerusalem in the Nineteenth Century.* Boulder, Colo.: Westview Press, 1991.

Halpern, Ben. *The Idea of the Jewish State.* Cambridge, Mass.: Harvard University Press, 1961.

Hamilton, Robert W. *Khirbat Al Mafjar: An Arabian Mansion in the Jordan Valley.* Oxford: Oxford University Press, 1959.

————. *The Structural History of the Aqsa Mosque: A Record of Archaeological Gleanings from the Repairs of 1938–1942.* Oxford: Oxford University Press for the Government of Palestine, 1949.

Hansen, Miriam. "Mass Culture as Hieroglyphic Writing: Adorno, Derrida, Kracauer." *New German Critique* 56 (spring/summer 1992): 43–73.

Hattis-Rolef, Susan. "Sir Herbert Samuel's Policy of Economic Development." *Cathedra* 12 (1979): 80–90.

Hays, K. Michael. "Allegory unto Death: An Etiology of Eisenman's Repetition." In *Cities of Artificial Excavation, The Work of Peter Eisenman, 1978–1988,* ed. Jean-François Bédard. Montreal: Canadian Center for Architecture, 1994.

Hegel, Georg Wilhelm Friedrich. *Phenomenology of Spirit.* Trans. A. V. Miller. Analysis and foreword by J. N. Findlay. Oxford: Oxford University Press, 1977.

————. *The Philosophy of History.* Trans. J. Sibree. Buffalo, N.Y.: Prometheus Books, 1991.

————. *Philosophy of Right.* Trans. S. W. Dyde. Amherst, N.Y.: Prometheus Books, 1996.

———. "The Spirit of Christianity and Its Fate." In *On Christianity: Early Theological Writings*, trans. T. M. Knox, intro. Richard Kroner. New York: Harper, 1948.

Heller, Joseph. *British Policy towards the Ottoman Empire, 1908–1914*. London: Frank Cass, 1983.

Herbert, Gilbert, and Sylvina Sosnovsky. *Bauhaus on the Carmel and the Crossroads of Empire, Architecture and Planning in Haifa during the British Mandate*. Jerusalem: Yad Itzhak Ben-Zvi, 1993.

Hertz, Neil. "Medusa's Head: Male Hysteria under Political Pressure." In *The End of the Line: Essays on Psychoanalysis and the Sublime*. New York: Columbia University Press, 1985.

Herzl, Theodor. *Altneuland*. Trans. Lotta Levensohn, intro. Jacques Kornberg. New York: Markus Wiener Publishing and Herzl Press, 1960.

Heynen, Hilde. "Architecture between Modernity and Dwelling: Reflections on Adorno's 'Aesthetic Theory.'" *Assemblage* 17 (April 1992): 78–91.

Hines, Thomas S. *Richard Neutra and the Search for Modern Architecture*. New York: Oxford University Press, 1982.

Hobsbawm, Eric. *The Age of Empire, 1975–1914*. New York: Vintage Press, 1989.

Hobsbawm, Eric, and Terence Ranger, eds. *The Invention of Tradition*. Cambridge: Cambridge University Press, 1992.

Home, Robert K. "British Colonial Town Planning in the Middle East: The Work of W. H. McLean." *Planning History* 12, no. 1 (n.d.): 4–9.

———. "Town Planning and Garden Cities in the British Colonial Empire, 1910–1940." *Planning Perspectives* 5 (1990): 23–37.

Horkheimer, Max. "Traditional versus Critical Theory." In *Critical Theory: Selected Essays*, trans. Matthew J. O'Connell et al. New York: Continuum, 1972.

Horkheimer, Max, and Theodor W. Adorno. *Dialectic of the Enlightenment*. Trans. John Cumming. New York: Continuum, 1989.

Hourani, Albert. *Europe and the Middle East*. London: Macmillan, 1980.

Howard, Ebenezer. *Garden Cities of Tomorrow*. Ed. F. J. Osborn. Cambridge, Mass: MIT Press, 1965.

Hudson, Michael C., "The Transformation of Jerusalem, 1917–1987 AD." In *Jerusalem in History*, ed. J. K. Asali. New York: Olive Branch Press, 1990.

Huhn, Thomas, and Lambert Zuidervaart, eds. *The Semblance of Subjectivity: Essays in Adorno's Aesthetic Theory*. Cambridge, Mass.: MIT Press, 1997.

Hullot-Kentor, Robert. "Back to Adorno." *Telos* 81 (fall 1989): 5–29.

———. "Suggested Reading: Jameson on Adorno." Review of *Late Marxism: Adorno, or the Persistence of the Dialectic* by Fredric Jameson. *Telos* 89 (fall 1991): 167–177.

Huntley, Frank Livingstone. *Bishop Joseph Hall, 1574–1656: A Biographical and Critical Study*. Cambridge: D. S. Brewer, 1979.

———. "Bishop Joseph Hall and Protestant Meditation in Seventeenth-Century England: A Study with Texts of the Art of Divine Meditation" (1606) and "Occasional Meditations" (1633). In *Medieval and Renaissance Texts and Studies*, vol. 1. Binghamton, N.Y.: Center for Medieval and Early Renaissance Studies, 1981.

Hurewitz, J. C. *The Struggle for Palestine*. New York: W. W. Norton, 1950.

Al-Husayni, Muhammad Amin. *Haqaʾiq ʿan Qadhiyyat Filastin*. Cairo: Maktab al-Haya al-ʿArabiyya al-Ulya li-Filastin, 1954.

Husserl, Edmund. *Experience and Judgement*. Trans. J. S. Churchill and K. Ameriks. Evanston, Ill.: Northwestern University Press, 1973.

Ingrams, Doreen, ed. *Palestine Papers, 1917–1922: Seeds of Conflict*. London: John Murray, 1972.

International Commission for the Wailing Wall. *The Rights and Claims of Moslems and Jews in Connection with the Wailing Wall at Jerusalem*. Institute for Palestine Studies Basic Documents Series, no. 4. 1931; Beirut, Institute for Palestine Studies, 1968.

"The Islamic Congress, Views of Sayed el Husseini." *Egyptian Gazette* (Cairo), 14 November 1931, 5–6.

Jakobson, Roman, and Morris Halle. *Fundamentals of Language*. 2d rev. ed. The Hague: Mouton, 1971.

Jameson, Fredric. "Architecture and the Critique of Ideology." In *Architecture, Criticism, Ideology*, ed. Johan Ockman, Deborah Berke, and Mary McLeod. Princeton: Princeton Architectural Press, 1985.

———. "Imaginary and Symbolic in Lacan." In *The Ideologies of Theory: Essays, 1971–1986*, vol. 1: *Situations of Theory: Theory and History of Literature*. Minneapolis: University of Minnesota Press, 1988.

———. *Late Marxism: Adorno, or The Persistence of the Dialectic*. London: Verso, 1990.

———. *Marxism and Form: Twentieth-Century Dialectical Theories of Literature*. Princeton: Princeton University Press, 1971.

———. "Marx's Purloined Letter." *New Left Review* 209 (January/February 1995): 75–107.

———. *Signatures of the Visible*. New York: Routledge, 1990.

Jay, Martin. *Adorno*. Cambridge, Mass.: Harvard University Press, 1984.

———. *Downcast Eyes: The Denigration of Vision in Twentieth-Century French Thought*. Berkeley: University of California Press, 1994.

———. *Marxism and Totality: The Adventures of a Concept from Lukács to Habermas*. Berkeley: University of California Press, 1984.

Jeffries, J. M. N. *Palestine: The Reality*. London: Longmans, Green, 1939.

Jervis, Robert. *The Logic of Images in International Relations*. New York: Columbia University Press, 1989.

Johnson, Nels. *Islam and the Politics of Meaning in Palestinian Nationalism*. London: Kegan Paul International, 1982.

Jones, Philip, ed. *Britain and Palestine, 1914–1918: Archival Sources for the History of the British Mandate*. Oxford: Oxford University Press for the British Academy, 1979.

Kant, Immanuel. *The Critique of Judgement*. Trans. Werner S. Pluhar. Indianapolis: Hackett Publishing, 1987.

Kapitan, Tomis, ed. *Philosophical Perspectives on the Israeli-Palestinian Conflict*. Armonk, N.Y.: M. E. Sharpe, 1997.

Kark, Ruth. *Jerusalem Neighborhoods, Planning and By-Laws, 1885–1930*. Trans. Michael Gordon. Jerusalem: Magnes Press, 1991.

———. "Pe'ilut Iriyat Yerushalayim Besof Hat'kufa Ha' Otomanit." *Cathedra* 6 (1977): 74–94.

Katz, Yossi. "Me'afianim Merkazi'im Behakamatan Shel Sh'chunot Hevrot Hab'niya Hechalutziyot B'Yirushalayim: Mishkenot Israel, 1875–1914." In *Mechkarim Begiographia Historit-Yishuvit Shel Eretz-Israel*, vol. 2, ed. Y. Katz, Y. Ben-Aryeh, and Y. Kaniel. Jerusalem: Yad Ben-Zvi, 1991.

Katzburg, N. "Kavim Lehitpatchuta Shel Yerushalayim Michutz Lachoma." In *Yad Yosef Yitzhak Rivlin, Sefer Zikaron*, ed. H. Z. Hirshberg. Ramat-Gan: Machon Rivlin, 1954.

Kedourie, Elie. *The Chatham House Version and Other Middle-Eastern Essays*. Hanover, N.H.: Brandeis University Press, 1984.

———. "Sir Herbert Samuel and the Government of Palestine." *Middle-Eastern Studies* 5, no. 1 (1969): 44–68.

Keegan, John. *The Face of Battle*. New York: Penguin Books, 1976.

Kendall, Henry. *Jerusalem, The City Plan: Preservation and Development During the British Mandate, 1918–1948*. London: HMSO, 1948.

———. *Village Development in Palestine during the British Mandate*. London: Crown Agents for the Colonies, 1949.

Khaldûn, Ibn. *The Muqaddimah: An Introduction to History*. Bollingen Series. Trans. Franz Rosenthal, ed. and abridged by N. J. Dawood. Princeton: Princeton University Press, 1967.

Khalidi, Rashid, ed. *From Haven to Conquest: Readings in Zionism and the Palestine Problem until 1948*. Beirut: Institute for Palestine Studies, 1971.

———. *Palestinian Identity*. New York: Columbia University Press, 1997.

al-Khalil, Samir [Kanan Makia]. *The Monument: Art, Vulgarity and Responsibility in Iraq*. London: Andrew Deutsch, 1991.

Khoury, Philip S. *Syria and the French Mandate, The Politics of Arab Nationalism, 1920–1945*. Princeton, N.J.: Princeton University Press, 1987.

Kim, Jay. "Hierophany and History." *Journal of the American Academy of Religion* 40 (September 1972): 334–348.

King, A. D. *The Bungalow: the Production of a Global Culture*. London: Routledge and Kegan Paul, 1984.

———. *Colonial Urban Development: Culture, Social Power and Environment*. London: Routledge and Kegan Paul, 1976.

Kisch, Frederick, H. *Palestine Diary*. Foreword by Rt. Hon. D. Lloyd George. London: Victor Gollancz, 1938.

Kohl, Phillip, and Clare Fawcett, eds. *Nationalism and the Practice of Archeology*. Cambridge: Cambridge University Press, 1995.

Kolinsky, Martin. *Law, Order and Riots in Mandatory Palestine, 1928–1935*. London: St. Martin's Press, 1993.

Kracauer, Siegfried. *The Mass Ornament: Weimar Essays*. Trans., ed., and intro. Thomas Y. Levin. Cambridge, Mass.: Harvard University Press, 1995.

Kramer, Martin Seth. "The Congress in Modern Islam: On the Origins of an Innovation." Ph.D. diss., Princeton University, 1982.

——. *Islam Assembled: The Advent of the Muslim Congresses.* New York: Columbia University Press, 1986.

Krauthammer, Charles. "A Desecration of Truth: Israel Is Maligned While Palestinians Get a Free Pass." *Time* 148, no. 18, 14 October 1996, 104.

Krautheimer, Richard. "Introduction to an 'Iconography of Medieaeval Architecture.'" *Journal of the Warburg and Courtauld Institutes* 5 (1942): 1–33.

Kristeva, Julia. *Powers of Horror: An Essay on Abjection.* Trans. Leon S. Roudiez. New York: Columbia University Press, 1982.

Kroyanker, David, curator. *Chalom Behakitz, Yerushalayim Halo B'nuya.* Exh. cat. Jerusalem: Tower of David, Museum of the History of Jerusalem, 1992.

——. "Phases in the Orientalism of Modern Jerusalem Architecture." *Adrihalut Israelit* 11 (1991): 4–8.

Kupferschmidt, Uri M. "The General Muslim Congress of 1931 in Jerusalem." *Asian and African Studies* 12, no. 1 (1978): 123–163.

——. *The Supreme Muslim Council: Islam under the British Mandate for Palestine.* Leiden: E. J. Brill, 1987.

Kutcher, Arthur. *The New Jerusalem: Planning and Politics.* London: Thames and Hudson, 1973.

Lacan, Jacques. *Écrits.* Trans. Alan Sheridan. New York: W. W. Norton, 1977.

——. *The Four Fundamental Concepts of Psychoanalysis.* Trans. Alan Sheridan. New York: W. W. Norton, 1973.

Lacan, Jacques, and the *École Freudienne. Feminine Sexuality.* Ed. Juliet Mitchell and Jacqueline Rose, trans. Jacqueline Rose. New York: W. W. Norton, 1985.

Lacoue-Labarthe, Philippe. "The Caesura of Religion." In *Opera through Other Eyes,* ed. David Levin. Stanford: Stanford University Press, 1993.

Lacoue-Labarthe, Philippe, and Jean-Luc Nancy. *Retreating the Political.* Ed. Simon Sparks. London: Routledge, 1997.

Lacqueur, Walter. *A History of Zionism.* New York: Holt Rinehart Winston, 1972.

Lamartine, Alphonse de. *Voyage en Orient.* 1835; rpt., Paris: Hachette, 1887.

Lanchester, H. V. "Town Planning in Southern India." *Journal of the Town Planning Institute* 3 (1916): 89–115.

Landau, Jacob M. *The Politics of Pan-Islam: Ideology and Organization.* Oxford: Clarendon Press, 1994.

Lang, Yosef. "Me'oraot Tarpat: Hafra'ot, Pra'ut, o Mered?" *Cathedra* 47 (1988): 134–162.

Laplanche, Jean. *Problematiques II: Castration Symbolisations.* Paris: Presses Universitaires de France, 1980.

Lavie, Smadar. *The Poetics of Military Occupation: Mzeina Allegories of Bedouin Identity under Israeli and Egyptian Rule.* Berkeley: University of California Press, 1990.

Lawrence, T. E. *Seven Pillars of Wisdom: A Triumph.* Harmondsworth, England: Penguin Books, 1962.

Leach, Edmund. *Claude Levi-Strauss.* Harmondsworth, England: Penguin Books, 1974.

League of Nations, Council for. *Mandate for Palestine.* Geneva: League of Nations, 1926.

Leavey, John P., Jr. *Glassary.* Lincoln: University of Nebraska Press, 1986.

Le Bon, Gustave. *Psychologie des Foules.* 1895; Paris: PUF, 1998.

Legal Aspects of Town Planning in Israel. Jerusalem: Institute for Legislative Research and Contemporary Law, 1966.

Lethaby, W. R. *Architecture Mysticism, and Myth.* London: Macmillan, 1892.

Lévi-Strauss, Claude. *Totemism.* Trans. Rodney Needham. Boston: Beacon Press, 1963.

Lewis, Bernard. *The Arabs in History.* Rev. ed. New York: Harper and Row, 1966.

———. *Islam and the West.* New York and Oxford: Oxford University Press, 1993.

———. *Islam in History: Ideas, Men and Events in the Middle East.* New York: Library Press, 1973.

Lewis, Thomas Hayter. *The Holy Places of Jerusalem.* London: John Murray, 1888.

Lukács, Georg. *History and Class Consciousness: Studies in Marxist Dialectics.* Trans. Rodney Livingstone. Cambridge, Mass.: MIT Press, 1968.

Lyotard, Jean-François. "Adorno as the Devil." *Telos* 19 (spring 1974): 127–137.

———. *The Differend: Phrases in Dispute.* Trans. George Van Den Abbeele. Theory and History of Literature 46. Minneapolis: University of Minnesota Press, 1988.

MacGregor-Hastie, Roy. *Never to Be Taken Alive: A Biography of General Gordon.* New York: St. Martin's Press, 1985.

Maguire, Penny. "A Great and Golden City." *Architectural Review* 165 (1979): 343–350.

Mairet, Philip. *Pioneer of Sociology: The Life and Letters of Patrick Geddes.* London: Lund Humphries, 1957.

Makover, Rachela. *Shilton Uminhal Be'Eretz-Israel, 1917–1925.* Jerusalem: Yad Ben-Zvi, 1988.

Mallock, W. H. "General Gordon's Message." *Fortnightly Review* n.s. 36 (July 1884): 57–74.

Maoz, Moshe, ed. *Studies on Palestine During the Ottoman Period.* Jerusalem: Magnes Press, 1975.

Marcuse, Herbert. "On the Affirmative Character of Culture." In *Negations: Essays in Critical Theory,* trans. Jeremy J. Shapiro. London: Free Association Books, 1988.

Marlowe, John. *Rebellion in Palestine.* London: Cresset Press, 1946.

———. *The Seat of Pilate: An Account of the Palestine Mandate.* London: Cresset Press, 1959.

Massey, W. T. *How Jerusalem Was Won.* London: Constable, 1919.

Mattar, Philip. *The Mufti of Jerusalem: Al-Hajj Amin al-Husayni and the Palestinian National Movement.* New York: Columbia University Press, 1988.

Maundrell, Henry. *A Journey from Aleppo to Jerusalem, at Easter,* A.D. 1697. Reprinted in *Early Travels in Palestine, comprising the Narratives of Arculf, Willibald, Benard, Saewulf, Sigurd, Benjamin of Tudela, Sir John Maundeville, De la Brocquiere, and Maundrell,* ed. Thomas Wright. New York: Ketav Publishing, 1968.

McClintock, Anne. *Imperial Leather: Race, Gender and Sexuality in the Colonial Contest.* New York: Routledge, 1995.

McKenzie, John L., S.J. *Dictionary of the Bible.* New York: Macmillan Publishing, 1965.

McLean, William Hannah. *Regional and Town Planning in Principle and Practice.* London: Crosby Lockwood and Son, 1930.

McTague, John J. *British Policy in Palestine, 1917–1922.* Lanham, New York, London: University Press of America, 1983.

Meinertzhagen, Richard. *Middle East Diary, 1917–1956.* London: Cresset Press, 1959.

Melchett, Lord [Henry Ludwig Mond]. *Thy Neighbor.* New York: H. C. Kinsey, 1937.

Meller, Helen. *Patrick Geddes, Social Evolutionist and City Planner.* London: Routledge, 1990.

Mendes-Flohr, Paul. "Fin-de-Siecle Orientalism, the Ostjuden and the Aesthetics of Jewish Self Affirmation." In *Studies in Contemporary Jewry I,* ed. Jonathan Fraenkel. Bloomington: Indiana University Press, 1984.

Mendes-Flohr, Paul, and Jehuda Reinharz, eds. *The Jew in the Modern World: A Documentary History.* New York: Oxford University Press, 1980.

Merleau-Ponty. Maurice. *Phenomenology of Perception.* trans. Colin Smith. London: Routledge and Kegan Paul, 1962.

Miller, A. V., trans. *Hegel's Phenomenology of Spirit.* Analysis and foreword by J. N. Findlay. Oxford: Oxford University Press, 1977.

Mishal, Shaul, and Reuben Aharoni. *Speaking Stones: Communiqués from the Intifada Underground.* Syracuse, N.Y.: Syracuse University Press, 1994.

Misrad Habitachon. *Hashoter Ha'ivri Bit'kufat Hamandat.* Tel-Aviv: Alef Moses, 1974.

Mitchell, Timothy. *Colonizing Egypt.* Cambridge: Cambridge University Press, 1986.

Mitchell, W. J. T. *Picture Theory.* Chicago: University of Chicago Press, 1994.

Mockaitis, Thomas R. *British Counterinsurgency, 1919–1960.* London: Macmillan, 1990.

Modern Architecture in Jerusalem. Ed. Ora Ahimeir and Michael Levin. Discussion Paper no. 4. Jerusalem: Jerusalem Institute for Israel Studies, 1984.

Monk, Daniel Bertrand. "The Dimensions of History: On Architecture, between 'Constructive Phenomenology' and Apotropaism." *AA Files* 35 (spring 1998): 46–55.

———. "Orientalism and the Ornament of Mediation." In *Design Book Review* [Orientalism Issue] 29/30 (summer/fall 1993): 32–34.

Morris, Benny. *The Birth of the Palestinian Refugee Problem, 1947–1949.* Cambridge Middle East Library. Cambridge: Cambridge University Press, 1987.

———. *1948 and After: Israel and the Palestinians.* Oxford: Clarendon Press, 1990.

Mosely Lesch, Ann. *Arab Politics in Palestine, 1917–1939: The Frustration of a Nationalist Movement.* Ithaca, N.Y.: Cornell University Press, 1979.

"Mr. Richmond." *Sawt al-Sha'b,* February 1924.

Nashashibi, Nasser Eddin. *Jerusalem's Other Voice, Ragheb Nashashibi and Moderation in Palestinian Politics, 1920–1948.* Exeter, England: Ithaca Press, 1990.

Neillands, Robin. *The Dervish Wars: Gordon and Kitchener in the Sudan, 1880–1898.* London: Murray, 1996.

Nielsen, Alfred. "The International Islamic Conference at Jerusalem." *Moslem World* (London), Nile Mission Press by the Christian Literature Society for India, 22, no. 4 (October 1932): 340–354.

Nietzsche, Friedrich. "On Truth and Lies in a Nonmoral Sense." In *Philosophy and*

Truth: Selections from Nietzsche's Notebooks of the Early 1870's, ed. and trans. Daniel Breanzenle. Atlantic Highlands, N.J.: Humanities Press, 1979.

Nora, Pierre. Les Lieux de memoire. Paris: Gallimard, 1984.

Nordau, Max. Degeneration. Lincoln: University of Nebraska Press, 1993.

———. Zionistische Schriften. Cologne: Juedischer Verlag, 1909.

Ofer, Pinhas. "The Commission on the Palestine Disturbances of August 1929: Appointment, Terms of Reference, Procedure and Report." Middle-Eastern Studies 21, no. 3 (1985): 349–361.

Oke, Mim Kemal. "Young Turks, Freemasons, Jews and the Question of Zionism in the Ottoman Empire, 1908–1913." Studies in Zionism 7, no. 2 (1986): 199–218.

Osborn, Frederic J. Green-Belt Cities. New York: Schocken Books, 1969.

Owen, Roger. State, Power and Politics in the Making of the Modern Middle East. London: Routledge, 1992.

Palestine Exploration Fund. The Survey of Western Palestine. General index to the memoirs, vols. 1–3; the special papers; the Jerusalem volume; the flora and fauna of Palestine; the geological survey; and the Arabic and English name lists; comp. Henry C. Stweardson. London: Committee of the Palestine Exploration Fund, 1888.

Pappé, Ilan. The Making of the Arab-Israeli Conflict, 1947–51. London: I. B. Tauris, 1992.

Parzen, Herbert. The Hebrew University, 1925–1935. New York: Ktav Publishing House, 1974.

———. "The Magnes-Weizmann-Einstein Controversy." Jewish Social Studies 32, no. 1 (1970): 187–209.

Patai, Raphael, ed. The Complete Diaries of Theodor Herzl. Trans. Harry Zohn. New York: Herzl Press and Thomas Yoseloff, n.d.

Patton, Paul. "Conceptual Politics and the War Machine in Mille Plateaux." SubStance 44/45 (1984): 61–80.

Penslar, Derek J. Zionism and Technocracy: The Engineering of Jewish Settlement in Palestine, 1870–1918. Bloomington: Indiana University Press, 1991.

Peters, F. E. Jerusalem. Princeton, N.J.: Princeton University Press, 1985.

———. Jerusalem and Mecca: The Typology of the Holy City in the Near East. New York University Studies in Near Eastern Civilization. New York: New York University Press, 1986.

———. "Who Built the Dome of the Rock?" Graeco-Arabica 2 (1983): 119–138.

Plesner, Ulrich. "Holy City Girdled in Green." Architectural Review 165 (1979): 351–354.

Podro, Michael. Critical Historians of Art. New Haven, Conn.: Yale University Press, 1982.

Pollock, John Charles. Gordon: The Man behind the Legend. London: Constable, 1993.

Ponte, Alessandra. "Building the Spiral Stair of Evolution: The Index Museum of Sir Patrick Geddes." Assemblage 10 (1990): 47–63.

———. "Architecture and Phallocentrism in Richard Payne-Knight's Theory." In Sexuality and Space, Princeton Papers on Architecture, ed. Beatriz Colomina. New York: Princeton Architectural Press, 1992.

221

Porath, Yehoshua. *The Emergence of the Palestinian-Arab National Movement, 1918–1929.* London: Frank Cass, 1974.

———. *The Palestinian Arab National Movement: From Riots to Rebellion, 1929–1939.* London: Frank Cass, 1977.

Qureshi, M. Naeem. *Pan-Islam in British Indian Politics: A Study of the Khilafat Movement, 1918–1924.* Leiden: Brill, 1999.

Rabat, Nasser. "The Meaning of the Ummayad Dome of the Rock." *Muqarnas* 6 (1990): 12–21.

Rabinow, Paul. *French Modern: Norms and Forms of the Social Environment.* Cambridge, Mass.: MIT Press, 1989.

Renan, Ernest. *The Life of Jesus.* Intro. John Jaynes Holmes. New York: Modern Library, 1927.

"Report of Annual General Meeting." *Quarterly Statement of the Palestine Exploration Fund* [PEFQ] (1869): 90–99.

"Resignations." *The Near East,* 21 February 1924.

Richmond, Ernest Tatham. "Aggression." *G.K.'s Weekly,* 25 November 1937, n.p. [published under pseudonym Nemo].

———. "As Others See Us." *G.K.'s Weekly,* 16 December 1937, n.p. [published under pseudonym Nemo].

———. "British Policy in Palestine and the Mandate." Parts 1–3. *The Near East* (1925) 26 March, 329–330; 2 April, 350–352; 9 April, 381–382.

———. "The Church of the Nativity: The Alterations Carried Out by Justinian." *Quarterly of the Department of Antiquities in Palestine* 6, no. 2: 67–72.

———. "The Church of the Nativity, The Plan of the Constantinian Church." *Quarterly of the Department of Antiquities in Palestine* 6, no. 2: 63–66.

———. "Dictatorship in the Holy Land." *Nineteenth Century* 123 (February 1938): 186–192.

———. "Diktaturiyya fi'l 'Ard al-Muqaddasa" [Dictatorship in the Holy Land]. Trans. George Antonious. *Al-Muqattam,* 31 March 1938.

———. *The Dome of the Rock in Jerusalem: A Description of Its Structure and Decoration.* Oxford: Clarendon Press, 1924.

———. "'England' in Palestine." *The Nineteenth Century* (July 1925): 46–51.

———. "'England' in Palestine." Paper presented to Near and Middle East Association, Summer 1926.

———. "Fair Play." *G.K.'s Weekly,* 18 November 1937, n.p. [published under pseudonym Nemo].

———. "The Man Who Knew Everything." *G.K.'s Weekly,* 27 January 1938, n.p.

———. *Moslem Architecture 623 to 1516: Some Causes and Consequences.* London: Royal Asiatic Society, 1926.

———. "Palestine To-Day, the Old Order, and the New." *Guardian,* 9 April 1926, n.p. [published anonymously].

———. *The Sites of the Crucifixion and the Resurrection.* London: Catholic Truth Society, 1939.

———. "St. George of Lydda." *G.K.'s Weekly*, 18 November 1937, n.p. [published anonymously].

Richmond, John. "Prophet of Doom: E. T. Richmond, F.R.I.B.A., Palestine, 1920–1924." In *Arabic and Islamic Garland: Historical, Educational, and Literary Papers Presented to Abdul-Latif Tibawi*. London: Islamic Cultural Center, 1977.

Ricoeur, Paul. *Manifestation et Proclamation*. Paris: Aubier, 1974.

Robinson, Edward, and Elihu Smith. *Biblical Researches in Palestine, Mount Sinai and Arabia Petraea: A Journal of Travels in the Year 1838*. Vols. 1 and 2. London: John Murray, 1841.

———. *Later Biblical Researches in Palestine*. London: John Murray, 1852.

Rosenau, Helen. *Vision of the Temple: The Image of the Temple of Jerusalem in Judaism and Christianity*. London: Oresko Books, 1979.

Rosen-Ayalon, Myriam. *The Early Islamic Monuments of al-Haram al-Sharif, An Inconographic Study*. Qedem, Monographs of the Institute of Archaeology, Hebrew University of Jerusalem 28. Jerusalem: Institute of Archaeology, 1989.

Rosenblum, Nancy. *Romanticism and the Reconstruction of Liberal Thought*. Cambridge, Mass.: Harvard University Press, 1987.

Rubin, James. "Disorder/Order: Revolutionary Art as Performative Representation." In *The French Revolution, 1789–1989: Two Hundred Years of Rethinking*, special issue of *The Eighteenth Century: Theory and Interpretation*, ed. Sandy Petrey (1989): 83–111.

———. "Jacques-Louis David et la main du peuple: Saisir le site de la représentation." In *David contre David: Actes du Colloque du Musée du Louvre* 2:783–803. Paris: Documentation Française, 1993.

Rubinstein, Elyakim. "Yehudim Ve'aravim Be'iriyot Eretz-Israel (1926–1933) Yerushalayim Ve'arim Acherot." *Cathedra* 51 (1989): 122–145.

Sachar, Howard. *A History of Israel: From the Rise of Zionism to Our Time*. New York: Knopf, 1976.

Said, Edward. *Culture and Imperialism*. New York: Vintage Books, 1994.

———. "In Search of Palestine." Videocassette. London: BBC, 1999.

———. *Orientalism*. New York: Vintage Books, 1979.

———. "Palestine, Then and Now, an Exile's Journey through Israel and the Occupied Territories." *Harper's Magazine* (December 1992): 47–55.

———. *The World, the Text, and the Critic*. Cambridge, Mass.: Harvard University Press, 1983.

Samuel, H. B. *Beneath the Whitewash: A Critical Analysis of the Report of the Commission on the Palestine Disturbances of August, 1929*. London: Hogarth Press, 1930.

Samuel, Maurice, *What Happened in Palestine: The Events of August, 1929, Their Background and Their Significance*. Boston: Stratford, 1929.

Sanbar, Elias. *Palestine 1948: L'expulsion*. Paris: Institut des Études Palestiniens, 1984.

———. "Le Vécu et l'écrit: Historiens-réfugiés de Palestine. Quelques propositions pour la recherche." *Revue d'Etudes Palestiniennes* 1 (fall 1981): 62–75.

Sanders, Ronald. *The High Walls of Jerusalem: A History of the Balfour Declaration and the Birth of the British Mandate for Palestine*. New York: Holt, Rinehart and Winston, 1983.

Sandler, P., ed. *Hizionei Medinah: Yalkut Utopiot Tzioniot*. Tel-Aviv: M. Newman, 1954.

Sayigh, Rosemary. *Palestinians: From Peasants to Revolutionaries*. Foreword by Noam Chomsky. London: Zed Press, 1979.

Schatz, Boris. *Yerushalayim Hab'nuya: Chalom Behakitz*. Jerusalem: 1924.

Schelling, Thomas C. *The Strategy of Conflict*. Cambridge, Mass.: Harvard University Press, 1960, 1980.

Scholch, Alexander. "Jerusalem in the 19th Century (1831–1917 A.D.)." In *Jerusalem in History*, ed. J. K. Asali. New York: Olive Branch Press, 1990.

Segal, Jerome, ed. *Negotiating Jerusalem*. SUNY Series in Israel Studies. Albany: State University of New York Press, 2000.

Shaffer, E. S. *"Kubla Khan" and the Fall of Jerusalem: The Mythological School in Biblical Criticism and Secular Literature, 1770–1880*. London: Cambridge University Press, 1975.

Shapiro, Shaham. "Planning Jerusalem: The First Generation, 1917–1968." In *Urban Geography of Jerusalem: A Companion Volume to the Atlas of Jerusalem*, ed. D. H. K. Amiran, Arie Shachar, and Israel Kimhi. Berlin: Walter de Gruyter, 1973.

Sharon, Arieh. *Planning Jerusalem*. Jerusalem: Weidenfeld and Nicholson, 1973.

Shaw, Stanford J., and Ezel Kural Shaw. *History of the Ottoman Empire and Modern Turkey*, Vol. 2: *Reform, Revolution, and Republic: The Rise of Modern Turkey, 1808–1975*. Cambridge: Cambridge, University Press, 1977.

Sheffer, G. "British Colonial Policy-Making towards Palestine (1929–1939)." *Middle-Eastern Studies* 14, no. 3 (1978): 307–322.

Shepherd, Naomi. *The Zealous Intruders: The Western Rediscovery of Palestine*. London: Collins, 1987.

Sherman, A. J. *Mandate Days: British Lives in Palestine, 1918–1948*. New York: Thames and Hudson, 1997.

Shiloh-Cohen, Nurit, ed. *'Bezalel' Shel Schatz, 1906–1929*. Exh. cat. no. 23. Jerusalem: Israel Museum, 1983.

Shlaim, Avi. *The Politics of Partition: King Abdullah, the Zionists and Palestine, 1921–1951*. New York: Columbia University Press, 1990.

Shragai, Nadav. "Olmert: The Behavior of the Palestinian Authority—'Maniacal Incitement.'" *Ha'aretz*, 26 September 1996, 3.

Shragai, Nadav, Sami Sokol, Gai Behor, Aluf Ben, and Sharon Sade. "Arafat Calls upon the Palestinians to Carry Out Protests and a Commercial Strike." *Ha'aretz* 25 September 1996, 1.

Silberman, Neil Asher. *Digging for God and Country: Exploration in the Holy Land, 1799–1917*. New York: Doubleday, 1982.

Siebers, Tobin. *The Mirror of Medusa*. Los Angeles: University of California Press, 1983.

Silverman, Kaja. "The Lacanian Phallus." *Differences* 4, no. 1 (spring 1992): 84–115.

———. "Lost Objects and Mistaken Subjects: Film Theory's Structuring Lack." *Wide Angle: A Film Quarterly of Theory Criticism, and Practice* 7, nos. 1/2 (1985): 14–29.

Simmel, Georg. *The Philosophy of Money*. Ed. David Frisby, trans. Tom Bottomore and David Frisby. London: Routledge, 1990.

Simpson, William. "Transference of Holy Sites." *Palestine Exploration Fund Quarterly Report* [PEFQ] (1879): 18–32.

Smith, Charles D. *Palestine and the Arab-Israeli Conflict.* New York: St. Martin's Press, 1988.

Smith, Joseph H., and William Kerrigan, eds. *Taking Chances: Derrida, Psychoanalysis, and Literature.* Baltimore, Md.: Johns Hopkins University Press, 1984.

Smith, William. *Dictionary of the Bible: Comprising Its Antiquities, Biography, Geography, and Natural History.* Rev. ed. H. B. Hackett, with Ezra Abbot. 1858; Boston: Houghton Mifflin, 1881.

Sokol, Sami, and Nadav Shragai. "Tens of Palestinians Threw Stones; the Western Wall Square Was Cleared." *Ha'aretz,* 25 September 1996, A2.

Spence, Johnathan D. *God's Chinese Son: The Taiping Heavenly Kingdom of Hong Xiuquan.* New York: W. W. Norton, 1996.

Spivak, Gayatri Chakravorty. "Can the Subaltern Speak?" In *Marxism and the Interpretation of Culture,* ed. Cary Nelson and Lawrence Grossberg. Chicago: University of Chicago Press, 1988.

———. *In Other Worlds: Essays in Cultural Politics.* New York: Methuen, 1988.

Stein, Kenneth W. *The Land Question in Palestine, 1917–1939.* Chapel Hill: University of North Carolina Press, 1984.

Steiner, George. "Our Homeland, the Text." *Salmagundi* (winter/spring 1985): 4–25.

St. Laurent, Beatrice, and Andras Riedlmayr. "Restorations of Jerusalem and the Dome of the Rock and Their Political Significance, 1537–1928." *Muqarnas* 10 (1993): 76–84.

Storrs, [Sir] Ronald. *The Memoirs of Sir Ronald Storrs* [previously published as *Orientations*]. New York: G. P. Putnam and Sons, 1937.

Strachey, Lytton. *Eminent Victorians: Cardinal Manning, Florence Nightingale, Dr. Arnold, General Gordon.* New York: Harvest/HBJ Books, 1980.

Strappini, [Rev.] William Diver. "The Religious Opinions of General Gordon." *Month* (May 1884): 29–38.

Tafuri, Manfredo. *Ideology and Utopia.* Trans. Barbara Luigia La Penta. Cambridge, Mass.: MIT Press, 1976.

———. *The Sphere and the Labyrinth, Avant-Gardes and Architecture from Piranesi to the 1970's.* Trans. Pellegrino d'Acierno and Robert Connoly. Cambridge, Mass.: MIT Press, 1987.

Tafuri, Manfredo, and Francesco Dal Co, *Modern Architecture.* Vol. 1. Trans. Erich Wolf. Milan: Electa-Rizzoli, 1976.

Taggar, Yehuda. *The Mufti of Jerusalem and Palestine Arab Politics, 1930–1937.* New York: Garland Publishing, 1986.

Tannous, ʿIzzat. *The Palestinians: A Detailed Documented Eyewitness History of Palestine under the British Mandate.* London: IGT, 1988.

Tash, Dr. Abdul Qader. "A Distortion of History and Truth." Rpt. in *Arab View,* 20 October 1996. <http://www.arab.net/arabview/articles/tash4.html>

Taussig, Michael. *Mimesis and Alterity: A Particular History of the Senses.* New York: Routledge, 1993.

Tavin, Eli, and Yonah Alexander. *Psychological Warfare and Propaganda: Irgun Documentation 24*. Wilmington, De.: Scholarly Resources, 1982.

Taylor, Ronald, ed. *Aesthetics and Politics*. By Ernst Bloch et al. London: NLB, 1977.

al-Tibawi, Abdul-Latif. *Arab Education in Mandatory Palestine: A Study of Three Decades of British Administration*. London: Luzac, 1956.

Tiedemann, Rolf. "Concept, Image, Name: On Adorno's Utopia of Knowledge." In *The Semblance of Subjectivity: Adorno's Aesthetic Theory*, ed. Thomas Huhn and Lambert Zuidervaart. Cambridge, Mass.: MIT Press, 1997.

Todorov, Tzvetan. *Theories of the Symbol*. Trans. Catherine Porter. Ithaca, N.Y.: Cornell University Press, 1982.

"The Topography of Jerusalem." *Quarterly Statement of the Palestine Exploration Fund* [PEFQ] (1869): 3–5.

"A Tribute to the Rev. Father Denis Fahey, C.S. sp." *Candour*, 26 February 1954.

Tsahor, Ze'ev. "Nitzachon Atzuv, Ben-Gurion Veq'dud Ha'avoda." *Cathedra* 43 (1986): 333–351.

Tuchman, Barbara W. *Bible and Sword: England and Palestine from the Bronze Age to Balfour*. New York: Ballantine Books, 1956.

Turner, Ralph E. *James Silk Buckingham, 1786–1855: A Social Biography*. New York: McGraw-Hill, 1934.

Unwin, Raymond. *Town Planning in Practice*. London: T. Fisher Unwin, 1909.

Vattimo, Gianni. *The End of Modernity: Nihilism and Hermeneutics in Postmodern Culture*. Trans. and intro. Jon R. Snyder. Baltimore, Md.: Johns Hopkins University Press, 1988.

Vidler, Anthony. *The Architectural Uncanny: Essays in the Modern Unhomely*. Cambridge, Mass.: MIT Press, 1992.

———. "The Scenes of the Street: Transformations in Ideal and Reality, 1750–1871." In *On Streets*, ed. Stanford Anderson. Cambridge, Mass.: MIT Press, 1986.

Vilnai, Ze'ev. *Madrich Yerushalayim*. Jerusalem: Ariel Press, 1946.

Vincent, L. H., O. P. "Garden Tomb: L'histoire d'un mythe." *Revue Biblique* 34, no. 3 (1 July 1925): 401–431.

Volney, Constantin, Comte. *A New Translation of Volney's Ruins; or Meditation on the Revolution of Empires*. Vols. 1 and 2. Paris: Levrault, 1802. Rpt. in *A New Translation of Volney's Ruins*, ed. Burton Feldman and Robert D. Richardson. New York: Garland Publishing, 1979.

———. *Travels through Syria and Egypt*. Vols. 1 and 2. London: Robinson, 1787.

Wardle, J. *A Tour of Palestine and Egypt and Back*. Nottingham, England: H. B. Saxton, 1907.

Wasserstein, Bernard. *The British in Palestine: The Mandatory Government and the Arab-Jewish Conflict, 1917–1939*. London: Basil Blackwell, 1991.

———. " 'Clipping the Claws of the Colonisers': Arab Officials in the Government of Palestine, 1917–1948." *Middle-Eastern Studies* 13, no. 2 (1977): 171–194.

Wedeen, Lisa. *Ambiguities of Domination: Politics, Rhetoric, and Symbols in Contemporary Syria*. Chicago: University of Chicago Press, 1999.

Weisgal, Meir, gen. ed. *The Letters and Papers of Chaim Weizmann*. Jerusalem: Transaction Books; Rutgers University, Israel Universities Press, 1977.

Weizmann, Chaim. *Trial and Error, the Autobiography of Chaim Weizmann*. Philadelphia: Jewish Publication Society of America, 1949.

White, [Rev.] Bill. *A Special Place: The Story of the Garden Tomb, Jerusalem*. Grantham, England: Stanborough Press, 1989.

White, Hayden. *Metahistory: The Historical Imagination in Nineteenth-Century Europe*. Baltimore, Md.: Johns Hopkins University Press, 1973.

Wigley, Mark. "Theoretical Slippage: The Architecture of the Fetish." In *Fetish, Princeton Papers on Architecture*, ed. Sarah Whiting, Edward Mitchell, and Greg Lynn. Princeton: Princeton Architectural Press, 1992.

Williams, Raymond. *Culture and Society*. New York: Columbia University Press, 1983.

Wilson, Andrew. *The Ever-Victorious Army: A History of the Chinese Campaign under Lt.-Col. C. G. Gordon, C.B. R.E. and of the Suppression of the Tai-ping Rebellion*. Reprint Series: Chinese Materials Center 63. Ed. with notes by John Holland. San Francisco: Chinese Materials Center, 1977.

Wilson, Charles, and Charles Warren. *The Recovery of Jerusalem: A Narrative of Exploration and Discovery in the City and the Holy Land*. New York: D. Appleton, 1873.

Wilson, C. W. *Golgotha and the Holy Sepulchre*. London: Committee of the Palestine Exploration Fund, 1906.

Wilson, Kathleen. *The Sense of the People: Politics, Culture, and Imperialism in England, 1715–1785*. 1995; Cambridge: Cambridge University Press, 1998.

Wolin, Richard. *Walter Benjamin: An Aesthetic of Redemption*. New York: Columbia University Press, 1982.

Yanait, Rachel, Itzhak Avrahami, and Yerach Etzion. *Hahagana B'Yerushalayim, Eiduyot Vezikhronot Mipi Chaverim*. 2 vols. Jerusalem: Kiriyat Hasefer, 1973.

Yavuz, Yildirim. "The Restoration Project of the Masjid al-Aqsa by Mimar Kemalettin (1922–26)." *Muqarnas* 13 (1996): 149–164.

Yogev, Gedaliah, and Yehoshuah Freundlich, eds. *Haprotokolim shel Hava'ad Hapo'el Hatsiyoni, 1919–1929*. [Minutes of the Zionist General Council]. Vol. 2. Trans. Menahem Dorman and Yedidiah Fels. Jerusalem: Hasifriya Hatziyonit, 1984.

Young, Robert J. C. *Colonial Desire: Hybridity in Theory, Culture and Race*. London: Routledge, 1995.

Žižek, Slavoj. *For They Know Not What They Do: Enjoyment as a Political Factor*. London: Verso, 1991.

———. *The Sublime Object of Ideology*. London: Verso, 1989.

Zipperstein, Steven J. *Elusive Prophet: Ahad Ha'am and the Origins of Zionism*. Berkeley: University of California Press, 1993.

Zuidervaart, Lambert. *Adorno's Aesthetic Theory: The Redemption of Illusion*. Cambridge, Mass.: MIT Press, 1994.

n.23, 187 n.49; restoration of tile program of, 48–50, 52, 60–64, 68, 159 nn.11, 12, and 15, 160 nn.17–19, 161 n.21, 162 n.26, 168 n.60, 169 n.71. See also Haram al-Sharif/ Temple Mount (Jerusalem): restoration of; Holy places (Jerusalem); Richmond, Ernest Tatham: and survey of the Dome of the Rock, Jerusalem; Spirit (Geist): architecture perceived as raiment of; Supreme Muslim Shariʿa Council (Majlis al-Sharʿi al-Islami al-Aʿla)

Dramaturgy (as reflexive accusative framework of political actors), 71, 85–87, 90, 93–96, 103, 106–107, 115–118, 130, 135–136 n.14, 181 nn.10–11, 182 n.18, 184 n.30, 187 nn.49–50. See also Adequation: "reflexive" theory of; Goffman, Erving

"Eastern Question," 27–29, 146 n.35
École biblique (Jerusalem), 35, 37, 149 n.4. See also Archaeology; Vincent, Louis Hughes
Eder, David Montagu, 53, 88, 182–183 n.23
Egypt, 27, 51, 156 n.1, 157 n.2, 161 n.22
Eliade, Mircea, 6
Eliash, Mordechai, 111–114, 191 n.32
Elpeleg, Zvi, 91, 150 n.10, 185 n.33. See also Israel/Palestine conflict, historiography and periodization of
England. See Great Britain, government of

Fahey, Dennis (Rev.), 38, 153 n.22
Fascism, 153 n.24
Fergusson, James, 22, 25, 27–28, 144 n.29, 150 n.8
Fitzmaurice, G. H., 51, 161 n.21. See also Great Britain, government of: Foreign Office (FO)
Flags. See Architecture: contested political instrumentality of representations of

Frame (analysis), concept of. See Dramaturgy
Franco, Francisco, 153 n.24
Frazer, George James, 126
Freud, Sigmund, 9–10, 41, 138 n.1, 139 nn.36–38, 155 n.36. See also Apotropaism

Gallop, Jane, 137 n.24
Garden Tomb. See Gordon, Charles George: and Golgotha
Garstang, John, 67. See also Palestine, government of: Department of Antiquities (ANT)
Geddes, Patrick, 157 n.1, 161 n.21
Geist. See Spirit (Geist)
Geography, scriptural, 9–11, 18, 22–25, 27, 30, 42; and role of "intriguers" in, 24–24, 143 n.23. See also Adequation, "magical" theory of; Benjamin, Walter: theory of allegory of; Hierophany, concept of; Manifestations, logic of
George, David Lloyd, 18
George V, King of England, 51
Gestures, menacing. See Apotropaism
Gibb, H. A. R., 179–180 n.1
Goethe, Johann Wilhelm von, 23, 142 n.16
Goffman, Erving, 85, 93, 136 n.14, 139 n.39, 181 n.11, 184 n.30, 187 n.50. See also Adequation "reflexive" theory of; Dramaturgy
Golgotha (Place of Skulls): as cipher of history, 22–23, 28–30, 142 nn.15–16; identification of, 18–19, 24–25, 26–27, 35, 144 nn. 27–29, 145 nn. 23–33, 149 nn.3–6, 155 n.33. See also Benjamin, Walter: theory of allegory of; Gordon, Charles George: and Golgotha; Holy places (Jerusalem); Toponymy

Gordon, Charles George, 18, 34, 115, 141 nn.1–2, 142 n.6; and Golgotha, 19, 22–23, 26–30, 142 n.7, 145 n.34, 148 n.2, 155 n.33. See also Golgotha

Gospels (Christian), 25-26, 41, 144 n.28. See also Bible (Hebrew); Toponymy

Grabar, Oleg, 172 n.88

Gramsci, Antonio, 178 n.22

Grand mufti (al-Mufti al-Akbar). See al-Husayni, Kamil; al-Husayni, (Hajj) Muhammad Amin

Granger, Terence, 137 n.23

Great Britain, government of, 71, 74, 147 n.43; Colonial Office (CO), 50–52, 57, 67–68, 89–91, 170 n.76, 171–172 n.82, 173 nn.92–93, 183 n.24, 184 nn.25, 28, and 30; Foreign Office (FO), 50–52, 57, 61, 92, 159 n.11, 160 nn.17–19, 161 n.21, 162 nn.24–25; India Office, 160 n.19, 162 n.24, 167 n.57; and League of Nations Mandate over Palestine, 4, 65, 70–71, 73, 91–92, 106, 135 n.11, 140 n.41, 172 n.84, 174 n.103, 182 n.21, 183 n.24, 184 n.25, 186 n.43; War Office (WO), 158 n.6. See also Commission on the Palestine Disturbances of August 1929 (Shaw Commission); Palestine, government of

Guha, Ranajit, 75, 176 n.6, 185 n.38. See also Subaltern studies (subaltern historiography)

Guy, P. L. O., 67, 173 n.92

Habermas, Jürgen, 163 n.34

Hakeren Lemoreshet Hakotel Hama'aravi. See Western Wall Heritage Foundation

Hall, Joseph (Bishop), 18, 141 n.2, 142 n.4

Hamilton, Robert W., 168 n.59. See also Palestine, government of: Department of Antiquities (ANT)

Haqa'iq 'an Qadhiyyat Filastin. See Truths

Concerning the Question of Palestine (al-Husayni, 1954)

Haram al-Sharif/Temple Mount (Jerusalem), xii, 28, 45, 48, 53, 56, 77, 88, 105, 116, 131, 136 n.9, 182 n.21; restoration of, 50–52, 60–64, 68–69, 71, 158 n.6, 159 nn.11, 12, and 15, 160 nn.17–19, 161 nn.21–22, 162 nn.26–27, 167 nn.54, 57, and 58, 169 n.71, 173 n.93. See also Aqsa Mosque; Dome of the Rock

Hasochnut Hayehudit. See Jewish Agency for Palestine

Hassan (Bin Talal), Crown Prince of Jordan, 2, 124 n.5

Haycraft, Thomas, 156 n.42

Hebrew University (Jerusalem), 161 n.21

Hegel, Georg Wilhelm Friedrich, 11, 60; Aesthetics, 104; Phenomenology of Spirit, 7, 38–39, 42, 55–56, 58, 69, 79–80, 134 n.5, 136 n.20, 164 nn.38–39, 166 n.49, 174 n.100; Philosophy of Right, 60, 167 n.55; "Spirit of Christianity and Its Fate," 34, 38–39, 147, 154 n.27. See also Derrida, Jacques; Richmond, Ernest Tatham: and Christian idealism

Herzl, Theodor, 105–108, 110, 190 nn.20–21

Hierophany, concept of, 6, 11, 30, 136 n.2. See also Geography, scriptural

Hijaz, 51

Historiography. See Israel/Palestine conflict, historiography and periodization of

Hobsbawm, Eric, 10, 137 n.23

Hogarth, David George, 49, 61, 159 nn.11, 12, and 15

Holliday, Clifford, 173 n.96

"Holy Fire," feast of. See Holy Sepulchre, Church of

Holy places (Jerusalem), 11, 173 nn.92–93, 174 nn.101–103; Aqsa Mosque, xi,

Jay, Martin, 138 n.27
Jeffries, J. M. N., 175 n.106. *See also* Israel/Palestine conflict, historiography and periodization of
Jerusalem, 6, 9–10, 22, 34–35, 66, 70–71, 84, 93, 106–107, 131, 137 n.24, 162 n.16, 179–180 n.1, 182–183 n.23, 187 n.48; governorate of district of (1918–48), 53, 63, 170 n.72, 177 n.9 (*see also* Storrs, Ronald); municipality of, town planning commission (JTPC), 173 n.96; topography of, 25–26, 30, 144 nn.25, 27, and 29, 145 nn.30–31
Jewish Agency for Palestine (Hasochnut Hayehudit), 84–85, 98, 101, 107–108, 130, 180 nn.2–3, 189, n.10
Jewish National Council (Hava'ad Hale'umi), xii, 71, 73, 78, 175 n.108, 178 n.21
Judaism: and aniconism, 35, 38, 45–46, 56–57, 112–113, 154 n.27, 171 n.80. *See also* Symbol(s)

Kapitan, Tomis, 7–8. *See also* Adequation: "reflexive" theory of
Kedourie, Elie, 150 n.9, 161 n.22, 162 n.27, 163 n.33, 171 n.82, 182–183 n.23. *See also* Israel/Palestine conflict, historiography and periodization of
Kemalettin, Mimar, 61, 63, 167 n.58, 168 n.59
Kenyon, Frederick, 67
"Kernel and shell." *See* Ahad Ha'am; Spirit (*Geist*): architecture perceived as raiment of
Khalidi, Rashid, 6–7, 136 n.23. *See also* Adequation: "operative" theory of; Israel/Palestine conflict, historiography and periodization of
Khalifa. See Caliphate
Khartoum, 141 n.2
Khilafat Committee (India), 51–52, 162 n.24, 179–180 n.1

Kisch, Frederick Hermann, 53, 93–97, 103, 119, 186–187 n.48, 187 nn.49 and 51
Kishani (tile). *See* Dome of the Rock: restoration of tile program of
Kitchener (of Khartoum), Horatio Herbert, 146 n.43
Kolinsky, Martin, 140 n.41, 176 n.1. *See also* Israel/Palestine conflict, historiography and periodization of
Kramer, Martin Seth, 91. *See also* Israel/Palestine conflict, historiography and periodization of
Krauthammer, Charles, 2–3
Kupferschmidt, Uri, 91, 166 n.47, 179–180 n.1, 181 n.5, 185 n.33. *See also* Israel/Palestine conflict, historiography and periodization of

Lacan, Jacques, 137 n.24
al-Lajna al-ʿArabiyya al-ʿUlya. *See* Arab Higher Committee
Lajnat al-Difaʿ ʿan al-Buraq al-Sharif. *See* Defense Committee for the Noble Buraq
Lamartine, Alphonse de, 23–24
Landscape of Palestine. *See* Jerusalem: topography of
League of Nations, 135 n.11, 154 n.24, 157 n.1, 172 n.84, 174 n.103. *See also* Great Britain, government of: and League of Nations Mandate over Palestine
LeBon, Gustav, 155 n.36
Lesch, Ann Mosely, 140 n.41, 174 n.102, 177 n.11, 179–180 n.1. *See also* Israel/Palestine conflict, historiography and periodization of

Mahdism (Mahdi), 18, 141 n.1 *See also* Gordon, Charles George
al-Majlis al-Sharʿi al-Islami al-Aʿla. *See* Supreme Muslim Shariʿa Council (SMC)

239

166 n.49, 167 n.55, 174 n.100 (*see also* Manifestations, logic of; Spirit [*Geist*]: architecture perceived as raiment of); and "Richmondism," charges of, 37, 53, 65, 71–72 152 n.17; and *The Sites of the Crucifixion and the Resurrection* (1935), 34, 40–44, 47, 149 nn.4 and 6; and survey of the Dome of the Rock, 33, 45–46, 48–50, 71, 158 nn.6–7, 159 nn.11, 12, and 15, 160 nn.16–19, 161 n.21 (*see also* Dome of the Rock: restoration of tile program of); and Zionism, critique of (as Anglo-Judaic cabal against Islam and Christianity), 62–66, 68, 150 n.13, 153 n.22, 164 n.39, 169 n.71, 170 nn.74 and 76, 171 n.80, 172 nn.84–85. *See also* Palestine, government of (1917–48): Department of Antiquities (ANT) *and* secretariat (CS)

Richmond, Herbert W., 67, 173 nn.92–93

Richmond, William Blake, 147–148 n.1

Riots and rebellions (Israel/Palestine), 74; Jerusalem, March 1920 (Easter/Nabi Musa), xii, 51, 73–74, 162 n.28, 172 n.83, 176 n.2, 187 nn.48 and 51; Jerusalem, August 1929 (Buraq/Wailing Wall), 11, 36, 54, 55, 65, 70–72, 75–78, 84–85, 98, 100, 106, 130, 150 n.12, 151 n.15, 152 n.17, 174 nn.101–103, 176 n.1, 177 n.11, 178 n.21, 189 n.6 (*see also* Commission on the Palestine Disturbances of August 1929); Jerusalem, September 2000 (*Intifadat al-Aqsa*), 131; Palestine, 1936–39 (*al-Thawra al-Kubra*), 11, 140 n.41, 177 n.11 (*see also* Qassam, 'Izz al-Din)

Robinson, Edward, 25. *See also* Geography, scriptural

Romanticism, 23, 139 n.41

Ruin. *See* Allegory; Benjamin, Walter: theory of allegory of

Rumor. *See* Agency: role of rumors and

Russia, 28, 38, 146 n.42, 153 n.22

al-Sahyuniyya wa'l-Amakin al-Islamiyya al-Muqaddasa fi Filastin. *See* Zionism and the Islamic Holy Places in Palestine (1931)

Said, Edward, 4, 23–24, 27–28. *See also* Orientalism

Samuel, Herbert, 36, 45–46, 50, 52–53, 65, 67, 89, 150 n.9, 163 n.28, 167 n.57, 171–172 n.82, 172 n.83, 183 n.24, 184 n.25. *See also* Palestine, government of: high commissioner (HC)

Sanbar, Elias, 140 n.41. *See also* Israel/Palestine conflict, historiography and periodization of

San Remo Conference, 135 n.11. *See also* League of Nations

Saunders, Alan, 75, 77–78, 176 n.4

Schatz, Boris, 168 n.60

Schick, Conrad, 26

Second nature, concept of (in critical theory), 5, 23, 143 n.19

Sensus communis. *See* Agency: as collective will

Şeyhüulislâm. *See* Shaykh al-Islam

Shari'a Courts (Palestine), xii, 57–58, 166 nn.46–47, 169 nn.67, 70, and 71. *See also* Supreme Muslim Shari'a Council (SMC)

Sharon, Ariel, 131

Shaw Commission. *See* Commission on the Palestine Disturbances of August 1929 (Shaw Commission)

Shaykh al-Islam, xii, 51–52, 161 n.22

Shepard, Naomi, 28, 146 n.42. *See also* Israel/Palestine conflict, historiography and periodization of

Shomrei Hakotel Hama'aravi. *See* Society for the Defense of the Kotel

Shuckbrugh, John, 68, 171–172 n.82

Silberman, Neil Asher, 27. *See also* Ar-

243

DANIEL BERTRAND MONK is Associate Professor of Art
and Architecture at the State University of New York,
Stony Brook, and teaches at Harvard University's Graduate School of Design. A practicing architect, he has
also been the recipient of an SSRC-MacArthur Foundation Fellowship in International Peace and Security and
the Samuel H. Kress Fellowship from the American
Schools of Oriental Research.

■

Library of Congress Cataloging-in-Publication Data
Monk, Daniel Bertrand.
An aesthetic occupation : the immediacy of
architecture and the Palestine conflict / Daniel
Bertrand Monk.
p.   cm.
Includes bibliographical references and index.
ISBN 0-8223-2803-8 (cloth : alk. paper)
ISBN 0-8223-2814-3 (pbk. : alk. paper)
1. Palestine—Politics and government—
1917–1948.   2. Monuments—Political aspects—
Palestine.   3. Religion and politics—Palestine.
4. Religion and geography.   5. Sacred space—
Palestine.   I. Title.
DS126.M62   2001
956.9'04—dc21   2001040726